Good Housekeeping

COMPLETE

HOME BOOK

LINDA GRAY

HarperCollins*Illustrated*

First published in 2000 by
HarperCollins*Publishers*
77–85 Fulham Palace Road
London W6 8JB

The HarperCollins website address is:
www.**fire**and**water**.com

This edition first published in
paperback in 2001

05 04 03 02 01
9 8 7 6 5 4 3 2 1

Published in association with The
National Magazine Company Limited
Good Housekeeping is a registered
trade mark of The National Magazine
Company Limited.

The Good Housekeeping website
address is: www.goodhousekeeping.com

The expression Good Housekeeping as
used in the title of the book is the mark
of the National Magazine Company
Limited and the Hearst Corporation,
registered in the United Kingdom and
the USA, and other principle countries
in the world, and is the absolute
property of the National Magazine
Company and the Hearst Corporation.
The use of this trade mark other than
with the express permission of the
National Magazine Company Limited
or the Hearst Corporation is strictly
prohibited.

Copyright © 2000
HarperCollins*Publishers*

A CIP catalogue record for this book is
available from the British Library.

ISBN: 0-00-713280-8

Colour reproduction:
Colourscan, Singapore

Printed and bound:
Printing Express Ltd., Hong Kong

contents

foreword

Over the past few years, there's been a revolution in the way we view our homes. Paint, wallpaper and accessories ranges have expanded to take in fashion trends and more eclectic ideas and the cost of furnishings has come down in real terms. For the first time ever it's possible for everyone of us to create a home that reflects our personality and individual style. The only problem with so much choice is, well, there just is so much choice. Where do you begin?

Good Housekeeping magazine is the leading authority on everything to do with the home. We know that interior design is about so much more than simply choosing paint, fabrics and furnishing styles. It is working out what you want from your home and how your surroundings affect you. This is why our experts have produced this comprehensive home bible covering every facet of interior design – from room planning and colour schemes to choosing furniture, soft furnishings and home appliances – providing the perfect source of creative ideas and information, whatever your chosen style.

Beginning with an introduction to room planning and decoration and an overview of all the issues to consider when decorating the home, the chapters of this book form a guided tour of the home. Room-by-room we start with living rooms, move on to kitchens and dining rooms, continue through to halls and stairways, bedrooms, children's rooms and finally bathrooms. Chapters on home offices and conservatories are also included to reflect the increasing importance that these areas now have in our homes. Throughout the book are special directories that look in detail at the range of appliances and furniture available today, and case studies, featuring interior solutions taken from real homes.

Whether you are starting from scratch in a new home, decorating a single room in your existing home, or simply want to change your living room curtains, the *Complete Home Book* offers practical advice and inspiration, in fact everything you need to create a stylish and practical home.

Lindsay Nicholson
Editor-in-chief, *Good Housekeeping*

room planning

It's your home, your space, and the only ones who matter here are you and your family. So move the kitchen to the front if you wish, or the living room up to the first floor where it will catch the light. Open up the space if you like open-plan living or divide it into a series of self-contained rooms. The most important thing is to plan the space to suit your way of living.

Using the space

Take a good tour of your home and try to look at it with fresh eyes, walk around it as a potential buyer, noting all of its good and bad points. Then think how you could best adapt the space to make it work harder for you.

Above *The dining room of this Edwardian house has moved to the conservatory and the original now combines with the former front room to make a single large living area. The doors in between can be left open or closed, making the space flexible.*

Right *One side of a former stable block, this living space is divided by two freestanding walls that split it into kitchen, dining and living areas, complete with fireplace.*

A SENSE OF INTEGRITY

Respecting the original architecture of a house is important but it need not conflict with modern design. There is nothing authentic about using a traditional-style lampshade in a house that was built before electricity was invented. You might equally well opt for a very modern lamp, or for discreet architectural lighting where the effect is more important than the source. This applies to bathrooms, kitchens and even living rooms. Equally, there is no point in being dogmatic. Swapping fitted carpet for wooden flooring is one thing, but giving up the comfortable sofa for a set of upright wooden chairs simply because it was the usual form of seating prior to Victorian times is quite another.

Perhaps the best way forward is to keep original architectural features where they exist – windows, fireplaces, doors and details such as decorative plasterwork, picture rails and deep skirting – but to rearrange the internal space to suit present-day requirements. That applies even to unfashionable styles of architecture. Houses built in the 1960s, at a time when energy was inexpensive, often have single-glazed picture windows and minimal insulation, with perhaps a built-in stone fireplace-cum-storage unit. If you can use secondary glazing or replace the windows with double-glazed copies and cover up rather than remove the fireplace, the important features of the house will be retained until they become desirable again – which they will.

New plans for living

Sometimes rooms simply acquire a new function. A 19th-century scullery often makes an ideal utility room, a box room can be converted into an en-suite bathroom or shower room, and a roomy understairs cupboard is a good place for a downstairs toilet. At other times, more radical action is required. Although the whole point about barns and lofts is their breathtaking size, a few partitions are essential around bedrooms and bathrooms for privacy. In contrast, a tiny terraced house might be transformed if small rooms are knocked together to increase light and space.

Try playing with different ideas – from a loft extension to a cellar conversion – to see what they would offer. Open up the house, extend it or turn the whole thing upside down in your mind, to see how it could really work for you. The study at the back that catches the evening sun might be better used as a sitting room that opens on to a conservatory leading to the garden. That tiny bedroom could make a perfect second bathroom – and what about the garage? Perhaps you could turn it into a home office or playroom, or extend over the top to create another bedroom.

PRACTICAL MATTERS

It is worth repeating the obvious: the more people that live in a house, the greater the number of separate rooms you need. Open-plan loft living, for example, is wonderful for one or two, but families that want to work, watch television, study and listen to music at different times need time and room apart. And although people crave space, it can diminish the value of your house if you do away with a separate kitchen, lose the garage or reduce the number of bedrooms.

Open-plan homes need first-class insulation to prevent heating bills soaring, as well as excellent ventilation to minimize cooking smells. It is also essential to identify load-bearing walls, that hold up the house.

One indication is if there is another wall in exactly the same position above or below, and floorboards that run parallel to the wall. If one of these walls is removed, a special steel or concrete joist has to be used to take the weight of the structure above. This usually protrudes into the room, so if this would bother you, think about keeping part of the wall as a frame and possibly adding double doors instead.

Extra level

It may be possible to squeeze an extra floor into a home with very high ceilings – for example, in a barn, a large 19th-century house or even a mansion flat. A mezzanine level creates a vast internal balcony, taking light from the existing windows. It is especially useful space for sleeping or studying and can look spectacular, despite drawbacks with regard to noise from below.

On a simpler level, rethinking the layout of furniture can make an immediate difference to the amount of usable space. To save your back, instead of physically trying out different positions for the furniture, draw a plan of the room, marking on it doors, windows and features such as fireplaces that you don't intend moving. Cut templates of every piece of furniture you want to include so you can try out as many arrangements on paper as possible. Less is usually better than more, so don't be afraid to discard anything that does not add to the look.

Top left *Bringing the sofa forward in this room creates an intimate seating area close to the fireplace, which benefits from extra warmth in winter and offers decorative interest in summer.*

Left *A load-bearing wall cannot be knocked out unless a special joist is inserted. Here, enough of the wall is left as a support, while creating an open-plan effect between dining room and kitchen.*

***Left** This bed fits exactly across a deep window, which becomes the focal point of the room. The curtains form a softly draped background at night.*

Furnishing the space

Although it is tempting to arrange furniture around the walls, this is not necessarily the best way to make the most of space. Sometimes it is better to draw furniture into the centre of the room. Screens, cupboards, a bookcase or a table can be used to define the sitting area in an open-plan room, and you can also use furniture to create a traffic 'lane', keeping it away from the kitchen, eating and seating areas. Furniture that fits into an alcove or along a wall increases the impression of space.

structural checklist

▓ There are certain rules and guidelines for domestic structural alterations, which will vary between countries according to national building regulations. Many building regulations are enforced in order to ensure the inhabitants' safety – contact your local authority for advice.

▓ A bathroom is the one room where a window is not necessarily essential. An internal bathroom can be ventilated by an extractor fan that works in conjunction with the light switch.

▓ To be a 'habitable room', the living space will probably require ceilings to be a minimum height

– at least 2.3m (7½ft) high in the UK, with window space equivalent to at least one-tenth of the floor area to provide sufficient light and ventilation.

▓ Some national regulations stipulate the need for a ventilated lobby or hall between a bathroom/ WC and a living room or kitchen. It might be that a bathroom can open directly off a bedroom – as long as there is a second set of facilities elsewhere in the house.

▓ If you are planning a loft extension or wanting to add a third storey, you will usually need special fire doors at each level.

Cool in cream

Stripping the floors and keeping to a limited number of colours throughout preserves the feeling of space and light in this elegant upper ground-floor flat in a Regency house.

Above *Cream is the theme for this calm-looking bedroom, with its elegant shutters. Serena renovated the junk shop chest of drawers by rubbing it over with candle wax then painting it with cream eggshell, for a 'distressed' look. She also made the soft drape over the bed, which helps accentuate the ceiling height.*

Below right *The purple-walled dining room is a theatrical contrast with the rest of the flat. A large mirror on one wall reflects what light there is and helps foster a feeling of space. The screen reflected in it was retrieved from a shop window display.*

Far right *The purity of the colour scheme preserves the elegance of this high-ceilinged living room. A trio of Serena's mosaic boules sit on the sideboard, which has been painted to match the walls and hides the television. The purple velvet cushions add a splash of colour to the room's otherwise cool tones.*

Simplicity was the key note for the way in which Serena has decorated her two-bedroom flat. Not wanting to detract from the rooms' generous proportions and handsome features – such as shutters, cornices and fireplace – she has opted for a pared-down but comfortable look, using a cool colour scheme throughout.

Serena has recently given up her hair-dressing business for a more precarious but more fulfilling existence as a mosaic artist and has therefore had to decorate and furnish her flat on a shoestring. At the same time she has radically revised her taste in furnishings: 'I used to collect antiques and have them all out on display around the flat,' she says, but she now prefers the simpler, minimalist look. Since she uses the flat as a gallery for her own work and for that of other local artists and crafts-people, it has to retain a spacious feel and remain free of clutter.

The ash floorboards were stripped and varnished and a light cream was chosen as the predominant colour throughout the flat. All the walls and ceilings were painted with egg-shell paint, a time-consuming task given the height and decorative detail of the ceilings. This cool colour has been followed through the flat in most of the furniture, with cream rugs, upholstery fabric and painted chests.

The only room in which strong colour has been used is the dining room – a through area between the hallway and kitchen where the walls are a vibrant, specially mixed shade of purple. 'I didn't see the point of trying to make a naturally dark room any lighter,' says Serena of her colour choice. To link the area with other rooms in the flat she has purple velvet cushions on the pale sofa in the living room.

Examples of Serena's work are in all the rooms. A dramatic mosaic mirror above the fireplace in the sitting room is made from glass cut to precise shapes and sizes. In fact, it was designing a mosaic panel for the pink bathroom she had inherited that inspired her to make ceramics her new career.

'It was just like walking into candy floss,' says Serena. 'I couldn't wait to rip it all out and start again. But the bathroom initiated my interest in mosaic art. I wanted to do something simple but effective so I designed

a mosaic around the bath. I enjoyed doing it so much that I went on to make similar mosaics for other surfaces in the flat, then an artist friend of mine encouraged me to exhibit at the local Festival – and it just went on from there.'

The art of restoration

Courage, hard physical work and an eye for bargains sustained Paula through the restoration of her huge Victorian house. Its original condition was such that the council declared it 'uninhabitable', but her now inviting home has made all the hard work and financial hardship worthwhile.

When Paula embarked on the renovation of an 'eight-bedroom derelict Victorian monstrosity' with a budget that was half the estimated cost of restoration, she knew the following year would be a living nightmare. Luckily, Paula and her 13-year-old son Luke were able to envisage the finished house, which helped them see past the squalor, damp and rubble they had to put up with for over a year. A combination of recycled materials, helpful builders working for a day rate, her own hard labour, some luck in the form of an improvement grant from the local council, and a series of Premium Bond windfalls, got Paula through and she now has a lovingly restored family home with plenty of space.

Much of her budget was spent on unglamorous necessities such as a new roof, treating the house for dry rot, repairing all the windows and having the whole house rewired. Once these basics were taken care of, Paula spent the remaining money on fitting a new kitchen and bathroom. After that, she had to rely on her own hard work and hunting for second-hand furnishings. Junk shops and skips were scoured for bargains or rubbish that could be recycled. Paula had a rule: the items had to be of good quality and preferably outside her normal price range when new. Among her more valuable finds were a batch of school radiators, two pairs of beautiful French windows for the kitchen, a quantity of old but unused lino tiles for a fraction of their value and enough 'old stock' paint to decorate the whole house at a 75 per cent reduction.

Much of the sanitaryware came from ends of ranges or salvage depots – although she drew the line at second-hand WCs. Finding a 'rusting heap' of fire surrounds in a builder's yard, Paula struck a deal and bought them as a job lot. Her star bargain was the nearly new boiler removed from a doctor's surgery and sold to her for a very small sum. The underlay for six flights of stairs and landings came from an optician's that was being recarpeted; the contractor gave it to Paula for nothing.

Her refusal to be daunted and her determination to keep going have certainly paid off and she now has a wonderful home.

Above *Painting the walls in the entire house represents months of Paula's labour of love. The rich red used here offsets beautifully the walnut bed head and Arts and Crafts bedside table in one of the bedrooms.*

Far left *One of the fire surrounds found in a builder's yard and lovingly restored now features in a small sitting room; a reclaimed school radiator sits in an alcove. Painting the floor is an imaginative way of cutting costs and doing without carpet; the blue border gives the room a stylish finishing touch.*

Below left *The decorative French doors were perhaps the most exciting of Paula's second-hand finds and give the kitchen an enhanced elegance. Simple quarry tiles make a practical floor covering and the café curtain is one of Paula's economical window treatments.*

living rooms

The living room serves many functions in modern-day life. It is a space in which to relax, to read, to watch television or to work. It is where you will entertain visitors and it may well have to accommodate the needs of children. It is the public face of your private life so it must look good, but it must work efficiently too.

A place to relax

Creating a balanced and beautiful living room requires careful initial assessment. The role of this room varies from household to household and the space must be tailored to suit your personal needs before any paint effects and fabric swatches enter into the equation.

Using the space

A living room should be comfortable, warm and well lit. It will probably be required to house a full range of home-entertainment equipment – from television and video to music system and computer. It is also likely to contain books, toys, magazines, pictures, assorted *objets* and treasured family heirlooms. It is the place where you can relax and entertain yourself, your family and your friends and will need to accommodate many different moods.

Your first priority must be comfort. The living room must fit in with your lifestyle, not restrict it, so start by making a realistic appraisal of the available space and how you want to use it. An all-white living room is a haven of peace and tranquillity only if children and pets are permanently banished. And the most stylish showplace could prove to be a complete waste of space if it is never used. So look at the shape and proportions of your living space. The position of doors, windows or a fireplace will naturally dictate a certain style and layout of furniture. Don't fight any such restrictions too hard, but work with them instead.

Living rooms must be warm enough for comfort and have flexible lighting that will allow a number of different activities in the room. The style of chairs and sofas is less significant than how the seating is grouped. And storage in the living room should allow the household to deal with its conflicting interests. Storage should contain the necessities, like the television, while keeping them readily accessible. It is the things we use most often that we must work hardest to incorporate into the overall scheme.

Once you have a clear understanding of the structure and function of the living room you can move on to build mood and atmosphere with colour, print and texture, confident in the knowledge that the room will not only feel comfortable, but also look wonderful.

Above *Make a focal point of strong architectural features. Here, beautiful windows serve as display space and reflect and enhance the mood of the room as a whole.*
Left *Armchairs enhance seating flexibility in the living space. Mix different styles and upholstery fabrics to bring a touch of individuality to an otherwise co-ordinated room. Neutral fabrics always maintain decorative harmony.*
Below *Your living space should be inviting, offering cushions for comfort, a safe site for food and drink, and somewhere to put your feet up.*

living room checklist

▨ Start collecting pages from magazines, paint cards and fabric swatches to determine the colours and styles that appeal.

▨ Get the basics right first – electrics, lighting, heating and flooring must suit your requirements.

▨ A few pieces of furniture on wheels allow you to adjust seating, storage and table arrangements to suit the occasion. Position chairs to allow for ease of conversation and remember that a three-seater sofa is comfortable for only two people.

▨ When grouping furniture and tables, allow room for outstretched legs.

▨ A dimmer switch on central lighting will allow you to control the mood of the living space.

Hearth and home

Where facilities allow, there is nothing to beat the sheer beauty and primeval pleasure of an open fire. No matter how efficient modern heating systems may be, the hearth retains its appeal and provides a natural focus for a group of seats, even when not in use.

Burning up

Central heating, once a luxury, is now regarded as the norm. In the first flush of central heating fervour many fireplaces were sealed up, but today the appeal of the working fireplace is once again recognized and it features in most new homes.

The charm of a real fire is hard to define. An open fire is hardly a labour-saving option – the fuel has to be brought in and stored, dust and dirt are generated and the fireplace requires endless cleaning. But there is no denying the pleasure derived from sitting in front of an open log fire; the sensory flicker of the flames and snap of the logs are deeply satisfying.

Fuel your pleasure

Wood burning stoves are less trouble to clean and are less of a fire hazard – there is no chance of a spark or stray log damaging the hearth rug. Smokeless coal is more environmentally friendly than wood fuel and is a requirement in certain areas.

Coal-effect gas fires offer the look, but they do lack the atmosphere of a real fire. They don't give out a great deal of heat, but they can prove a good compromise if a real fire is not for you.

It does not matter that a fireplace is not in use all the year round, but you should pay some attention to what you will do to fill the space off-season. Fire screens or decorated panels offer a solution. Hunt them down in markets and antique shops or make your own. Alternatively, you can fill the hearth with driftwood, fir cones, shells or even dried flowers.

The mantelpiece is a great decorative surround, although it's too easy to load it up with favourite pieces and leave it like that for ever. Displays should be flexible. As a rule of thumb, opt for either the stark minimalist approach of one or two simple striking pieces, or a colourful assortment of textures and styles.

Lighting up

If you want to unblock a fireplace or fit a wood burning stove then seek expert advice. Getting a fireplace working again may not be as simple as merely unblocking it and you could have a considerable financial outlay. For example, chimneys may need to be lined to prevent smoke seeping into other parts of the house. Remember to have chimneys swept at least once a year to prevent a build-up of soot. If children use the living room you must fit a fireguard to prevent accidents. Smoke alarms should be fitted in all homes as a matter of course. If you don't have them already, then get them now.

Right *This contemporary hearth shows that open fires need not be traditional in approach.*

Above *This beautiful fireplace remains a strong focal point, even out of season. A fire screen conceals the dead space but is unassuming enough to allow other features to draw the eye away.*

Below *Fireplaces automatically attract the eye even when out of commission. Here, tall striking plants make a clean and modern design statement in an empty fireplace.*

Seating and loose covers

Comfortable seats are of great importance in a living room, whatever style you opt for. Seating should be positioned to look sociable yet to allow a little privacy when required. It must look and feel fabulous.

Group positions

The placement of chairs and sofas within a room is as significant as the style of the furniture itself. Seating has an impact on how people behave. Two sofas facing each other can feel formal. One sofa is acceptable if you are alone, but can be too intimate if you are sharing it. A mix of seating, combining both sofas and armchairs, offers the best choice, allowing people to sit where they will feel most comfortable. Mixing different kinds of furniture will achieve a distinctive and individual signature style. The contemporary approach to living is less formal and more creative, so you really can please yourself.

Furniture can also be used to create different areas within a room. This is especially important in the living room, which can have so many functions in a family home. Not everyone will want to watch the television at once, for example, so a separate space where it is pleasant and light enough to read or work in comfort will keep all the family happy.

Old and new

If you are buying a new item, take a little time to test out different styles. Once you have found something you like, sit down and don't move for 10 minutes. This is an

Left Old chairs, here painted and reupholstered, have a style and charm of their own that suit the contemporary as well as the traditional living room.

important purchase and must please your physique as well as your eye. Of course, you don't have to buy a contemporary design, it is deeply satisfying to track down a wonderful old sofa and have it reupholstered to your specifications. A sheet thrown over it can act as a temporary cover if funds are low.

Covering up

Upholstery in the living room will have to withstand considerable wear and tear so buy the best materials you can afford and if you are on a tight budget look for sale items or special lines. Loose or slip covers are practical, easy to clean and flexible. By changing the covers you change the style – the Victorians used to do this seasonally. Moreover, loose covers are not hard to make at home and can range from simple styles with self-ties to more complex constructions.

No matter how careful you are, accidents always happen, and ruby red fruit juice dribbled over the back of a cream sofa can make quite an impact on your decor. If you are buying new, try to make sure that parts of the upholstery can be removed for cleaning. It is also advisable to have furniture treated against stains so that they will throw off rather than absorb spills. Retailers can advise if this facility is on offer. This, of course, is where investing in loose covers really pays. If your family are accident-prone, or you are throwing a party, a few artfully arranged blankets and throws will offer some short-term protection.

Above Loose covers can dramatically transform chairs in a moment. Here a heady mix of blue and white checks blend together for real impact.

Below Warm, soft and inviting, this sumptuous pink upholstery introduces a strong design statement. Mix patterns and textures with confidence.

Armchairs

The days of the three-piece suite are over and armchairs can make as individual a statement as you like. The two main requirements are that an armchair should be comfortable to sit in and that its lines should complement the overall style of your living room.

Armchairs are more mobile than sofas, especially if fitted on castors, and the best seating plans comprise a mixture of the two, offering a flexibility that allows you to cater for different occasions – from family television viewing to entertaining visitors.

Whereas the lines of a sofa are often simple and quite formal, a single armchair can make a bolder style statement, or be quirky. You can mix and match styles, but it is best if an individual armchair is linked with the overall scheme in some way – perhaps in colour or the upholstery design.

Try out a new armchair for seat depth, height and the firmness of the springing, as you would a sofa (see page 28); upholstered armchairs may have a separate seat 'cushion', filled with feather or foam. Some modern armchairs are more streamlined in style, with the shape of the seat moulded for comfort.

New life for an old armchair

If your living room gets a lot of wear, and especially if used by young children, loose covers may be the answer. It is often the details that count – a valance or edging can do much to reinforce the style of loose covers. A squashy old armchair can be smartened up with a firm new cushion and neatly tailored covers piped at the seams. An upholstered wing chair with exposed legs will look less formal clad in loose covers, with a valance reaching to the ground. A gathered valance around the lower edge of an armchair gives it a country look, while box pleats indicate a smart, urban style.

Cover-up ideas

▨ When choosing an upholstery fabric, look for durability, closely woven texture and fade resistance.

▨ Think about a stain-resistant finish for fixed upholstery, especially if you opt for pale or neutral colours. Or spray with a fabric protector to make it easier to sponge off dirty marks.

▨ If you are having an armchair re-covered, have a separate set of arm covers made for where the chair gets most wear. Keep these in place for everyday use and remove them for washing or dry cleaning when they become grubby.

▨ Prolong the life of loose covers by having two sets and changing them over from time to time – perhaps with the seasons.

▨ Draping a throw – in tartan, plaid or paisley – over the back of an armchair will soften its appearance and give a warm, cosy look for winter.

A contemporary classic swivel armchairs combine form and function beautifully in a design that is as appropriate for the modern living room as it is for the office.

Recliner on metal frame *has an adjustable footrest; it is upholstered in dark blue cotton.*

Wooden-framed upholstered *wing chair has feather-filled seat cushion; 'flamestitch' fabric enhances its traditional appeal.*

Budget armchair *with solid beech legs is covered with a washable slipcover in durable cotton.*

Curvaceous cane-frame *'tub' chair mixes easily with modern and with traditional seating. It has a removable feather-filled seat cushion.*

Traditional straight-backed *'library' chair is upholstered in spongeable velour.*

Thickly plaited coir weave *gives this classic wing chair a new twist; it has a solid wooden frame and removable foam-filled cushion.*

Square-frame 'reading' *armchair is designed for comfort, with a solid oak frame and multi-density foam-filled seat and back.*

Wide-seat upholstered *armchair is fitted with castors for manoeuvrability. Although traditional in style, the checked fabric gives a contemporary look.*

Contemporary 'club' *armchair has beech frame with foam-filled cushions and stainless steel legs; it is perfect to curl up in.*

Sofas

Nothing makes a more immediate statement about your style than your choice of sofa. Classic or cutting-edge, patterned or plain, damask or calico – whatever you choose sums up the look you want. But since there is more to a sofa than its cover, it is worth finding out what's underneath to make sure that you're sitting pretty.

Of course, you won't use your sofa in isolation, so how it relates to the other seating in the room is important, too. If you already have a couple of eye-catching pieces – a bright 'tub' chair or a sculptural chaise longue for example – it might be a good idea to choose a simple shape for the sofa. The same applies if you want to buy a pair of sofas. Two unusual styles might look great if you live in a loft but could compete with each other in the average living room.

Put your feet up

Comfort is essential unless your sofa is strictly for occasional use, so it is important to try before you buy. The seat should be deep enough for you to sit without your feet dangling; a good tip is to choose a higher seat for each decade of your life. And beware the very long sofa. Few people like to play piggy-in-the-middle so, however many they are designed for, most sofas will, in practice, seat only two.

Fillings and frames

■ Most sofas are filled with foam and polyester fibre for comfort and resilience. Check the depth of the filling in both seat and back cushions; too little and you may feel the sofa frame through the padding.

■ Check the frame for excess movement, which indicates poor workmanship. It needs to be robust enough to take your weight every evening for up to 10 years.

■ Luxury sofas may have feather or feather and down cushions (wonderfully comfortable but need plumping up to stay in shape), a sprung base and hardwood frame.

■ Look for a seat that reclines at 110 degrees to follow the natural slope of your back and give lumbar support.

A budget sofa with a removable washable cover has large squashy scatter cushions to lean back on.

Long, feather-filled *lumbar cushion gives unexpected comfort to this sleek modern style.*

Curved back and skirt *give a sculptured look to this simple sofa.*

Modern classic design *fits into a variety of settings. The sofa's minimal arms are a useful space-saving device.*

Low arms *are a feature of this traditional-style sofa; its feather-filled seat cushions, beech frame and hand-tied springs put the accent on quality.*

Brocade-covered *Georgian-style sofa has the slim seat and walnut pad feet typical of the period.*

Two and a half-seater *sofa with gently curved arms and back has feather-filled seat cushions and turned wooden feet, with castors.*

Loose cushions *add support to a low-back sofa and soften the look. The box-pleat 'skirt' gives a particularly smart finish.*

End cushions *add comfort to this neat, compact style of sofa with narrow arms.*

Deep-pile velvet *upholstery and wide arms make this design a natural for lounging on.*

Contemporary ideas

The inspired use of colour has transformed an industrial space into a vibrant contemporary home in which the open-plan living area is as comfortable as it is eye-catching.

Above The clean, modern lines of the curvaceous sofas and glass-topped coffee table stand out against the stark walls and metal ceiling.

Below right Sliding glass doors open on to the decked roof terrace, which acts as an outdoor dining room in summer.

The generous sitting area is the main focus of the airy first-floor living space in this two-floor apartment. Penny, a successful florist, has a wonderful eye for colour and has used it to ingenious effect to create a stylish yet welcoming living room, dominated by two shapely sofas. The use of colour is dramatically set off against the almost industrial backdrop favoured by husband Paul, an architect. 'Paul had a strong feeling for building in the style of 1950s California,' explains Penny. 'There's no plaster on the walls and the ceilings are corrugated metal.'

While the apartment was being built, on the site of a disused garage which they had bought and had demolished, Penny admits she had doubts about living there. The empty interior seemed harsh, with its exposed steel columns and stairs that looked like fire escapes. But the use of primary colours has energized the space and makes it work; warm wooden flooring and a wall of bookshelves at one end make it feel like a home. Penny and Paul planned the colour scheme around their bright red sofas and Paul painted a large, dramatic canvas that pulls all the primaries together. An equally strong blue is used for the dividing unit that separates off the kitchen area and is picked up in the rug that softens the hardwood floor. Yellow appears throughout in a minor key – in cushions and lampshades.

The wide open space of this unconventional apartment meets the needs of both home and business. Penny's workshop and studio are at ground level. Above is the living area, where Penny likes to try out new ideas with her flowers, and from here, galvanized metal stairs lead up to bedrooms on the upper floor. A wall of sliding glass windows opposite the kitchen end of the living room opens on to a decked roof terrace. The iroko flooring of the interior simply continues through to the terrace, where it has weathered to a soft, silvery grey. In good weather, the terrace becomes an outdoor dining room, with its climbing plants such as jasmine and Virginia creeper softening the industrial outlines of the building.

Right Opposite the glass doors, a cobalt blue unit, made in stainless steel, divides the kitchen from the living area. In front of it are Marcel Breuer chairs, a design classic perfectly suited to the contemporary lines of this elegant living space.

Old and new

This sophisticated living room, decorated and furnished on a budget, owes its charm to the mix of old and new furniture, combined with the restored original features in the room and the use of a cool, pale colour scheme to pull it all together.

Above The pale leather sofa and cream silk curtains set the tone for this elegant living room. The painted cupboard and scrolled metalwork chair are among Josie's successfully renovated junk-shop finds, and the original fireplace has been burnished to a soft sheen.

Right Modern ceramics from Josie's collection sit on the ornate French console table she found at an antiques market. Wall sconces holding candles on either side of the pier-glass mirror match the beautiful chandelier that hangs from the ceiling.

It was the generous size of the living room that sold the large Edwardian house to Josie and her husband Matt. 'When I stepped into the sitting room I knew this was my dream home – the proportions were perfect,' says Josie.

The room's original features, such as the fireplace and deep cornices, clinched it. However, it was many months before the couple could enjoy their lovely living room since the whole house, which had been empty for three years before they bought it, had first to be completely renovated from top to bottom.

By the time the necessary structural work on the house had been carried out, Matt and Josie were left with a limited budget for decorating and even less for furniture. Fortunately, Josie has a passion for finding and restoring junk, which, she says, 'grew out of necessity. Worn furniture that needs renovating is my thing.' A further setback occurred when the couple discovered dry rot in the newly decorated living room.

'The whole building was soaked when we bought it as the roof was leaking. It had to be replumbed, rewired and re-roofed.' The water penetration had resulted in the dry rot, which had permanently damaged several of the floorboards in the living room.

So, the second time around, Josie, who says she is 'not a carpet person', opted for wall-to-wall matting and an antique-style needlepoint rug.

Apart from the flooring, the couple restored their original decorating scheme, using a soft grey shade for the walls above the dado rail because it had the right period feel. Also, it fitted well with Josie's collection of modern ceramics from California and with the pale leather sofa, which was the first piece of furniture she and Matt bought. Cream silk curtains edged with shades of pink and raspberry were made up by a specialist firm and give the room an opulent sense of luxury. Although Josie adores dark reds and purples, she always opts for pale curtains to let in as much light as possible. The pinks are picked up in the room's lampshades and cushions.

Most of the furniture in the room is French, including the large console table and the cupboard in the alcove, which Josie repainted to blend with the room's colour scheme. The elegant pier glass above the console table reflects light from the windows back into the room. Since the house has a separate family room, with space for toys and games as well as sofas and a television, this living room, with its luxury fabrics and pale tones, is a room firmly designated for adult use.

Timeless style

The simplest decorating schemes are often the most effective and certainly the most tranquil ones. The clever use of inexpensive natural fabrics brings style and comfort to this living room without trying to be fashionable.

Above *Striped cushions adorn the simple modern sofa, which is covered in a natural upholstery fabric, while the soft throw in another of Edward's fabrics picks up the blue. The floor-length curtains are something he now wishes to change.*

Below right *Built-in shelves house favourite books and the wall above makes a good display space for some of Edward's collection of paintings.*
Right *The old Indian cupboard hides the stereo system. Next to it, the reading chair is upholstered in a simple striped cotton fabric. The subdued wall and floor colours allow the bright hues of the large canvas to shine out.*

The simplest and most inexpensive of fabrics can be turned into designer furnishings for the living room, or for any other room in the house. This is admirably demonstrated in the home of a successful owner of furnishing fabric shops in London.

'Bright colours have become more acceptable in this country, but my business isn't about fashion,' says Edward. 'It's about natural, inexpensive fabrics and showing people how to make utility materials like calico and ticking look stylish for both curtains and upholstery.'

In the three-storey family home he shares with his wife, Kirsty, a mixture of simple, natural fabrics and furniture create restful, unfussy rooms that are easy on the eye. No particular period style prevails; 'I don't favour a particular era, although I feel I relate best to the 1930s style, with its curved lines, because I dislike hard edges,' says Edward.

Kirsty, a graphic designer-turned-painter, is comfortable with her husband's design ideas and happy to let him deal with the house. 'I like his style,' she says. 'It's not chintzy with lots of bits and bobs around.' She generally lets Edward deal with the house although they do make

joint decisions, too. She recalls that it particularly amused the builders, who are used to asking women about colour schemes, to see the reverse situation in this household.

Kirsty concentrates on painting portraits and is preparing for her first exhibition, while Edward has collected paintings for many years and has a fascination with people. As a result, many of the pictures adorning the walls of their living room are in fact portraits.

Edward cannot bear clutter and prefers everything to be functional, without being starkly minimal. The striking grille-fronted cupboard in the living room, with its original paint, is used to house the stereo system. The cupboard came from India, where a good proportion of the fabrics that Edward sells are manufactured.

These natural fabrics – ginghams, tickings, muslin and calico – are used in the living room, as well as throughout the rest of the house, for curtains, blinds and upholstery. 'My fabrics and colourways are easy to live with. I hate to see people buying fashionable colours only to wonder why, when they're no longer in vogue,' says Edward. 'I concentrate on timeless style.'

Loft living

Living in a converted loft apartment in the city centre demands a single-minded approach to how the space is used and how it is furnished. The light, uncluttered space, minimally furnished using contemporary materials, is a perfect place to relax at the end of a hectic working day.

When bachelor Robin Frost bought his top-floor apartment in a newly converted department store, he knew that none of his furniture would look right in it. He had, in the past, bought traditional and period furniture but realized that this stark, contemporary environment dictated a new approach. He responded to the challenge in a radical way by giving away most of his existing pieces to family and friends, and sticking to a modern theme when he went shopping for new furniture. His idea was to mix contemporary styles of furniture in glass, metal and chrome with bold panels of single colour. 'I was trying to avoid clutter and leave as much clear space as I could,' he says. 'So moving here was as much about having a lifestyle clear-out and throwing away everything I had no use for.'

When Robin came to visit the show flats, he had been dazzled by the expanse of light and space in the building. He loved the combination of sand-blasted brick, white-painted walls and natural wood but, above all, was struck by the imaginative use the architects had made of the space. The main living area in his top-floor apartment is light and airy, with three windows overlooking the street. It has a kitchen to the rear and an open-plan bed deck-study above it. Although the living space is generous, there is no storage, so Robin drastically pruned his personal possessions as well as his furniture. This meant ditching clothes he no longer wore, books he had already read, CDs he no longer played and an accumulation of out-of-date paperwork. He found the experience a challenge but 'very liberating'.

The brand new apartment came with white-painted walls and floor covering throughout: Robin chose seagrass over wood for the floors because of its affinity with bare brick walls and wooden beams, and he felt it would add warmth to a rather stark environment. He considers lighting one of the most important aspects of furnishing a loft: 'My white walls can look cream or magnolia or soft grey, depending on the light.' The galvanized light fittings were bought in a sale just before moving in. After much deliberation, Robin decided on silver Venetian blinds for the windows, since curtains would have looked out of place, but he only closes the blinds on wild winter nights. 'Where I live is very personal. It doesn't worry me that the apartment does not look what some may consider to be homely. For me the flat is more to do with finding peace and tranquillity after work.'

Above left *Ornament is kept to a minimum, but the glass coffee table is used to display a few favourite objects.*
Below *Above the kitchen end of the living room steep steps lead up to the bed deck, a second 'bedroom', which is also used as a study. White folding chairs are space-savers and blend with the white walls.*

Right *Robin kept to a modern, minimalist theme when furnishing his living space. A pair of blue sofas provide broad slabs of colour, while occasional tables are made of either glass or metal. The metallic-looking silver slatted blinds at the windows have a clean, uncluttered look and let in maximum light.*

Flooring options

The key to success in selecting your floor covering is simply to choose the most suitable material for your environment. Cost, maintenance, durability, comfort and style are all important factors to take into account.

Above *Rugs can be used to introduce pattern and colour to a decorating scheme. This exotic rug acts as a focal point for the room.*

Right *Wooden floorboards are a superb choice for living rooms, being durable and stain resistant, as well as warm and pleasant to the touch.*

Natural finishes

The style of flooring you choose, its colour and its texture, is the start of your decorating scheme. The choice will have an impact on your home for years and a good flooring will see out several changes of decor in the course of its lifespan. It should make a statement, but should not dominate the room.

Soft- and hardwood flooring are both popular options. Floorboards stripped bare and either painted or varnished have classic appeal and are wonderfully durable. Flooring specialists can transform old, dilapidated boards in a few hours and can seal the gaps between them. Alternatively, you can hire a sanding machine and do the job yourself. It is dirty and noisy but very cost-effective. Wooden flooring is especially desirable for households in which someone suffers from allergies or asthma.

However, if you don't already have floorboards, such flooring can prove to be an expensive option. Matting offers an equally natural approach. It can be fitted wall to wall, like carpet, or the edges can be bound and it can sit within the room's boundaries. Matting comes in many different forms. Seagrass is smooth to the touch and comfortable underfoot. More heavyweight matting such as coir and sisal can be useful where greater durability is required.

Carpets and rugs

Carpet is soft and luxurious and there is a massive array of styles on offer. Begin by deciding what type of carpet you require – do you want wool, twist, shag pile, linen, cotton, nylon or tufted? Familiarize yourself with the range, then narrow down your choice. A good dealer will let you take home a sample for a few days to make sure it looks good *in situ*. Don't scrimp on underlay just because it cannot be seen – it will help to keep your carpet in shape. If you are buying a good-quality carpet to last, or opting for a pale shade, invest in a stain inhibiting treatment. It won't prevent staining, but should help you clear up spills more efficiently.

Rugs provide spectacular focal points. There are some beautiful contemporary designs on offer as well as exquisite antiques. They can inject a dash of much needed colour, texture or luxury.

Sound considerations

Sound insulation or acoustics may contribute to your final decision. Sound will bounce in rooms with ceramic or stone floors, whereas carpets will absorb and deaden noise. Wooden floors reflect sound and are regarded as a good choice of flooring for rooms with sound systems.

Vacuum cleaners

What used to be a simple choice between cylinder and upright models is now much more complicated as vacuum cleaners have become more sophisticated and the selection gets ever wider.

The basic difference between the two kinds of vacuum cleaner was that the cylinder model relied mainly on suction, while the upright model used a beater bar (a rotating brush in the cleaning head). Now the technologies are merging, with each style taking some characteristics of the other. The beater bar is key to this: while it is effective in lifting dirt, dust and pet hairs from cut-pile carpets, its disadvantage is that it can damage delicate floors such as polished wood, loop-pile carpets and natural floor coverings such as coir or seagrass. While the beater bar can now be switched off on some uprights so that they function more like

cylinders, some cylinders now come with a turbo brush attachment, which works in a similar way to the beater bar, to give them the advantages of upright vacuum cleaners.

Because there is now such flexibility, what you choose comes down to personal preference. With the cylinder, the cleaning head is in constant contact with the floor, so you have to push against the strength of the suction, whereas the upright has a raised floor head that glides along on wheels, requiring less effort. Uprights are more awkward to use along edges and on stairs, although they have separate tools to tackle this. Cylinders usually have smaller dustbags

that fill up more quickly, although you can choose a bagless model. Bagless cleaners rely on filters, which need replacing every so often – bear in mind the cost of filters or of bags when making your choice. If you have stairs or suffer from arthritis, choose a lightweight machine. For house-holds with pets, a cleaner with a beater bar or turbo brush will help lift hairs – but never use these on loop-pile or natural floor coverings.

What type of floor?

■ If your floor coverings comprise mainly cut-pile carpet, choose an upright or a cylinder with a turbo brush attachment.

■ If you have loop-pile carpeting, natural floor covering like coir, or hard floors such as tiles, stone, wood, lino or vinyl, you need a cylinder or an upright whose beater bar can be turned off.

■ If your floors are a mixture of coverings, choose an upright with optional beater bar or a cylinder with turbo brush attachment.

This hand-held, cordless *cleaner is rechargeable and can be fixed to a wall. Accessories, including crevice tool and upholstery brush, are mounted underneath.*

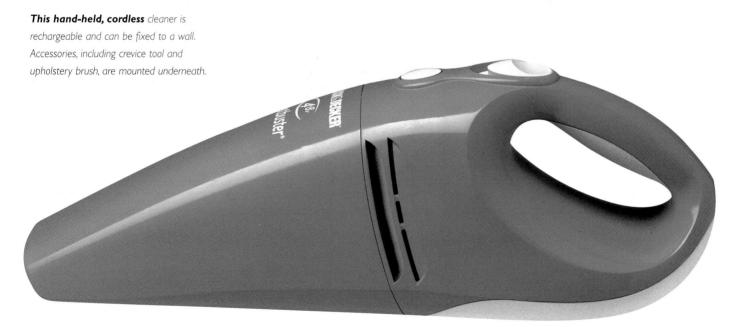

Improved upright *Dyson has a washable filter; although bulky to manoeuvre, it is a good all-rounder with a long hose for stairs.*

Conventional upright *performs well on carpet and hard floors and is good at removing pet hairs; bags and filters need replacing.*

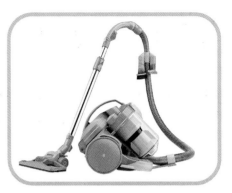

Compact version *of bagless Dyson cylinder has a washable filter and tools attached to flexible hose, but it is an untidy shape to store.*

Cleverly designed upright *converts to an over-the-shoulder cylinder; it has separate cleaning heads for delicate floors and for shampooing carpets.*

Cylinder with turbo brush *and a large-capacity dustbag performs well on all floors; the flexible hose has an integral handle.*

Bagless upright *with washable filter is heavy to manoeuvre but good for getting under furniture; it has automatic cord rewind.*

Space-age bagless 'cylinder' *cleaner, designed so that hose and electric cable are stored inside it; it is excellent for hard floors.*

Versatile cordless *model – use as an upright for carpets, or detach hand-held cleaner and fit with a small brush for stairs and upholstery.*

Chrome finish *makes this cylinder with turbo brush a stylish choice for a household with lots of hard floors and no pets.*

Dressing windows

Curtains and blinds are your shield from the world outside. They control light, keep out the sun and screen your private life from public scrutiny. They must frame your outside view and complement your internal decor.

STYLED TO SUIT

To some extent, your choice of window dressing should be dictated by the window itself. An attractive window is an architectural feature that should be displayed to best effect rather than concealed by great swathes of fabric, while a badly proportioned window can be dressed up to look better. Large rooms with high ceilings can take more elaborate window treatments; smaller rooms demand cleaner, purer lines. Narrow windows can appear wider if curtain poles and curtains extend beyond the frame. Whatever style you choose, it should either harmonize with a few select colours or provide a dramatic contrast with the decor.

Choosing curtains can be a daunting task because there are so many permutations in style, shape or colour. A good first step is to start saving pictures of window treatments that appeal and make decisions from there. You can make curtains from virtually any fabric, including sari lengths, sheets or calico. However, investing in good furnishing fabric and selecting one cohesive look will affect the room as a whole. If in doubt, a good rule of thumb is to keep things simple and allow fabric and architecture to speak for themselves. Curtains should be either window sill or floor length.

Measuring up

To calculate the amount of fabric required, measure the desired length of curtain (allowing extra for headings and hems) and multiply this by the number of curtain widths. To achieve the right degree of fullness, allow between two and three times the width of the window. Final quantities will depend on your choice of fabric and heading. Measure your window accurately on all four sides and check the fall to the ground. Windows can become distorted and there can be a surprising disparity in fall. Such factors can affect your choice of plain or printed fabric. Never scrimp on fabric quantities, as your economy will result in mean-looking curtains and will spoil the finished effect. If necessary, pick a less expensive fabric that will allow you to purchase the correct lengths.

Curtain headings – the gathering at the top of the curtain – dictate style. Tape sewn on at the back determines the shape and size of the gathers and pleats. Your choice of heading will be decided by the mood you want to create and the weight of your fabric.

Making curtains is less complicated than you might think, and haberdashers can advise you on tapes and linings. If you hate sewing or are worried by headings, then curtain clips could be a solution. These attach to the fabric like clothes pegs and thread on to a pole like curtain rings. There are plenty of contemporary curtain headings, including looped, eyelet and cord, if traditional headings are not for you. Whether you hang your curtains from poles or tracking, make sure that they pull smoothly and meet evenly in the centre.

Above Original window shutters leave beautifully proportioned windows undressed for maximum light. They also offer increased security.

Below Slatted Venetian blinds allow you to create different moods with light and shade effects.

Right A plain fabric blind, featuring a border and red trim edge, displays a quiet elegance in keeping with the structure and mood of the room.

BLINDS AND SHUTTERS

Blinds and shutters suit virtually all window shapes. Their clean-lined simplicity works equally well in both contemporary and traditional settings. Moreover, they are very cost-effective compared with curtains.

The humble blind controls light, ensures privacy, helps temperature control and takes up no space at all. Blinds are especially suited to smaller rooms since their clean lines do not eat into the limited space and they maximize light levels. Larger windows are usually best fitted with two or more blinds rather than one vast one. This multi-blind approach allows greater flexibility in the control of light.

In terms of style, there are blinds to suit all environments. Stark Venetian blinds offer great versatility in light and shade control, and suit a minimalist interior. Roman blinds pull up into a series of broad flat folds. They can be made from various fabrics and are equally pretty in lightweight fabrics for low levels of light control. Roller blinds move up and down on a simple roll apparatus –tightly woven materials provide the smoothest finish. Scalloped Austrian or festoon blinds combine the drapery of a curtain with the motion of a blind and require twice the amount of fabric in ratio to window drop. These styles work best when the choice of fabric is kept plain and simple – anything else can rapidly become overblown and fussy. You can also find plenty of ready-made blinds in bamboo, wood, metal and paper for a natural, unassuming statement.

Function and fantasy

Making blinds is much less daunting than tackling curtains. There are kits available for all the different blinds, and tapes, nylon pulls and wooden stops can be bought from haberdashers. It is easier to be creative with a blind than it is with a curtain – mix and match fabric on each side of the fall or create your own ties with strips of material or ribbons. You can even roll a blind by hand and hang it on a piece of dowelling. Hardware stores and ironmongers can be helpful in tracking down custom-made fittings.

The top of a blind can be concealed behind a pelmet or valance. Similarly, windows can be dressed with beautiful swags and drapes and feature poles and finials for purely decorative effect, while a sturdy blind, tucked out of sight, deals with the day-to-day practicalities of privacy and light levels.

Timeless and clean-lined, shutters allow the architectural structure of a window to speak for itself. Traditional shutters made of solid wood can be bought from reclamation sites and cut to size. Louvred plantation shutters fold back on hinges and filter light. It is a straightforward enough job for a carpenter to make some simple wooden shutters to fit your windows.

curtains checklist

▨ When calculating curtain lengths allow an extra 150–250mm (6–10in) overall for heading and hems on sheer and lightweight fabrics, and allow 250mm (10in) for heavier materials.

▨ Never skimp on curtain fabric – for a full effect, curtains should be at least twice as wide as the window they conceal.

▨ If you are making curtains or blinds from fabric prone to shrinkage, wash the fabric beforehand so that perfectly fitting ones won't get spoiled.

▨ Simple blinds can be made inexpensively from a short length of fabric with dowelling top and bottom. Roll up by hand and tie with ribbon or braid. A simple socket and screw mechanism will allow you to fit it inside a deep window recess.

▨ The depth of a pelmet should usually be one-fifth of the curtain drop.

▨ Swing arms, carrying plain screening lengths of fabric, combine function and style in deep recessed or dormer windows.

Displays

A living room must inevitably fulfil many functions: it must be fit for work, rest and play, accommodate vast quantities of household equipment and, at the same time, retain a relaxing atmosphere. The secret lies in great storage and carefully chosen displays.

PRECIOUS MEMORIES

We spend our lives gathering around us things that are precious and pieces that we want to enjoy. This could be anything from photographs to pebbles from the beach. They make a statement about our personality and our sense of style. Mementos and cherished possessions change in emphasis over the years, and the stark purity of displays in a bachelor apartment might later have to make room for a child's first efforts at pottery.

Chaos management

What prevents a group of objects tipping over into complete chaos is careful and considered arrangement. A variety of photographs in a jumble of frames will look messy when scattered around a room so, instead, hang them all together on one area of wall. Either re-frame them for unity, or mix and match artfully to make an individual display, perhaps re-framing the odd photograph.

A collection of like objects acquires weight and gravitas – balanced displays are pleasing where disparate pieces are confusing. However, you also need to maintain some clearly defined areas of space. The room must still be lived in and it is essential that you have tables on which to place cups, snacks, glasses of wine and books. Blanket chests make wonderful tables and double up as storage space.

Showing off

If you have a great many personal effects you may need to consider special display units. Glass cabinets will clear the decks and allow you to show off treasured collections while reducing dusting.

Lighting adds the finishing touch and shows your treasured possessions to best effect. Table-top collections can be highlighted by a table lamp, pictures by overhead picture lights and bookcases can house discreet strip lights, either below or at the sides of the shelves.

Top left *Do not cram storage units to capacity; try to break up uniform lines wherever possible.*
Below left *Groups of similar objects make a wonderful display whatever their individual worth, as seen in this homely collection of jugs.*
Right *Symmetry is pleasing to the eye, so instead of scattering pictures pull them together for a strong visual impact.*

STORAGE SOLUTIONS

The living room usually houses the home-entertainment systems and the television tends to be a focus of attention. For some people, the position of the television dictates the layout of their living space; others like to minimize its impact. Either way it should be integrated into the room so that it does not dominate. A perfect solution is to house the television on a mobile platform, perhaps with the video recorder tucked underneath, so you can easily wheel it about as required. The rule is that it must be trouble-free to operate – yards of trailing wires or lots of lifting will be a disincentive, and the dreaded box will invade your space permanently.

Out of sight

As changing technology influences our day-to-day lives, storage must be carefully planned. It should be easy to link up the

music centre with the television so you can enjoy dual coverage of big events, or to indulge in some home shopping with your cable facilities close at hand. CDs should be housed close to music systems, likewise videos to the video recorder, but while CDs can make an acceptable display, videos always look ugly and should be kept out of sight in a cupboard or a drawer.

Everything in its place

List everything you need to house in your living space – from sewing kit to books, videos and CDs. Look at how much space they currently occupy to help you assess the storage space required, then design your new system and get a carpenter to help you build it. Alternatively, you could build a deep window seat and create a fantastic hidey-hole for bits and pieces underneath. The recesses either side of the chimney breast can be a good space for storage, but do not regularize every nook and cranny. A room should not be boxed into extinction.

Storage units do not have to be modern in style. Old cupboards, desks, chests and wardrobes can all be lovingly restored or painted and their interiors redesigned to suit requirements. Don't fill shelves to bursting from the start; instead, give the living room time to grow with you. Utilize boxes of all descriptions to contain play bricks, drawing materials, pens, paper or seed catalogues so that it is easy to maintain order.

---

shelving and storage ideas

● A few short lengths of staggered shelving are not only more visually appealing than one or two long lengths but also less likely to buckle under heavy weights such as books.

● Add wooden beading or scalloped leather library trims to decorate plain wood shelves.

● Break up lines of books with a picture, a vase or some solitary artefact to stop horizontals becoming oppressive.

● Group like objects together for impact, be it collectibles or pictures.

● Blinds or screens can be used effectively to conceal banks of electrical equipment needed for a home-entertainment system or a home office.

● Ensure power points are conveniently sited and that you have enough to suit demand. Organizing your life in terms of storage is pointless if the back-up systems are inadequate.

Above A small
decorative piece like
this découpage drawer
unit is both functional
and appealing.

Left A dual-purpose
low, mobile drawer
unit offers both storage
and display.

Far left Use every
inch of space with
imaginative storage
and tuck the dreary
basics out of sight;
this ottoman houses
a collection of CDs.

Tables

Coffee tables, occasional tables or side tables – every living room needs one or more small tables on which to display books or objects, stand a lamp or a vase of flowers, set down a glass of wine or rest a coffee cup.

Occasional and side tables are generally used for displaying flowers, photographs or china. Position them carefully, as you don't want them to block traffic routes through a room. If they hold a lamp, they are best sited against a wall and near to a power point so the flex does not trail across the floor. These tables are usually a conventional height, place lower models next to a sofa or armchair for convenience when people are seated. They may be made of solid wood, wood and glass, wicker or metal – choose materials and style to fit with the rest of your furniture and the mood of the room.

Coffee tables

Low coffee tables are often part of a seating group and hold magazines or books. When you are entertaining, they come into their own for glasses and plates of nibbles; if the surface is not heatproof you will need to supply mats for hot drinks. You can improvise by using a large footstool, blanket box, antique trunk or butler's tray on folding legs.

Space-saving ideas

■ A glass-topped table looks lighter and less space-consuming so is ideal for a small room.

■ Folding tables offer the most flexible solution as they can be stacked against a wall to be opened out when required.

■ Since a single large coffee table can dominate a room, it may be better to scatter several small tables more or less in front of a sofa.

In a design based on space and motion, *this triple occasional table in glass and steel is a work of art in itself.*

Curvaceous glass-topped steel coffee table with scrolled ends has a magazine rack underneath.

Traditional-style side table with lower shelf is elegantly crafted and veneered in walnut.

One of a series of modernistic side tables in grey powder-coated steel.

Budget-range folding table in stained wood brings colour to an informal room.

Solid pine table is sturdy and of a simple enough design to fit with any style of room.

Two-section pine coffee table has open magazine storage below the toughened glass top and a drawer concealed beneath the wooden top.

Round occasional table has a steel stand, while the top is made of aluminium-coated MDF.

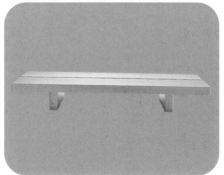

Sleek, elegant design in maple veneer particleboard could suit a minimalist interior.

Castors and a lower shelf make this contemporary aluminium table useful and extremely flexible.

Lights and lamps

The whole atmosphere of a living room is affected by the way it is lit, so you need to think carefully about overhead lighting, wall lights and table lamps. There is as wide a range of shades as there is of fittings, make a choice that is in keeping with the style of your room, and fit a dimmer to the main lighting to vary the mood.

Good illumination in the living room entails using several different types of lighting. Seating areas need general background lighting in the form of ceiling or wall lights that cast a warm, inviting glow, in addition to special 'task' lighting, provided by table or standard lamps. These may be supplemented by 'accent' lighting, to focus on a particular highlight such as a picture, a plant, a shelf display or an architectural feature.

In a large living room, especially one that includes a dining area or that doubles as a home study, it is a good idea to install several different lighting circuits so that you can 'fade out' the part of the room not in use. Connect at least one of the lighting circuits to a dimmer switch to adjust the light levels. For flexibility, include some table lamps, standard lamps and uplighters that can easily be moved around – this will mean fitting plenty of power points.

Fashions in lampshade styles come and go, and range from tall, slim ones to wide, 'coolie' shades that need a lot of space. Paired lamps with matching shades have a formal look.

Lighting tips

■ Always use 'candle' bulbs (of the right wattage) in chandeliers to simulate the original look.

■ Use clip-on spotlights as display lighting on the edges of shelves to illuminate book titles or decorative objects.

■ In a room with period features, light friezes and cornices unobtrusively from below using small low-voltage spotlights.

■ If you have a low ceiling, avoid pendant lights and fit recessed downlighters instead.

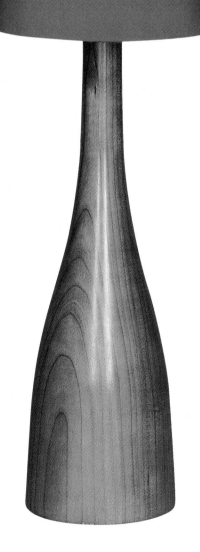

A retro-style table lamp with a tapering cherry wood base and a slim shade made of card.

Ceiling-mounted halogen *spotlights on tracks allow light to be angled where it is needed.*

Bistro-style pendant *lamps with large globe bulbs have enamel coloured or metallic shades.*

Tripod table lamp *in stained beech with a cream cotton shade.*

Futuristic table lamps *on slim chromed-steel bases have cone-shaped shades in various colours.*

Simple chromed steel *wall lamp with black shade gives subdued background lighting; it is moveable, so the shade can hang down.*

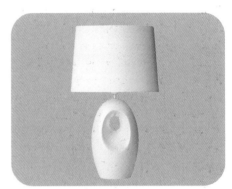

Pierced white ceramic *lamp base with white shade is perfect for a clean, modern interior.*

Slim 'cone' *table light in coated steel with a natural cork shade that comes down to its base.*

Creamy yellow ceramic *base with matching shade; neutral tones gives the best light and complement most colour schemes.*

Square column lamp *has a hand-finished bronze-effect base and a parchment shade.*

Colour schemes

Selecting the best colours for your living room decor may appear a daunting task. It is easy to be overwhelmed by the sheer range of choice and weight of responsibility – after all what delights one person may horrify another. Don't just play safe though – you must enjoy your living space. Think in general terms about rooms that you like or colours and colour mixes that please you to help kick-start the process.

Above Mix bright contrasting colours for dramatic effect, but allow one colour to dominate. Here, a warm hyacinth blue scheme is offset by flashes of lime green and scarlet.

Left Save neutral walls and floors from becoming bland by introducing blocks of colour. Here the bold blue sofa and patterned cushions inject life and texture into the scheme.

Below A sunny yellow treatment bathes the room in a warm glow and provides a superb backdrop for a stark display of keys.

BRIGHT IDEAS

It is only over the last century that we have become more reticent in our use of colour. Look at the amazingly rich tones used in stately homes: the deep red dining room, the sulphur yellow living room, the warm blue study or the violet parlour. The ranges of heritage paints now available show our ancestors' enthusiasm for bright tones.

Using bold colour is an extremely effective way of making a strong decorative statement. It shouts confidence and panache and even if everyone else hates it, they'll be impressed by your strength of mind.

Hot and cold

The sheer variety on offer today is incredibly tempting. Don't be influenced by trends as these simply restrict your choice – this season's hot colour will look dreadfully *passé* in a year's time. Basically, anything goes, as long as it is tackled wholeheartedly. If you feel it's right, it probably will be right.

If you are nervous of colour, the safest way to introduce it to a room is to make the statement on just one wall. A splash of orange or purple surrounded by white will have a powerful effect. The colour can be picked out in other soft furnishings to create a link. Once you've introduced strong colour it becomes quite addictive. Subtle pastels look washed out in comparison.

Minute changes in tone will totally affect the impact of a strong colour, for example, too much yellow in a green paint and it can become dangerously acidic and harsh on the eye. Select your colour carefully, look at it in your home environment and view it in isolation. Buy a small amount to begin with and paint a test area first. Check how it looks in daylight and at night and, if at all possible, in different weather conditions.

Opposites attract

Mixing bright colours together in a room creates a vibrant, exciting scheme. As a rule of thumb, use contrasting colours from opposite sides of the colour wheel – mix green with red, blue with orange, lime with fuchsia and so on.

Don't panic if your choice of colour doesn't seem quite right when it's on the wall. Sometimes adjusting the tone fractionally is all that is required. If the colour is too dark, or too bright, you may be able to tone it down by adding either white or black to the pot. Simply repaint, or sponge over the top for a mottled effect. Mix up a small amount and do a test run first.

NATURAL SHADES

If you are looking for a colour scheme to help you relax and unwind, then you might find neutral tones are your best option since they do create a very calm and soothing environment. The range of neutrals is vast, and a neutral colour scheme provides you with great flexibility and versatility.

Having opted for neutrals, go one step further with the use of exclusively natural materials in the decor – the atmosphere cannot help but be peaceful and serene. A gentle mixture of tones also throws the role of textures into prominence.

Whiter shade of pale

Choosing a neutral colour palette makes a distinctive style statement. Although you may not have to agonize over dramatic colour contrasts, just as much thought and consideration should go into the choice of neutral tones. Deciding to paint a room white, for example, is no easy option, because even white comes in different tones – egg white, milk, bone and so on. If you are working with whites you should mix different tones together to create a link with your furnishings. You want to show off the beauty and purity of the colour, not feel as though you've walked into a blizzard.

Neutral and earthy tones are easy on the eye and suit many different lifestyles. Depending on the treatment and how they are handled they can look sleekly modern or downright rustic.

A bit of rough

Textures seem to reinforce our links with nature, emphasizing purity and simplicity. A lovingly polished piece of wood, some slub silk, a leather cushion or a length of unbleached cotton all blend together for an atmosphere of peaceful calm. To create such a gentle ambience, each element of the room must be carefully considered. Each must pull its weight, yet no one item can be allowed to dominate the overall scheme. You also need to establish a balance between the varying elements of the room. Rough textures must be mixed with smooth – offset a coarsely woven log basket or rush matting, for example, with the perfect smoothness of a weathered stone or the semi-transparent beauty of a voile curtain. In such understated decorating schemes different materials and finishes bring depth and interest to the scene.

Going green

It is possible to take the natural scheme through to its ultimate conclusion and try to create an eco-friendly environment. Use wooden furniture, notably fast-growing softwoods, and unbleached fabrics, such as cotton, linen, silk and wool. You can now buy organic paints that steer clear of the petrochemicals and plastics found in synthetic paints. Walls can be covered in fabric, or you can even recycle newspapers and magazines and create your very own individual wallpaper.

Left Subtle mixes of similar colours are gentle on the eye and focus attention on textural detail.

Below left The simple purity of natural colours and the combined textures of wood, wicker and calico offer a calm and serene decor.

Above Use pure materials to produce a peaceful interior. The pale tones of wood and creamy beeswax candles highlight the dark splendour of the marble mantle. Here, everything is understated and gentle.

USING BLUES

Blue spans a huge range of tones. It is often dismissed as being a cold colour, but this is a great over-simplification. It is in fact a most relaxing and peaceful colour and can range from lavender to hyacinth and from the palest ice blue to the deep, warm hues of the Mediterranean.

From sky to sea

Blue is a colour that is easy on the eye and easy to live with. What more harmonious inspiration could you choose than that of the sky and the sea? The colder shades of blue are the paler, washed-out tones and, while these will certainly seem chilly in a north-facing living room, in a sunny room there is nothing fresher or brighter. Here, an expanse of pale blue will give the room a sense of space and airiness and make it appear larger. It is also easy to energize pale blues by introducing some warmer tones in accessories, such as brighter blues, earthy terracottas and warm golds.

Besides tranquillity and airiness, decorating with blue can also create a vibrant and dramatic look. Using brighter and deeper blues such as turquoise or midnight blue will allow you to create a very individual-looking living room to suit your personality. A deep blue colour scheme can make a cold room feel warm and inviting, like diving into an azure sea, and at night the tones become sensuous and dramatic. Deeper blues mixed with greys or greens are very elegant and provide a wonderful backdrop for wooden floors, furniture and dramatic and classical furnishings.

Blue economy

Blue is a wonderfully homely colour and if you are on a budget it is very easy to co-ordinate and accessorize. What could be prettier than diaphanous white drapes teamed with sea blue walls or cheerful ginghams in red and blue combined with ticking? Calico blinds, shells and stones put together with beach-hut blue paintwork will hint at the seaside.

If it's versatility you are after, then blue is your colour – it goes well with unvarnished or painted boards, with slate or stone floors, seagrass matting or sensuous carpet. It is also a superb colour against which to display collections, since blue is very compatible with the rest of the colour spectrum.

Above Assorted shades of blue mix comfortably together and the clean-lined weaves allow various patterns and textures to harmonize.

Below Deep blue furnishings combine elegance with practicality. The strong colours enhance the warm tones of the polished wooden floor and contrast well with the buttery yellow walls.

Right Soft blue paintwork makes a feature of the door panels and picks up and reinforces the subtle link between vase, bowl and picture.

colour checklist

▨ Empty your living room before you make a final decision on colour and layout. A bare space will allow you to view the room with fresh eyes and can spark off new ideas.

▨ Harmonious schemes use several shades of the same colour, or closely related colours.

▨ Warm colours will counteract the cooling effect of a north-facing room.

▨ Use a dark colour under a dado rail to reduce the visual height of a room, but a light colour on the ceiling to make walls appear higher and to reflect light.

▨ Contrasting colour schemes mix bold colours that complement each other. One colour should dominate, and the other appear as an accent.

You can use neutral colours to blend the two tones together and unite the whole.

▨ Don't panic if the colour looks too pale as you work – paint always looks a little darker when dry.

▨ Cool (receding) colours like blue, violet and green increase the sense of space, while warm (advancing) colours like red, pink and yellow seem to bring walls closer.

▨ For a softer effect on woodwork try using an eggshell or satin finish instead of gloss. Skirtings and window frames do not have to be painted in white and can look stunning in colour.

▨ To make a ceiling look lower and the room cosier, paint the ceiling in a deep colour or add a picture rail.

One room – two schemes

One room can handle any number of decorative schemes subject to preferences in taste and style. The architecture provides the backdrop, you change the emphasis and the mood with paint and furnishing fabric. Here, one room responds to two entirely different treatments.

Above *Country-style cream furniture reflects the natural feel of this scheme; the mix of furniture styles reinforces the sense of easy informality.*
Below *The more textures and patterns – stripes, checks, crewel embroidery, slubs and weaves – that can be mixed together in a monochromatic scheme, the better.*
Above right *Patterned fabrics unify the colour scheme, and button details contribute to the overall effect.*

MONOCHROMATIC COLOUR SCHEME

This spacious south-facing room is light, sunny and airy enough to withstand a great variety of decorative approaches. Here, the treatment is monochromatic. This design principle utilizes a single colour with subtle variation of tone and plenty of textural interest. Blue is combined with creamy neutrals to add a touch of light.

The starting point for the scheme was the vibrant blue of the fireplace tiles. A strong Mediterranean blue emulsion paint covers the walls and totally disproves the old adage that blue is a cold colour. The warm feel is enhanced by the golden tones of the stripped and polished floorboards. The two colours complement each other perfectly, like sand and sea. White against blue can cool the atmosphere but, by utilizing a warm buttery-cream eggshell paint on the fireplace and cornice, the mood of warm intimacy is maintained. The ceiling is painted in the same soft yellow emulsion paint to maintain colour purity and reflect light.

Blue and cream

The crisp floral curtain fabric is within the blue and cream theme, but it introduces a darker shade of blue, that is echoed and reinforced in the sofa upholstery. The plain cream armchair provides a light-coloured contrast. A mixture of patterns, in varying shades of blue, has been chosen for the scatter cushions. Checks, weaves, stripes and embroidered fabrics all work well together and are essential elements in monochromatic schemes, providing a range of shades and textures. The more variety you have, the more successful a scheme can be. Even the little footstool has received singular consideration and features distinctive upholstery.

Group dynamics

The painted wooden furniture emphasizes the room's informal, relaxed mood. Clean-lined and simple, the pieces stand out very effectively against the deep blue paintwork. The artful display of interior accessories adds a touch of warmth. The overall effect is subtle but each piece reinforces the same colour message – the soft blue of the still life, the matt cream of the stencilled vase, the vibrant purple blue of the anemones and the close patterns of the china.

Right *The blue fireplace tiles influenced the choice of colour for the walls and furnishings in this mono-chromatic scheme.*

CONTRASTING COLOUR SCHEME

In this second treatment, contrasting colours are used to transform the atmosphere of the same room. This scheme is complementary and relies on the principle of combining colours that lie on the opposite sides of the colour wheel, for example, yellow with purple, blue with orange and, here, green with pink. By throwing the opposites together you create a bold and vibrant mood. Each colour emphasizes the strength of the other, but it is necessary that a single one should be allowed to dominate.

Think pink

The dominant tone in this scheme is pink, with a glorious mix of shades appearing in a positive riot of prints – each one offsetting the power of the other. Pink is a warm and relaxing colour, ideally suited to living areas, and should not be banished to the bedroom. The soft and pretty floral curtains provide the basis for the scheme. The curtain print is 1950s retro in feel, while the smoky pink sofa features a deeply traditional floral weave. The deep pink armchair, by way of contrast, displays a more contemporary floral design. The room would spill into boudoir-like softness if the walls were similarly rosy in hue, but the crisp contrast of the fresh spring green emulsion paint lifts

the mood and provides a very contemporary feel. The soft yellow paint on the fireplace, cornice and ceiling, enhances the green walls but stops the colour becoming over-powerful. The cushions unify the separate tones – a pink and green check with a mix of pink and green florals trimmed in contrasting tones.

The carpet provides a neutral backdrop to the soft pink tones in the opulent oriental rug. The rich brown of the cherrywood furniture reflects the warm hues of the overall scheme.

Opposites attract

The room accessories blend in with the mood: green lampshades are set against the green wall and a pink lampshade against the soft colours of the window dressing. The green glass vase introduces a stronger green and is topped by the sugary beauty of pink tulips and the pale green and yellow tones of the alchemilla. The fireplace is dominated by a gaudy pink hydrangea tucked into a wicker basket. The look is traditional, but the dynamic colour and print combination gives the scheme a modern handle.

Above *Cushions in contrasting checks and prints offset the floral patterns in the room. Mixing patterns in this way ensures that no one print is allowed to dominate the eye.*
Below *The room's colour scheme is reflected in decorative details such as lampshades and* bowls *and is further complemented by the rich tones of the cherry-wood console table.*
Right *Mix contrasting colours for real impact. In this room, green and pink are combined to give a fresh yet warm approach. Traditional prints work well when combined with modern colour mixes.*

colour scheme ideas

● In contrasting decorative schemes always allow one colour to dominate. The palette must be limited to four colours in total.

● Monochromatic colour schemes should combine many tones of the same colour and highlight textures.

● When combining prints don't go for unity, mix different styles together but ensure there is a colour link throughout.

● Striped and checked cushions and soft throws can provide the link needed in contrasting colour

schemes and bring further colour depth to monochromatic treatments.

● Details are important – room accessories must integrate with the overall scheme and a vase of flowers or a bowl of fruit or sweets in toning colours has surprising resonance.

● Furniture must stand out within a bold colour scheme. Make a sharp accent with deeper colours, pale neutrals or resonant floral prints and weaves.

● Bind cushions in contrasting trims to emphasize their proportions.

Paint effects

With a brush in your hand and a pot of paint at your feet there is no limit to what you can achieve. Paint is a fast, inexpensive and efficient way of transforming your walls and furniture. The only rule is to let your imagination run riot.

WALLS

Besides the joy of flat colour, paint offers a limitless range of design permutations for the enthusiastic decorator. If you cannot track down the exact shade or style of wallpaper you require, you have no option but to compromise or start again. Painting allows you to take complete control of the creative process – colours can be worked on until they are 100 per cent satisfactory, and textures and pattern can be introduced with a light or heavy hand, just as you wish.

To ascertain whether or not you have made the right colour choice, it is always advisable to buy a sample pot to see how it will look *in situ*. Colours change with light levels over the course of the day. Sunshine, for instance, will make a colour appear more yellow. Paint a test patch on your darkest wall, usually the one with the window, and look at it at different times of the day.

Endless possibilities

There are many paint techniques for the enthusiast to master: dragging, rag-rolling, stippling, marbling, sponging, splatter finishes, colourwashing and much more. Some of these techniques require patience, teamwork and precision workmanship; others will also require specialist materials such as translucent paints and glazes. Practise techniques before you begin so that you can work with a sure hand.

You do not have to stay with fancy paint techniques, however. The walls themselves can be turned into huge works of art if they are simply sectioned off and painted in varying blocks of colour. It's easier than it seems – make a scale drawing of the wall and plan what you want to do, then mark up the wall accordingly and set to work. Patterns can also be painted on to walls – like a highly personal form of wallpaper – or done in strips, segments or panels. Simple designs can be achieved with paint and a stamp or a stencil. Stripes and borders can be created by masking off sections of wall.

The rule is to keep any design in proportion to the scale of the room. When you mark up straight lines for painting, use a spirit level and metal ruler for accuracy and tape the line before standing back to view. Your perfectly level line can highlight irregularities on walls and skirtings and it may be necessary to adjust the design by sight.

Preparation

No paint job will look good unless you tackle the basics first. Preparation makes all the difference in achieving a professional finish and longer-lasting result. Remove all the furniture you can and protect what you can't. Take off door handles and curtain poles, and loosen power point fittings. Fill and sand down all cracks and holes and, finally, brush ceilings and wash down walls.

Left A simple but effective paint scheme creates broad stripes in a soft and gentle colourway. This classic technique is suitable for both contemporary and period homes.

Above Paint effects can be used to transform a room into something magical. Here, blocks of colour highlight the beauty of the wood panelling.

FURNITURE

Painting furniture introduces a personal touch to your overall decor. All kinds of items are suitable for paint treatment, from cast-iron beds to chests of drawers, shelving systems and display units – even the humble orange box can be pressed into service as a storage unit with a simple lick of paint. Dining and occasional chairs can be transformed with a little imagination, some paint and some furnishing fabric. Scour second-hand shops, junk shops and markets for suitable pieces – all that matters is that the shape has potential. It's a great way of furnishing your home on a budget and turns recycling into an art form. Shop-bought, purpose-built basics, low cost and simple in design, are also suitable items for treatment.

Get ready

Good preparation makes all the difference to the finished effect – items must be able to withstand everyday wear and tear. Untreated wood will simply require a little sanding down, but furniture already thick with layers of paint or varnish will need to be stripped back to the natural grain. Use heavy-grade sandpaper, wire wool or even an electric paint stripper. Old and new bare wood should be primed first. It is advisable to apply two or three coats of the main colour before the decorative detail is applied. This should be followed by at least two coats of

varnish for protection. Professionals advise you to rub down each coat of paint, except the final decorative one, for a smooth finish.

Paint techniques

Most paint techniques are quick to master – dragging, rag-rolling and sponging are among the easier effects – and the results that can be acheived with these are stunning.

Stencils are fun to apply; patterns should relate to the piece as a whole since isolated spots of colour will simply look out of place. If you stencil a table, for example, think about bordering the table top as well as stencilling the drawers and legs.

Stamping is another quick method. Simply paint the surfaces with a suitable paint (depending on ultimate use) then apply paint to your stamp motif.

Découpage is a brilliant way to revive hat boxes, biscuit tins and other items. Stick motifs cut from cards, giftwrap or newspaper on a painted surface using spray adhesive then seal with several coats of matt varnish.

Remember, when decorating furniture, not to go over the top since too much detail can look amateurish rather than stylish. Simple paintwork is effective too.

Above A previously gloomy-looking giant wardrobe, now painted blue, harmonizes with the room.
Right An old cupboard has been painted a soft blue and given the crackle glaze treatment. Even humble cardboard boxes look stylish when painted.
Far right A cupboard is painted to reflect the grandeur of the room. Details are picked out in contrasting tones and gilded with gold paint, and the door panels painted and stencilled.

---

painting checklist

■ Emulsion paint used for walls and ceiling is water-based. Finishes include matt, soft sheen (or subtle sheen) and silk.

■ One litre of standard emulsion paint will cover about 12m² (14sq yd) on smooth walls and ceilings.

■ Gloss and satin (eggshell) paint can be solvent- or water-based. Water-based gloss is low odour and quick drying. Solvent-based gloss has a glossier finish. Use either type for indoor woodwork, but metal requires a solvent-based paint.

■ Keep any surplus paint for touching up areas. Hammer down the lid of the tin and store upside down to prevent a skin forming on the top.

■ Furniture can be 'distressed' for a pleasing, worn appearance. First paint the item with a pale base coat. When the paint is dry, rub a candle around the areas most subject to wear and tear, for example, handles and door edges, to deposit wax. Apply the top coat and, when dry, sand the waxed areas. The base coat will show through as if caused by heavy use.

Special effects

Paint, paper and varnish have been used imaginatively to transform the rooms of this very individual apartment. Paint effects are not limited to the walls either: they extend to the furniture, fireplaces and the partitions that are moved around to divide the space in different ways.

Above *Marble effects characterize this sunny front room that doubles as a bedroom. Yellow marbled walls make a cheerful backdrop, while layers of paper and washes of blue paint have been used to create the 'marbling' around the fireplace.*
Right *The kitchen area is hidden from view by a tall, painted partition with a shelved, oval hatch cut into it.*

Far right *Paint effects extend from the walls to the front of the corner cupboard in Annie's living and workroom. The ornate fireplace has no need of further embellishment but Annie made the framed collage especially to hang above it. The velour-upholstered chair and sofa blend in perfectly with the colour scheme.*

Originally trained in textile design, Annie now runs her own company specializing in decorative paint effects. The scope of her commissions ranges from shop interiors and hotels to designs for fabric, wallpaper, furniture and lighting. Since Annie makes use of every surface in her own apartment to try out her latest decorating ideas, the look of her home might change several times a year. 'I'm always developing new techniques for customers and I can't wait to apply them to my own walls,' she says.

Annie's ground-floor apartment has large windows and effectively has two living rooms. The front room doubles as a bedroom and the airy back room as a workroom. 'The flat is my home, workshop and showroom,' says Annie. She makes good use of tall screens, which act as movable walls to create different spaces and hide work in progress when necessary.

In the front room, the rich variety of colours, textures and styles helps to create an opulent atmosphere. The bed is cleverly disguised as a large sofa, and is embellished with silk- and satin-covered cushions. No surface remains untouched: the mirrors were some of Annie's first decorated pieces, and

picture frames and small chests of drawers are covered in different stained papers and varnish. 'I love putting different materials together,' says Annie.

Unable to find the right shade of marble for the fireplace, she simulated the effect with layers of paper and washes of paint. A unifying feature of the whole flat is the floorboards, painted silver and sealed with heavy-duty varnish, which enhances the light, airy look. In this room the boards are scattered with sheepskin rugs.

The same passion for colour and design can be seen in the living room–workroom at the back of the flat. Annie designed a tall partition to stand behind the sofa and cleverly screen off the kitchen area. The coffee table is all her own work, too, and a bar that has been decorated with layers of bright paper and fitted castors holds her hi-fi equipment and music collection. Annie discovered the chair and two-seater sofa at a trade show and they work brilliantly with her colour scheme. Carefully disguised cupboards run the entire length of the inside walls of both rooms, holding all Annie's paper, fabrics, books and clothes: 'All my clutter is hidden away so as not to distract from the design.'

Floral ideas

Not so long ago it was *de rigueur* to pepper the home with a liberal application of floral prints. They appeared on upholstery, carpets, curtains, cushions – just about everything. The overall effect was at best overblown, at worst overpowering. Today, florals are used with a more judicious hand. Fashions come and go but florals have a timeless appeal – in many senses they are a furnishing classic.

Coming up roses

We are drawn to florals for complex reasons and not least because they are extremely pretty. It is perhaps their very prettiness that made them something of a dirty word in contemporary home design. It is hard to equate them with clean-lined modernity since they hint so much at the past. They speak nostalgically of bygone days and rural life, and remind us of long summers, hot days and our childhood. Yet florals do have a place in modern life. Using them in an unconventional setting can be particularly effective. The key is to choose the right floral pattern, to use them with restraint, and never mix them with frills or lace.

The strongest floral prints are unashamedly retrospective. Flowers and leaves grow across neutral or pale pastel backgrounds in soft, warm, muted tones. Tiny rosebuds march in serried ranks to make a formal pattern. Alone, such prints can look quaint, or lost, as if struggling to maintain an identity, but introduce other florals, or soft stripes and checks, and the style is reaffirmed, becoming a glorious blur of colour and form. For this scheme to work no single print should dominate or shout for attention. If background colours are cohesive, the overall effect will be harmonious.

Strength in simplicity

Bold floral prints on curtains can be overwhelming and for such designs to work successfully both curtains and room should be large. However, small dainty floral prints look very attractive on small windows. Make a blind out of a mass of different prints mixed together for a glorious patchwork of gentle prettiness. Prints with well-spaced sprigs of flowers, tone-on-tone patterning or embroidery can offer a subtle effect. On fine fabrics such as voile and muslin, white sprays of flowers can float across the lengths like shadows. Delicate cut embroidery on white linen curtains is another plain but effective approach.

Highlighting florals

It is also possible to introduce florals to an otherwise neutral scheme with a swathe of fabric. Throw an old patchwork quilt or embroidered floral tablecloth across the back of a sofa, or hide a tired old table top with a beautiful antique cloth sprigged with delicate floral appliqué. Paint wooden boxes and stencil them with flowers; perhaps develop a passion for china. What could be prettier than a collection of old tea plates, each with its own floral decoration, or a crazy pile of multi-patterned tea cups and saucers?

Above left Floral china has a timeless appeal. If you cannot afford a complete set, buy individual cups and saucers when you come across them.

Left A striking mix of florals on curtains, cushions and upholstery ensures that the overall look is lively but not overblown. Even the woven rug maintains the theme.

Below Old-fashioned floral prints work best against neutral backgrounds. A mix of prints and weaves of similar colours produce a pleasing blur of shapes.

Finishing touches

The last details that you add to a room can make or break the whole effect. The perfectly ordered scheme will be reduced to manic confusion if every surface is laden with bits and pieces and every chair stuffed with cushions. Details should accent your scheme, not hijack it. Exercise restraint: details stand out when they have sufficient space to shine.

CUSHIONS

There may be virtually identical sofas in every high street furniture shop window across the country, but it is how your sofa is dressed with cushions that makes it unique in your home. Cushions come in virtually every shape, size and pattern. Whether they are plain or fancy, shop bought or home-made, your choice of cushions makes a personal statement in your living room. These finishing touches can inject flashes of colour into a room scheme without overwhelming it.

Comfortably full

Cushions should enhance our comfort. They are what we reach for when we want to snuggle down in a chair or sofa. The fillings are important – feather- or kapok-filled pads are the most comfortable, while foam pieces can be somewhat lumpy. Never overfill a cushion: always make sure that the pad fits comfortably inside the cover or it will feel overstuffed and hard and will be uncomfortable to use. Whether you buy cushion covers or make them yourself, ensure that they will be easy to clean at home, or at the very least can be easily removed for dry cleaning – cushions do take a lot of wear and tear and can become exceedingly grimy.

Plain and fancy

It is shamefully easy to make cushions and they look good in most fabrics. Almost anything goes – plain calico is calm and inviting and can be dressed up with striking buttons or tie fastenings in colours that match or contrast. Checked and striped designs and tickings all mix beautifully, while floral cushions introduce a little old-fashioned prettiness. For an opulent look, choose cushions made of silk, velvet or chenille. Trimmed, piped, braided and fringed, these all look fabulous. Recycled fabric can be utilized and effective – for example, rust-spotted antique tablecloths, tea towels and even old knitted jumpers.

Cushions have different uses according to their shape and size. Some are merely decorative, others are provided for a purpose. You often want support and comfort from a cushion, but you may find that too many small cushions can be slippery and irritating. If you have a favourite view from a window consider creating a simple window seat. It will provide useful storage underneath and, with a tailor-made cushion, will become a favourite lounging place.

Above Mix different coloured and textured cushions to highlight aspects of your decor. Checks and stripes can break up strong colours and maintain the flow of the room.

Far left The green and aqua tones of textured cushions blend with the curtains and walls of this scheme – contrasting with the soft ivory of the chairs.

Above left Pale florals lighten the impact of a dark sofa while reaffirming the overall scheme. Fringe trims and piping add a touch of luxury.

DISPLAYING FLOWERS

All interiors, no matter how minimalist or contemporary in style, are improved by the addition of a vase or pot of flowers. They introduce colour, form and perfume to a room and create a link with the great outdoors, whether your environment is a country garden or a concrete jungle.

A la mode

There are fashions in flowers and plants as in any other area of interior or exterior design. Modern florists work sympathetically with flowers and foliage rather than contorting them into artificial arrangements. Simple displays work best and anyone can make a bunch of seasonal flowers look good. Cut the stems so that the flowers – daffodils, tulips, cornflowers, sweet peas, sunflowers or stems of winter-flowering blossom, for example – are roughly all the same stem length. Hold them in your hand as a bunch and drop them in the water: they will make their own wonderful arrangement. Small vases allow you to create displays with just two or three solitary flowers.

Supporting role

Specific flowers require different styles of vase. Tall, solid, chunky vases are best for displaying a few wonderful long stems, such as lilies. Middle-sized containers cope with daffodils or tulips, while smaller bowls are ideal for bunches of garden roses or hyacinths. A selection of very small containers – perhaps a row of test tubes – show off individual blooms to their best advantage. Glass vases act as a wonderful frame for flowers, but you can use anything from antique medicine bottles to the humble jam jar.

Pots of bulbs are similarly stylish and you can watch the bulbs grow, often out of their natural season, bringing us colour and perfume in the winter months when flowers are scarce. Keep containers simple, for instance, a terracotta pot or a rustic basket. For drama, combine the majestic beauty of a blood red amaryllis with a sleek aluminum pot and wait for the blooms to explode. Don't leave any soil showing: concealing it below a mulch of moss, pebbles, shells or glass nuggets is very attractive.

Outdoor elements

Window boxes and flowerpots on sills enhance your view of the world outside. You don't have to rely on seasonal bedding and bulbs. Shrubs such as lavender and rosemary will thrive in sunny spots. Herbs are delightful to rub between the fingers for fragrance, and on a warm day will fill the air with an intense and pungent smell. Ivy is tolerant of most aspects and can be grown over topiary shapes. Ornamental grasses work well in pots and bring an element of movement to a static display.

Above *Two or three strongly silhouetted flowers in a vase make a strong visual statement and require no skill in arranging.*
Left *The perfect simplicity of a repetitive display is easy to produce and devastatingly stylish. Two or more narrow-necked vases will make any flower arrangement look assured.*

Below *Pots of bulbs inject a room with life and colour and bring the smell of spring. Simple containers are best – terracotta or aluminum pots, lined baskets or even old pudding basins.*

flowers checklist

▨ Try to have at least three different vase shapes at home – ranging from the tall to the short – so that you can best arrange different types of flowers.

▨ Always cut flower stems by at least 12mm (½in) to enable the plant to take up fresh water.

▨ Use bulb fibre or special compost when potting bulbs so that they have the correct nutrients to grow and flower.

▨ Buy seasonal flowers for arrangements at home: they cost less and will look more natural.

▨ Always purchase an odd number of long-stemmed flowers – five, seven or nine stems – as it produces a more balanced display.

▨ If you are not keen on flowers and always forget to water pots, why not make space for a vase of dried twigs? Their stark and complex structures have a simple and pure beauty.

PICTURES AND MIRRORS

Whatever your taste in art, you want to display it to best advantage. This is more of a complex question than simply where to hang a work of art. Frames should never dominate a picture; as a rule of thumb, gentle, more moody colours show a picture off the best. It isn't always easy to tell what is going to look good so go to a picture framer's and let them show you some samples. Take your artwork along to get a real impression of how it will look.

Proportions are critical. How much space should a mount take up around the artwork and how does this balance with the depth of the frame? A good picture framer will advise you and might well get to know your likes and dislikes as well as the style of your home.

Think about how you want the frame to interact with the artwork. Intense pictures may need space around them. Textural pieces may need to be framed in boxes to show them off properly. Remember that frames do not have to sit flat against a wall: chunky frames thrust visuals forward, boxed in pictures draw in the eye.

A valuable piece of artwork is not necessarily any better than a framed photograph, but you should be honest in how you approach your material. Never pretend that a framed poster is anything other than that, do not apologize for it but make a feature of it.

Hanging pictures can be daunting as you pepper your freshly painted walls with nasty holes. Always enlist the help of a trusted friend with a good eye and you will make less mistakes. Pictures do not have to hang in solitary splendour. Themed groups can be very striking – black and white photographs, collections of postcards or a range of botanical prints, for example, have enormous impact *en masse*.

Reflecting views

Mirrors reflect light back into a room and open up small spaces. Mirror frames do not have to be bound by the same conventions as picture frames – with no central image to be contained, the surround can be as adventurous as you please.

Mirrors vary hugely in shape, size and style and can be decorative as well as functional. It is worth looking around and getting the best-quality mirror you can afford for your living room. Bevelled mirrors seem to reflect light and appear more sparkly but are better suited to more traditional, ornate frames.

Above *Mirrors draw the eye and reflect light. This carved wooden mirror, with the table below it, makes a strong focal point.*
Below *This huge ornate mirror maximizes light levels and blurs the concept of space with a repeat reflection in the opposite facing looking glass.*
Right *A quirky, contemporary mirror offers a new slant on traditional hearthside style.*

---

picture hanging ideas

● Large and medium picture frames maximize space, stretching the boundaries of the room. Small frames force the eye into the picture to view the detail.

● You can make your own picture frames with mouldings from do-it-yourself shops or timber merchants, then paint and decorate them to taste.

● Never panic buy a picture to fill a space or to suit your decor. Artwork should speak for itself – you will come across the right piece in time.

● Pictures do not have to be hung on walls or picture rails: they can be placed on shelves or hung from shelves to avoid damaging walls. They can also be simply propped up against walls instead of being hung.

● Don't leave a picture hanging in the same place for years. It is better to move artwork about to stimulate your eye.

● If you are hanging pictures in groups, lay them out on the floor before you begin to make sure the layout is working.

● Some large picture frames and mirrors can be extremely heavy so make sure you hang them from suitable brackets to prevent accidents.

dining rooms

A dining room can turn even the simplest of meals into an occasion, and makes a special one even more memorable. Good food, good wine and good company deserve the best setting possible so enjoy the convivial atmosphere to the full in comfortable chairs that encourage you to linger, and in stylish surroundings that provide a feast for the eyes as well as the tastebuds.

Top *A traditional country-style dining room takes on a modern look with carefully chosen furnishings – simple Windsor chairs, a Roman blind and a pair of prints.*

Above *A small glass-topped table gives a sense of space, while its curves (and those of the chair-backs) contrast with the rectangular shapes in the rest of the room.*

Dining areas

Take a long look at where you eat. Do you use the dining table regularly or do friends and family tend to eat anywhere except the place that's set aside for meals? If so, there's a lot you can do to make the dining room a more welcoming place.

The dedicated dining room

Furnishing a dining room is easy: all you need is a table and half a dozen chairs, plus somewhere to serve up perhaps. But there is one essential quality missing from this list – atmosphere, which takes a little more thought. Colour can be your ally here. Since you don't tend to spend as much time in the dining room as in other rooms, you can afford to be more adventurous here and opt for shades that you might tire of elsewhere. If the room is used mostly in the evenings, terracotta, deep blue or burgundy can look particularly effective, as can neutrals offset by one of the new metallic finishes for woodwork or accessories.

Of course, the table is usually the centre of attention, but it is worth creating a second focal point, too. For example, you could swathe a window in lengths of flowing tulle or voile, introduce a trend-setting light fitting such as a wirework chandelier or a dainty curtain of fairy lights, and fill a large empty fireplace with flowering plants, heavy church candles or pebbles.

Before you start, make sure that you want to keep your existing dining room. Ideally, it should be adjacent to the kitchen, but in older properties it may, in fact, be some distance away. If so, consider whether it is possible to convert a breakfast room, study, or part of the living room, into the dining room instead.

Sharing space

Using the dining room as a dual-purpose room can ease pressure on space in the house. Unless the room is very large, choose space-saving furniture such as a table that extends to seat 10 but can condense into a small circle or square to free space for a home office or perhaps a spare bed. (Remember that you will need somewhere to store the extension leaves and extra chairs.) It is worth organizing the room so that specialized furniture can be concealed when you have friends round. Book-lined walls are fine any time, but if the room is a part-time spare bedroom you might prefer to have a sofa bed rather than an ordinary bed on show; similarly you may want to hide a computer kept in the dining room behind a screen, curtains or doors.

Together yet apart

The living–dining room that is perfect for everyday meals is not quite so easy to manage when it comes to entertaining. Lighting is the invaluable thing here, throwing the table into focus during the meal and casting it into shadow afterwards. Ideally, seating and eating areas should complement each other but be separately defined. Screens or double doors can divide the two areas in a long, narrow room and, if the room is large, it may be worth separating them with a storage unit.

dining room ideas

● Where the focus is firmly in the centre of a room add interest to the walls with prints, china and collections in box frames.

● Changes in floor or ceiling materials can help define the distinct areas in a living–dining room.

● Wear and tear is less of an issue in the dining room than elsewhere, so you can afford to use delicate colours and fabrics. In a small dining room, keep the decor simple and colours light.

● Keep style consistent – tiles and marble for a Mediterranean look, polished wood for Victorian/Edwardian, birch and glass for contemporary style.

● A plain blind works best at small windows. For more drama, add voile side curtains or shutters.

Above *This small living–dining room places the emphasis on dining. Pale walls make the room seem spacious and the strong blue upholstery and accessories provide a good contrast.*

Stylish tables

Think ahead when choosing a table – this is not a purchase that is often repeated so it is worth forecasting your future lifestyle. Do you want a highly polished table for formal dining or a casual table for family meals, or both? Will you need a table that is larger, or smaller, than the one that is right for now? And should it be fashionable or a timeless classic?

Flexible dining

The space you have often decides the shape of the table. In a restricted space, a rectangular or square table may be best. Space-saving options include traditional gatefold tables with barley twist legs, tables with detachable flaps, and designs in sections that fit together like a jigsaw puzzle. A round table encourages convivial meals but one that extends to form an oval can cater for more guests. You can even buy a billiards table with a solid wood top, to create a dining table capable of seating a dozen or more.

Adaptable tables have their advantages. A circular wooden table perfect for a modern dining room could be equally at home in a large kitchen, while a glass-topped trestle table would look stunning in a home office. Polished wood is appealing, but surfaces should be easy-clean if the table is used every day. Sealed or oiled wood, laminate and glass are all possible: they may still need protecting from heat, so keep mats handy for hot dishes.

Old and new

Beautifully restored antiques aside, old dining tables are not usually in perfect condition, but this is part of their charm. Polished oak and mahogany gain a mellow patina with age, while large kitchen tables that have been scrubbed clean for decades can be perfect for family living if you don't

mind a few dents. Check that drawers don't interfere with your seating plans and that legs are stable or can be repaired.

Round pedestal tables are the easiest to sit at. For others, see if any extension mechanism or supports for flaps are likely to get in the way. The height is crucial too; make sure there is adequate leg room, although this should not be a problem if you are investing in a new table with matching chairs.

Below An art deco maple dining suite, complete with leopard-print seats, is the focus of this traditional dining room where it mixes happily with a variety of woods.

Right The simple pine table looks as much at home with the colourful moulded chairs, painted cabinet and metal chandelier that make up this eclectic setting as it would do in a country kitchen.

Flooring options

Any place where food is served needs flooring that is easily cleaned, and the dining room is no exception. It is hard to beat washable flooring if you eat at the table every day, although carpet is rarely a problem if the dining room is used less often. You can have the best of both worlds by choosing a rug to mark out the dining area and cover the floor beneath – whether it is carpet that needs protecting or hard flooring that could do with a softer touch.

Above *Warm and easy to care for, sanded and sealed floorboards provide a ready-made dining room floor.*
Below *Stone flooring is a versatile classic. Here it makes an effective background for dark wooden furniture, light cupboards and vivid blocks of colour.*

Right *A ponyskin rug puts the focus firmly on the floor in this simple setting. Plain white walls and drapes form a dramatic foil for the dark furniture.*

Hard choices

Any of the smarter kitchen floorings look good in a dining room setting, especially if the rooms lead into one another. Limestone and slate have a grand, baronial appeal when teamed with traditional furniture, yet look excitingly up to the minute when partnered by light woods. Red quarry tiles have a rustic charm that is perfect with rush seats or Windsor chairs, but quarry tiles take on an architectural look in autumnal browns, and go well with metal and glass or moulded shapes. Ceramic tiles are one of the most elegant floor coverings: choose large, plain, pale tiles for a modern look, black and white for a classic floor that suits all styles of furnishing, or create a border around the table or the perimeter of the room with patterned tiles. Good-quality vinyl tiles and linoleum are additional possibilities and, for a stylish option, look at solid vinyl flooring in a range of iridescent finishes.

Natural warmth

Sealed wood and cork are excellent choices for dining rooms, combining warmth and flexibility with hard wear. Stripped floorboards can be a budget-price solution if the existing floor consists of wide planks that simply need sanding. Remove and replace any cut boards for the best effect – any variations in tone usually disappear if you stain the floor. After sanding, use several coats of floor varnish on top to protect the surface. Polished wood is not such an easy option as it is constantly scraped by chairs, which makes maintaining a shine difficult. Placing a rug over the wooden floor beneath the table may be the best solution.

Soft answers

A single flooring used throughout a living–dining room creates an impression of space – an important effect if space is limited. If you opt for carpet, choose twist pile rather than velvet, which tends to show every mark, and stay away from long-pile carpet, which is not ideal for dining areas. A classic 80 per cent wool–20 per cent polyamide carpet is a safe choice. Pure wool tends to 'wear clean' and the advanced synthetic fibres combine improved looks with durability. Wine and food spills are inevitable in a dining room and some stains are tricky to shift. If you want a rug – as a design flourish or for practical reasons – choose one that is not too precious and that is relatively easy to clean (or remove it before your guests arrive).

Storage ideas

Keeping special glass and china separate from the things you use every day makes good sense, and it can look decorative, too. A gilt-edged dinner service in a glass-fronted cabinet, rows of jugs on a dresser, plates arranged on a shelf or hanging from the walls … all of these can be displayed to give pleasure, even when they are not in use. And, of course, there is always a need for purely practical storage where less attractive items can be hidden away.

Above *Glass doors show off decorative china while keeping dust at bay. Coffee cups and glasses are heaped together for a casual look and a tassel adds a stylish finishing touch.*

Below *A wall cupboard perched on top of a chest of drawers makes an unusual and effective substitute for a dresser in this country-style dining room.*

Right *Keep a look out for furniture that can be adapted to provide useful storage. Here, cream paint has been used to rennovate a sideboard.*

Behind closed doors

Cupboards were originally side-tables – the place where you kept cups. Only later did cupboards acquire doors to protect the contents from prying eyes and dust. It is therefore not surprising that sideboards, dressers and cabinets have always been important in the dining room. These are stow-away zones where the dinner service, large platters and dishes that you don't want on display can be stored. There is no need to be restricted by purpose-made furniture: a tall armoire or a decorative wardrobe fitted with shelves provides more storage when floor space is limited, and a chest of drawers is invaluable if you have a large amount of table linen to store.

For a modern look, choose cupboards that form part of a storage unit, or built-in designs, painted to match the walls if you prefer. All are well worth including in your plans if you want to limit what is on show.

If you prefer a decorative look but decide against open shelves, cupboards with glass doors will keep the china clean. Again, it is possible to utilize other pieces of furniture. If you want to show off a collection of glasses, a bookcase with clear doors is ideal and its narrow shelves are a positive bonus. If you prefer to display plates, however, fit plate shelves, which have a bar to stop the china sliding forward.

Shelve it

The simplest form of storage is often the most effective. It is hard to match the decorative appeal of a dresser crammed with china or shelves filled with books. Shelves in alcoves or self-contained units can take a variety of objects without looking too cluttered. For a clean modern look, opt for an asymmetric arrangement of wide shelves in light wood or bold colours and choose the contents with care. Glass shelves make the most of space visually, while curved metal wound into abstract shapes is a great conversation piece, even if its capacity is limited.

Collective charm

The dining room is the ideal place to store collections too fragile to keep elsewhere, whether they are button hooks, toy soldiers or scraps of lace. Large picture or box frames and shallow storage cabinets can be excellent ways of displaying the cream of the collection, while the rest can be kept in a plan chest with shallow drawers that make the contents easily accessible.

Dining chairs

If you have a separate dining room, it is quite likely that you will want a matching set of chairs to go around the table. But dining is informal these days and more or less anything goes when it comes to styles of chair – and there really is no reason why you cannot mix and match individual seats either.

The two most important requirements of a dining chair are that it should be a comfortable height for the table and its legs should be sturdily constructed. After a good meal, dinner guests are prone to expansive gestures, often leaning back in their seats, and you do not want a chair leg breaking at the joint. Unlike upholstered armchairs, squashy comfort is not the first priority – dining chairs generally have hard seats, which are conducive to sitting upright for eating.

With upholstered dining chairs, covers that can be removed for cleaning are useful. Otherwise spray them with a fabric protector so that any marks can be sponged off. To smarten up a set of old chairs, you could make removable cotton slipcovers that reach to the ground and fasten with ties.

Chair checklist

■ Measure seat widths before you buy dining chairs to ensure that they can be pushed under the dining table when not in use, without table legs getting in the way.

■ If you are short of space it is a good idea to buy folding chairs, which can be stacked against a wall or hung on pegs when not in use.

■ If your chairs stand on a wooden floor, it is a good idea to fix felt pads underneath each leg to prevent them scratching the floor. You can buy sets of adhesive-backed pads that peel off a card.

The simple lines of modernity: this birch plywood chair on a tubular steel frame is designed for stacking.

Minimalist lines of a moulded beech plywood chair on slim steel legs make this an ideal seat for a contemporary interior.

Solid wooden chair with a sprung seat and high, padded back is covered in calico; it is ideal for long evenings around the dining table.

Director's chairs convey a relaxed feel and can move easily between indoors and out. This luxury version has a leather seat and back.

Sturdy budget chair in solid pine, has an easy-care painted finish.

Ladder-back carver chair with natural rush seat has a painted finish. The 'carver', with arms, was traditionally reserved for the head of the household.

Timeless cane-seated bent wood chair with a new look, which would blend easily with a traditional or modern interior.

Folding 'high-tech' silver chairs in coated steel have a contoured seat for comfort; they can be stacked or hung on pegs when not being used.

Beech 'balloon' chair painted in red, this style of chair is easily adaptable to all different sorts of interior schemes.

Simple, sturdy pine chair with upholstered seat has good back support; it would look equally at home in a country-style kitchen.

Space and light

Opening up the internal space and adding a glass-walled extension has provided a spacious dining area that is serene and uncluttered, with superb views over the garden and beyond. The modern-looking area has been furnished with simple, well-designed furniture and natural materials.

Sheila and Robert chose their solid, well-constructed suburban house for its enviable position – facing fields at the front and with views over wooded hills at the rear. Not as keen on the interior, however, the couple then commissioned an architect to work on the house, with instructions to radically open up the interior.

Accordingly, the internal layout has been totally replanned along modernistic lines and two new extensions have been added to enlarge the living areas. The house is now a series of interconnecting serene spaces, which are bathed in natural daylight and furnished in natural materials and neutral colours. The owners specified that they wanted to use all of the house at all times, with no 'formal' areas kept only for entertaining.

One of the extensions is the spectacular garden room that opens on to the kitchen, where they dine informally with friends. With glass walls on three sides, the room is designed to be part-conservatory, but has a solid roof so the summer heat is never a problem. With views over the garden and of the woodland beyond, the architect's inspired

way of bringing the outdoors inside provides all the pleasures of alfresco dining without any of the inconvenience.

Having left all their furniture behind in their previous house, now rented out, Sheila and Robert had the enviable freedom of starting again from scratch. They wanted functional, well-designed furniture, in simple shapes and pale neutral shades that would create a restful environment. Consequently, throughout the living areas contemporary materials like glass, marble and chrome are balanced by natural wood and the soft textures of calico, sailcloth and seagrass. The seagrass floor covering in the dining room echoes the pale sycamore table, while the calico-covered chairs match the cream Roman blinds at the windows.

The transformation of the original living space, which Sheila and Robert had found bland and lacking in character, has helped create a house where the family now feel they have room to breathe, with no clutter or superfluous details. Nowhere is this seen more clearly than in the light-filled dining area, its simply designed furniture as easy on the eye as its clean lines and natural finishes.

Above *Contorted twigs combine with the textures of timber, glass and pottery to create a decorative still life on a sycamore console table.*

Far left *A glass-walled dining area has been added to the back of the house; its solid roof helps to keep the temperature constant. The glazed walls were designed to have minimum interference from metal uprights. The simple, classic dining table is made of sycamore, its* curving lines inspired by the design of the 'Mosquito' plane. The elegant high-backed chairs are covered in calico to match the cream blinds.

Below left *Natural light floods into the dining area, which opens on to the garden through sliding glass doors. Porthole windows in the ceiling provide overhead illumination day and night, aided by exterior suspended light fittings.*

Traditional elegance

Living in a Victorian house but with a fondness for Georgian pictures and furniture, art historians Margaret and John have found a way to blend the two, pushing the interior of the house back in time rather than recreating it in its original period style.

Above *The Victorian neo-classical chiffonier, is a triumph of renovation by Margaret who replaced the broken front panels with brass fretwork, backed by dark fabric, and added ornamental brasswork and columns to the front. Wall sconces on either side hold candles, which give an atmospheric, flickering light.*

Right *An 1825 mahogany sideboard, found years ago in Edinburgh, is perfect for displaying silverware and old china, such as this cheese dome and pair of tureens.*

Far right *The 'Regency' dining table, made in the 1920s, is the only reproduction piece in the room. The set of chairs date from the late-18th century. The ornate fireplace, topped by a lovingly restored gilt mirror, was made by Margaret using mouldings rom the fascia of an old shop.*

Margaret and John both lecture in art history and their favourite period for art and furniture is classical Georgian (late 18th to early 19th century). Yet they have chosen to live in a Victorian house as it is conveniently situated for work. Over the years they have found a comfortable way to mix Georgian furniture and pictures with the Victorian architecture. The couple have developed in confidence with their decorating style and are now prepared to take a few risks and trust their judgement. 'If it doesn't work you can always change it back,' says Margaret.

In the early days their use of colour was based on authentic Georgian schemes, using colours like mint green and sharp pink but 'they looked too crisp,' says John. They now use darker colours and find these a stronger background for old prints and paintings, which are often yellowed or faded with age.

The dining room is painted in a colour they refer to as 'stewed liver', a bluish-grey violet that was the result of a happy colour-mixing accident. The unusual shade makes a good foil for the pictures and gilt mirror. The use of dark colours results in a rather shadowy interior, at its best at night when the mahogany shines and the crystal gleams.

Margaret and John started collecting Georgian pieces of furniture in their student days, when antiques could be bought relatively cheaply. They love 'architectural furniture' – 'pieces that give height to a

room and have a presence of their own'. Nowhere is this more apparent than in the dining room, with its handsome mahogany dining table and sideboard. A bargain Victorian chiffonier, in need of renovation, has been given a neo-classical treatment to create a piece that looks perfectly at home with the Georgian furniture in this room.

The couple are used to restoring small pieces such as gilt frames, mirrors or *objets d'art*. Margaret even made the mantelpiece in the dining room. They didn't want a cluttered interior but 'some things are too good to miss,' they say, and have acquired a number of treasures as well as junk. John admits: 'The place does get rather dusty, by most people's standards. But Margaret has the answer: candles and 40-watt light bulbs.'

Sleek and modern

A dramatic extension turned a cottage by the sea into an idyllic weekend and holiday retreat for a hard-working couple nearing retirement. So successful has it been that they now cannot wait for the time they can live there permanently.

Above Silver-finish metal chairs complement the grey-blue colour of the ceiling and window frames; their contemporary lines are entirely in keeping with this pristine space.

Below The open area that leads into the kitchen and dining room is useful for entertaining. The oak chair is an Arts and Crafts piece found in a local antique shop (Pat and Kenneth love the well-crafted design of the Movement).

Far right The extension has provided a light-filled space for cooking and dining. Tucked away behind the panelled wooden wall are a utility room and cloakroom.

Pat and Kenneth bought the small and dilapidated farmer's cottage because of its location and the fact that a large plot of land behind it was also for sale at the same time. The cottage was in a bad state and its layout poorly designed, but it is situated right in the centre of a pleasant village, just behind the square, with the shop, pub and a good restaurant all within walking distance. Even more persuasive were the splendid views out to sea from the back. Their intention was to renovate the cottage, sell it, and then build a weekend house for themselves on the land.

The couple realized that they needed professional help and a local architect was recommended. He asked many questions about how they lived: where they liked to eat, where they enjoyed listening to music and how often they had family and friends round for meals, before he even began to talk about the space. And when he came up with an ingenious design to extend the

ground floor, pulling down an ugly back extension and putting a contemporary glass 'wing' in its place, Pat and Kenneth saw the great potential for the cottage as a permanent home after all.

The ground-floor extension now provides a bright, spacious area for cooking, dining and entertaining, plus a compact cloakroom and utility room. With its great quantity of glass, it is filled with light all the time. The contemporary beamed ceiling is designed to echo the original ceiling beams throughout the cottage but is painted a soft, grey-blue like the door and window frames. The zinc roof is constructed like an aircraft wing, with an overlapping flap halfway along to accommodate a change in ground level. Since there is no gutter, the effect is spectacular when it rains, creating a sheer wall of water beyond the glass.

Inside the extension, the decoration has a simple fresh feel, with a marked lack of clutter and white distemper-painted walls. The concrete floor has been covered with several layers of protective sealant, which gives it a polished-looking finish. And while the pale wooden dining table matches the simple beech kitchen units, the metal chairs echo the units' brushed aluminium knobs as well as the stainless steel of the cooker.

The couple now look forward to the day they can enjoy their cottage and the views of the sea and the big skies on a full-time basis.

Table settings

Nothing looks more inviting than a carefully laid table, whether it is set for a major celebration or for an informal supper with friends. It takes only a moment to arrange a bunch of sweet peas in a china jug and tie napkins with raffia, but small touches such as these turn a casual meal into an occasion to remember.

Above This fresh and summery setting for breakfast relies on lilac and white for flowers, cloth and china, with just a touch of yellow for contrast.
Below right Flowers tucked with the napkin into a silvery wirework napkin ring give a charming individual touch to each place setting.

Right Silky table runners used across rather than along the table create an unusual table covering in a setting that is made even more effective by the use of green – for flowers, food and textiles.

DAYTIME ENTERTAINING

Even breakfast and lunch can provide opportunities for imaginative dressing up of the table, and making an occasion of a meal, especially if you have guests.

Breakfast

Breakfast is so often eaten on the run that it is worth making a special effort when you can afford the time to sit down and enjoy it. Lay a small table with a fresh cotton cloth (gingham is a classic) and toning napkins, plus a spray of flowers in a glass – perhaps daffodils, apple blossom, marguerites or autumn crocus – to pick up a colour in the cloth. Choose strong porcelain or chunky earthenware crockery and simple stainless steel cutlery. A butter dish, toast rack, rolls in a basket under a cloth, jam in a pot with a beaded cover, and a pot of tea or a cafetière of hot coffee, are all you need add.

Lunch

This meal can be whatever you want it to be – from help-yourself salads on a scrubbed table with a stack of stoneware plates and a pot of wild flowers for decoration, to a formal affair

with a crisp cloth and matching napkins, fine china and silver. It is quite permissible to serve food on plates, but if you prefer guests to help themselves and don't want to bring out the full dinner service, choose unusual serving platters and dishes, such as a soapstone bowl for salad or a carved wooden leaf for fruit. Flowers should be arranged with a light hand, mixing unusual colours and shapes – gerbera, ranunculus and green chrysanthemums are all popular – with miniature vegetables like cabbages, peppers and vine tomatoes if you want. Flower heads can also be used to mark each place setting, and have extra impact if they colour co-ordinate with napkins or china.

Afternoon tea

This is an almost forgotten meal but one worth reviving, if only for the chance to serve tea in bone china cups. A cake stand comes into its own here but is equally useful for displaying fruit or supporting a bowl of flowers. China does not always have to match and a collection of different cups or plates all linked by colour or shape are an immediate talking point.

DRESSED FOR DINNER

A sense of theatre helps to set the scene for a great dinner party. With the trend towards deep bowls, pasta plates and mugs in earthenware rather than bone china, and for hot colours or smoky shades in place of elaborate multi-coloured patterns, the table setting need not be excessively grand. Whichever of these is your style, there are certain elements common to both, such as the vogue for large 'charger' plates that stay in place during every course. Metallic effects like hammered silver and gold are especially popular, but you can also buy china charger plates to co-ordinate with a dinner service. The accent is on height – charger, dinner and soup plates piled up at each place setting, accompanied by tall glasses with sinuous stems. Designs with a gold rim continue the metallic look, or you can use wirework napkin rings to carry on the theme.

Table coverings

Tablecloths are not mandatory at dinner (silver cutlery and crystal glasses look wonderful on a polished table), but white linen is the traditional choice. However, you can also create a wonderful setting with lengths of dress or furnishing fabric – white or gold tulle or sari braids – laid out as cloths or runners, with brilliantly coloured

remnants cut into large squares and frayed to form napkins. Other ideas are to stick shells on hessian place mats or shiny sequins on silky ones. Whatever you use, it is sensible to put a layer of felt and a second cloth beneath the top cover to protect the table from spills.

Table centres

Candles and flowers or even fruit play a part in most formal dinners, sometimes combined in a central table setting. On the whole, flowers should be kept low so as not to interfere with conversation and should not be highly scented or they will compete with the food – the same applies to candles. Strong shapes and colours look good, or opt for miniature topiary for a stylized effect. Look out for unusual, utilitarian containers that make an effective contrast to fine china.

Celebrations

Christenings, weddings and anniversaries deserve special attention. Use appropriately coloured netting or other fine material to swathe the table and the cake stand, keeping it in place with staples, disguised with ribbon or raffia. Write place-cards in metallic pen in a colour to suit the theme and wrap tiny presents – bonbons for a christening, sugared almonds for a wedding – in tissue, paper tied with coloured string.

Above *A single shade of vivid blue for both glass and china is offset by white to create a stunning table setting.*
Left *This classic table setting introduces a hint of tea rose in the cloth and napkin border to contrast with the white china and clear glass.*

Below *Shells drilled then sewn on to hessian mats repeat the seashell pattern of these china plates and are a simple way of decorating a special summer table.*

---

table setting ideas

▓ Use candle holders of different heights interspersed with flowers for a table centrepiece.

▓ You could decorate plain white charger plates by flicking them with paints in primary or metallic colours – but then you can only handwash them .

▓ Mix reflective materials such as chrome and steel, metallic-thread textiles and glass, as a change from a theme based on colour, and have large square or pyramid-shaped candles.

▓ Decorate the table with netting sprayed the colour of your choice – perhaps shocking pink or

marine blue for a christening, and gold, silver or ruby red for wedding anniversaries..

▓ Float tea lights and large flower heads, such as gerbera or chrysanthemum, in a dish of water for a flameproof table centrepiece.

▓ Edible centrepieces are dual-purpose arrangements. Try berry fruits dipped in chocolate or heaps of frosted grapes.

▓ Trim white cotton table linen with coloured borders using no-sew bonding to co-ordinate with china or flowers.

Seasonal tables

Christmas dinner is one meal that even the most divided family eats together, while Easter is another increasingly significant date for family reunions. These festival times touch many faiths, with Chanukah and Diwali marking the winter solstice and Passover coinciding with spring. So whatever your customs, consider these ideas for celebration tables.

NATURE'S BOUNTY

Foliage, fruit and flowers in the traditional Christmas colours of red and green look particularly effective teamed with frosty white for a fresh look or with bronze and gold for opulence.

Have a go at making a sumptuous-looking table centrepiece. Using a block of dry florist's foam and a few sharp sticks to hold the fruit in place, pile a golden bowl high with red apples or pears and bright pomegranates. Place a red cyclamen at the back and fill the gaps with red hypericum and purple viburnum berries. Then frame the arrangement with laurel leaves, pine branches, trailing ivy and gold-sprayed twigs. If liked, coat the fruit with thinned wallpaper paste then cover them in gold leaf, or simply rub them with gold wax crayon.

For a different, more natural look on the table, simply wind strands of ivy around the napkins and mark each place setting by writing a guest's name on a holly leaf, using a gold marker pen.

Festival of light

Candles are a must at Christmas time, which in many cultures is a festival of light. If they are to be part of a table setting, be sparing with the foliage for safety reasons. For a low arrangement, tuck sprigs of holly and ivy around red and gold pillar candles of different heights on an oval platter, or place candles in a glass votive or storm lantern filled with glass beads for colour and light.

Millennium looks

There is plenty of scope for a new approach to Christmas, and if you decide to return to old traditions, they will seem fresher after a rest. Try an oriental mix of lacquer red and purple, or combine blue and lilac with silver or gold. Arrange silver-sprayed pebbles and ivy around blue and silver baubles and a blue candle; or use silver only – spray sprigs of holly and tie napkins with silver string.

Far left A sari table cover and velvet runner in jewel-rich colours make an excitingly different festive table. Gilded pears and glasses and a beaded copper candleholder emphasize the eastern look.

Above left Silver dragees wrapped in organza and tied with silver ribbon make charming presents at each place setting and are an original alternative to crackers.

Left Serve guests colour-coordinated champagne – the ultimate look of luxury. Simply run a piece of lemon around the rim of a fluted glass and dip it in coloured sugar crystals.

THE RITE OF SPRING

Whenever Easter arrives, it is marked by seasonal flowers – often snowdrops and crocuses or bluebells and daffodils. These, together with the other signs of spring like buds and young green leaves, make wonderfully fresh table centres.

First flowers

Typical Easter flowers such as primroses, daffodils and narcissi often look better massed in a jug, a bowl hidden inside a basket, or a shiny tin, rather than in a formal arrangement. More suited to formality are tulips and mimosa, with their sculptural stems. Freesias and hyacinths are striking and can look splendid on the table but their heavy scent means that they are best moved before the meal begins. Cut spring flowers do not last long so, for a living display, plant everlasting pansies or primroses in an attractive trug lined with moss and keep them well watered.

Easter eggs

Eggs can play an important part in Easter table centrepieces. Unless you are planning a children's party, the combination of eggs, chicks and nests can look irredeemably twee, but there are some more grown-up ways to use them. A shredded paper 'nest' containing dark chocolate truffles on a bed of coloured tissue paper is one idea. Put a 'nest' beside each setting – the truffles are perfect with coffee. For candle holders, use food colouring to dye empty eggshells in soft pastel colours, pack them with sand or plasticine and lay a tea light on top of each. Place in eggcups and mass together for impact. Alternatively, use the eggshells as bud vases by filling them with tiny sprigs of lilac, lily of the valley, primrose or miniature narcissi.

Edible delights

Painted eggs look charming surrounding a display of spring flowers, or in a paper 'nest'. There is no need to blow them – just dip hard-boiled white eggs in paint. Unless they are purely for decoration, however, be sure to use food colouring or purpose-made egg dye from craft shops, because the shells are permeable. Brilliant jewel colours make a change from traditional yellow and green, and you can marble colours or mix them by dyeing one half of an egg in one shade and the other half in another. Marzipan eggs are a traditional part of a Simnel cake (they are supposed to represent the 12 apostles – 11 if you discard Judas). You can dress this up with miniature chicks and candy eggs, or, for a more sophisticated look, simply tie a length of broad green ribbon or a piece of yellow gingham around it and scatter primrose heads on top.

Above An assortment of candles in different heights, and in shades that suggest spring flowers and foliage, are surrounded by pebbles for a natural-looking display.

Right Yellows and greens are perfect for an Easter table setting. The contrast of curves (chrysanthemums and dishes) and angles (square candles) gives it a modern look.

festive table ideas

Winter:

● Make the most of scarce winter flowers by making miniature flower arrangements in tea cups, tumblers or eggcups.

● Heap clear glass baubles around a candle in a transparent dish and set them on a mirror to increase the play of light.

● Make a table runner from green or red satin, tartan or a festive print. Give it a border and sew tassels at each corner. It is the ideal way to transform a plain white cloth, especially if you make matching napkins with frayed edges.

Spring:

● To show off fragile blooms, float delicate single flower heads in a shallow dish.

● Place flowers in a glass vase filled with water coloured with food dye. Watch … and wait.

● Set a narrow glass jar filled with narcissi inside a tank vase and surround it with pebbles.

Glassware

Wine looks more tempting in an elegant glass, and water more thirst-quenching in an attractive tumbler. Glass is also moving into the dining room in other areas – plates, mugs and even teapots. Cared for properly, your glassware will gleam for years.

You need to know what you are buying when choosing glass. The most popular type of glass for everyday use is 'soda-lime glass', which is inexpensive and can be washed in the dishwasher. In time, the glasses may become cloudy, in which case they can be put through a dishwasher cycle with citric acid crystals or powder, omitting detergent. Delicate or hand-made glasses should always be washed by hand.

Know your crystal

High-quality glassware known as 'lead crystal' must contain at least 24 per cent lead oxide; glass with less than this is simply known as 'crystal'. The heavier the glass, the higher the lead content – which does not necessarily make the glass better quality. The hot water and detergents of a dishwasher will dull the appearance of lead crystal, so always wash it by hand, preferably separately in a plastic bowl, to prevent chipping.

Glass care

■ Take extra care when drying fragile stemmed glasses by hand – avoid holding the bowl and twisting the stem as you dry.

■ Do not stack glasses one inside the other or they may become stuck.

■ Always store wine glasses the right way up on a shelf – the rim is the most delicate part and is prone to chipping.

Glass tumblers come in all sizes; they are virtually unbreakable and ideal for everyday use.

Glass jug *and matching short and tall tumblers made of hand-blown lead crystal.*

Bee-embossed *wine tumblers, made from pressed glass, have broad bases that make them almost spillproof.*

Square glass plates *and bowls look smart in a contemporary setting and are dishwasherproof.*

Heatproof glass mug *makes an attractive vessel for herbal teas and infusions.*

Hand-made purple *wine glass with short stem has an unusual shaped bowl and is not easily knocked over.*

Lead crystal *wine glasses in generous sizes are individually craftsman-blown for superb clarity.*

Glass teapot *with heatproof black plastic handle and lid enables you to see the quantity of tea in the pot.*

Round hand-blown *blue water glass with heavy base sits comfortably in the hand.*

Hand-made goblets *in purple and pink with clear 'bubble' stems make elegant wine glasses.*

kitchens

In most homes, a new kitchen is often the focus of more thought and greater expense than any other room. While style and decor are important, what matters most is that the space works for you and the life you lead, whether you are a committed cook or a ready-made enthusiast, and whether the kitchen doubles up as a place to eat, to do the washing, or even to work.

Designing the kitchen

Installing a new kitchen has been likened to having a baby: the best parts are conception and delivery and the worst is the labour in between. Since it is something you will probably go through even less often (the average kitchen lasts for 15 years), it is worth spending as much time as you can at the planning stage.

Above *This freestanding unit is the perfect partner for a butler's sink. There is no need to set it into a worktop – traditional wooden draining boards are used each side instead.*

Below *A small kitchen has been extended to provide a dining area that overlooks the garden. The butcher's block serves here as an extension of the work surface.*

Make a wish list

Kitchen retailers can draw up computerized plans to show what the units will look like in place but they are not mind-readers and need an idea of what you want. Make yourself two lists – one noting what is essential and the other to remind you of what you would really like to include. The ideal kitchen should contain all of the first list and at least half of the second, so that it is satisfying as well as efficient and practical. At the same time, write down the good and bad features of your present kitchen and note any appliances you need to keep. Ask yourself how many people will be using the kitchen. If two people will be cooking at the same time, for example, you will need separate preparation areas and possibly a hob some distance from the oven.

Back to basics

Sketch a plan of the empty room, marking windows, doors, plumbing outlets, radiators and power points. Now see if any of these would be better changed. Is it possible to block off a doorway, for example? The fewer entrances the better, is the general rule. Do you want to move the sink? This is almost invariably under the window but you might prefer to move it along or turn it through 90 degrees so it faces the wall. If you put a worktop in its place, you could enjoy the view while chopping the vegetables. Can you move a radiator to free up wall space for more units? Do you want more power points, or flexible lighting? Looking at your kitchen as an empty room might prompt you to think about more radical improvements because the shape of the room invariably dictates the layout. If it is very small or awkward to use, you might want to extend it or combine it with another room. Equally, you might decide to settle for less and keep the framework as it is.

Filling the space

It is easy to believe from the brochures that all kitchens consist of fitted units; however, there is often a place for freestanding pieces, too. It can be a good idea to break up space with an island unit or butcher's block, for example, or you could equip your whole kitchen with separate pieces of furniture. Even more important than what you choose is its location, to make the most of the space see 'The best layout' overleaf.

kitchen checklist

▓ Store food near the preparation area but keep coffee and tea near the kettle.

▓ Decide whether you want china and cutlery stored close to the dishwasher, so that they are easy to put away, or near the eating area, so that they are close at hand when laying the table.

▓ Place tall units and fridge-freezers at the end of a worktop run.

▓ Mark the position of the mains stopcock on your plan and ensure there is easy access to it.

▓ Think hard about the cooker you want. If it is dual fuel, gas or LPG (liquid petroleum gas), you will need the appropriate fuel supply.

▓ Do not put a cooker in a corner (awkward), near a window (dangerous) or next to the fridge. Allow a worktop each side for hot pans.

▓ Who will install your kitchen? Some suppliers do it themselves, others recommend independent companies, or you can hire your own kitchen fitters (plus plumber, electrician and tiler).

Above *This Shaker-style kitchen in soft blue has two distinct areas, one for food preparation and the other for the actual cooking.. The island unit makes good use of space in such a large room.*

The best layout

Saving energy is what the modern kitchen is all about and that applies to those who use it, too. At the heart of kitchen planning is the 'golden triangle' that connects cooker, sink and fridge. Ideally, these items should be linked by a worktop, and unobstructed by a table or island unit for a smooth transition from one to the other. The exception is the very narrow kitchen with units along a single wall, where a linear arrangement is the only possible option.

Above An island unit is useful for breaking up space in a large kitchen. Positioned, as here, opposite the cooker, it provides a useful additional work surface. The wooden worktop of this one contrasts with the stainless steel cooker surround.

Top Fitted units have been used creatively in this awkwardly shaped kitchen and the oven has been set in the facing wall to create extra surface space. Painted chairs have been chosen to soften the effect of the polished wooden worktops and table.

Layout plans

It is worth sketching several plans to see how the different possible layouts apply to your kitchen. Allow space for all doors to open comfortably, and try to provide an unbroken sweep of worktop between cooker and sink, which will probably be your main food preparation and serving area. First mark the positions of the cooker, sink and fridge and measure the length of each side of the triangle that joins them. If the total length exceeds 6.6m (21½ft), it is too wearing; if it is less than 3.6m (12ft), it is too cramped.

U-shapes and L-shapes

The U-shape is the most flexible arrangement of all, and perfect for a square kitchen. However, in many houses this layout is prohibited by the position of the back door.

The L-shape is the next best layout, and more feasible in most kitchens. Units and appliances on two walls mean that cooking will not be interrupted by people passing through, and the third wall can be used for storage or as an eating area. A small L-shape allows too little room for food preparation so this layout is not ideal for tiny kitchens.

The island

An island unit can be an integral part of the work triangle, with a fridge underneath or hob and fan inset (although this can be costly), or used as an extra work surface outside the triangle. Whatever its function, it should not make the work triangle too narrow or turn it into a passageway.

The galley

Galleys are corridor kitchens, often with doors at each end. Although not always convenient, they can look extremely stylish. A double galley has units and appliances on facing walls, and needs at least 1.2m (4ft) clear floor space between them for access to the cupboards. For safety, keep the sink and cooker on the same side so you don't have to cross the room with hot pans. A single galley runs along one wall and needs to be at least 3m (10ft) long to accommodate the appliances and worktop and 1.8m (6ft) wide to give two people room to pass.

U-shaped layout

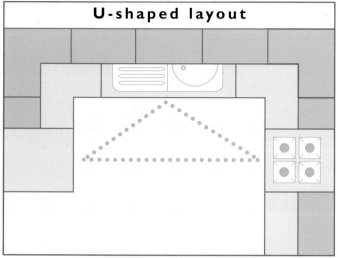

island layout

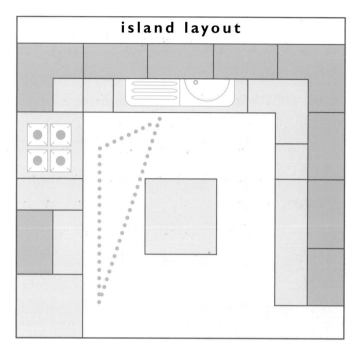

L-shaped layout

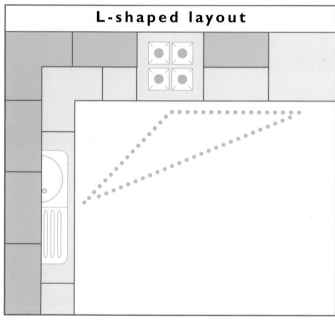

double galley layout

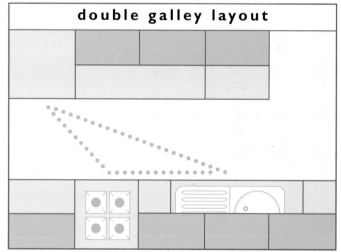

layout checklist

In a U-shaped layout (top left), units and appliances are placed along three walls, providing maximum work space.

An L-shaped layout (bottom left) has the units and appliances arranged along two adjacent walls.

An island kitchen (top right) is usually a U- or an L-shaped layout with an island unit or units in the centre.

In a double galley kitchen (bottom right) the appliances and units are lined up along facing walls, with the sink and cooker/hob on one side and the fridge and main storage area opposite.

If you have a narrow or galley kitchen, you can create extra storage and work surface space by using wall units, instead of standard base units, on the floor.

Above *All kitchens, except a single galley, should be planned using the golden triangle principle. The triangle is the shape that would be created if an imaginary line is drawn between sink, oven and fridge. These three areas should have working space in between, but should be uobstructed (by an island or table for example).*

The work zone

It is at the brochure-browsing stage that a kitchen starts to come alive. Flipping through photographs of different designs helps to clarify your ideas and sort the styles you like from those you don't. But don't make a final decision on kitchen units until you have had a chance to examine them by testing the drawers and doors and assessing the strength of the frame. Although visiting showrooms and the like can be tedious, it is essential in order to gauge what the kitchen is really like.

THE FITTED KITCHEN

It is easy to see why this is a popular choice. Fitted units are easy to clean (no gaps for crumbs to drop through) and make excellent use of space; and their streamlined effect can make the kitchen appear larger. The main drawbacks are price and inflexibility. Fortunately, all units conform to the same basic size so new doors can be used to update a kitchen that is ugly but sound. Alternatively, you could try painting the existing doors: sand them carefully, paint them, top with clear varnish and then fit stylish handles for a completely new look.

Shapes and sizes

A basic kitchen module, for example, a standard floor cupboard or a regular dishwasher, is 600mm (24in) wide by 600mm (24in) deep. Other units are variations of this size, so double units are 1200mm (48in) wide and narrow ones usually 300mm (12in) wide. Floor cupboards generally have adjustable legs, hidden by a plinth, to compensate for changes in floor level, and it helps if the door hinges are adjustable, too. Wall units are usually 300–350mm (12–14in) deep and available in a choice of heights. Short cupboards can be dust-traps and, while tall units to the ceiling look sleek, you may find the top shelves impossible to reach.

Construction

Units come either packed flat or rigid. Flat-packed units are often cheaper because they are easier to make and deliver, but they are not for do-it-yourself assembly unless you are really competent. The problem is not in putting the units together but in fixing them in place, making them level and filling the inevitable gaps at the rear and at the end of the run. The kitchen unit carcass is usually chipboard with a skim of melamine, although more expensive ranges may be made of solid wood.

Door styles and colours

These vary enormously but there are two main types: doors of chipboard or medium-density fibreboard (MDF), topped with plastic laminate, sprayed melamine or wood veneer, and doors of solid wood. Light woods, bright colours and simple Shaker styles are all fashionable but it may be better to opt for a design that will adapt to a number of different schemes than to choose a look that you love now but may soon tire of.

Top *Units, walls, shelves and Aga in a matching cream are offset by a light wood floor to make the most of the space in this small kitchen.*

Above *Natural wood is the classic choice for a farmhouse kitchen. The stainless steel cooker fits perfectly into the space once taken up by an old-fashioned range.*

Right *These eye-catching units have a hidden surprise – they are a vivid lime green inside. The soft blue doors are a good foil for the shiny granite worktop and stainless steel cooker.*

Above With its useful worktop and deep cupboards, the dresser base can be seen as the forerunner of today's fitted kitchen units. This one has been painted glossy white to contrast with the blue sink unit.

Below Freestanding furniture helps to humanize a fitted kitchen. A marble-topped chest serves as an island unit, a glass-fronted cabinet displays china, and the butcher's block provides mobile storage.

THE FREESTANDING KITCHEN

All kitchen furniture was originally free-standing, apart from the sink and the kitchen range. After the Second World War Formica surfaces and fitted cupboards became all the rage and, generally speaking, have been the accepted style ever since. Although the country house look, with its dark wood units, tiled worktops, carvings and bunches of dried herbs gave a traditional touch to kitchens of the 1980s and 1990s, minimalism has since put an end to nostalgia in decorating. Yet there is still something very seductive about a kitchen furnished with a dresser full of china, an Aga, a well-scrubbed pine table and a butcher's block.

The deceptive kitchen

Ideal for someone who is constantly house-moving is the kitchen that looks fitted but is not. Freestanding kitchen furniture tends to be found at the extremes of the price range. Costlier than many fitted kitchens are the craftsman-made pieces that are modern interpretations of traditional designs – the dresser, the work table or the settle, for instance. Far too precious to be left behind when you move, these can travel with you from home to home. At the other end of

the scale are budget kitchen units, which combine simple structures like side tables with freestanding cupboards. Although these lack the seamless appearance of a fully fitted kitchen, they are inexpensive and the perfect solution for anyone unwilling to invest in an expensive kitchen for a short-term home.

The eclectic kitchen

There is no reason, of course, why you cannot have both freestanding and fitted kitchen furniture. Many people find the clinical look of a fully fitted kitchen sterile, and an extra table, cabinet or comfortable chair can make all the difference to both style and comfort, if you have the space. You can mix and match classic and contemporary pieces. Open shelves, wicker storage baskets and racks for saucepans and tools all add an element of carefully controlled clutter, which makes a positive contribution to the look of the room. If your space is limited, you could go for narrow pieces like wall shelves, bookcases and side tables, with settles or church pews for seating.

Right Freestanding furniture need not be used alone. Here, open-fronted units on castors are combined with wall-mounted and glass-fronted cupboards for an eclectic, stylish look.

---

fitted kitchen checklist

▨ Look for a guarantee on kitchen furniture of at least five years. If you employ a separate company to install the units or fit them yourself, check that this will not invalidate the guarantee.

▨ Assess the thickness, strength and stability of the carcass before buying fitted units. The edges of chipboard should be properly sealed for protection from damp.

▨ Check that drawers have stops so that they cannot be pulled out too far. They should be full-height at the back to prevent things falling down the back of the unit.

▨ Look for hinges and drawer runners made of metal (plastic will not last). Runners with ball-bearings are the smoothest.

▨ Gas appliances should be fitted only by a qualified gas fitter, preferably one who is registered with the relevant national body.

▨ Do not sign an acceptance form for flat-packed units until you have had a chance to check that the right components have been delivered. After installation, it is wise to check the work and stipulate reassessment after a reasonable period of use before you sign to say that you are satisfied.

THE ISLAND UNIT

It takes as much thought to make good use of space in a large kitchen as in the tiniest galley. Endless trekking between the fridge, sink and cooker – the three elements of the work triangle – is tiring, which is why creating an island to bring food preparation or cooking closer to hand is so practical. Additionally, providing a barrier between the work area and the rest of the kitchen gives an opportunity to create two rooms in one. Beyond the island could be a dining area, a family den with sofa and TV, a mini home office with a computer, or a playroom, provided it is safe from kitchen hazards.

What will you use it for?

Although islands are often part of expensive 'bespoke kitchens', there is no reason why they should be limited to this part of the market. At its simplest, an island unit provides an additional worktop with storage beneath; there is often scope to create a breakfast bar on the other side. An island can also free up the cooking area by taking over a function of the work triangle. For example, it could be worth installing a fridge and extra food storage underneath so the island becomes the main food preparation area. Siting the hob there could create an impressive cooking area, especially with a large cooker hood overhead, which not only provides ventilation but also becomes a focal point. The island could also provide a site for the sink, perhaps with a dishwasher, for clearing dishes or for washing vegetables as an extension of the food preparation area.

The butcher's block

No room for an island? Then consider installing a butcher's block as a substitute. Essentially a chopping board on wheels, a butcher's block provides extra space for heavy-duty food preparation. It is practical because it also contains storage for utensils

or vegetables plus a rail for cloths, and of course it can be pushed to one side when not required. Butcher's blocks vary widely in quality and price. Many are flat-packed and some are frankly too flimsy to offer much more than extra storage. As when buying any form of kitchen furniture, make sure you see the finished product and, if you want it to be a serious workstation, make sure it is a comfortable height.

Left *Cleverly recessed cupboards create enough leg room for this island unit to double as a breakfast bar. A useful recess in the side provides shelving and storage space for cookbooks.*

Above *A two-tier unit for storage and food preparation shows how visibly effective as well as practical an island can be. Hardwood and granite work surfaces are an unbeatably hard-wearing duo.*

butcher's block checklist

▨ The way in which a butcher's block is described is often a guide to its purpose. Many are called kitchen workstations, butcher's trolleys or kitchen islands rather than butcher's blocks. If you want a block for chopping meat, you may have to hunt down an old butcher's block. These are now collector's items and are unlikely to provide a flat work surface if they've been well used.

▨ When buying new, a removable chopping board is probably the most hygienic option. Worktops on butcher's blocks are often not designed for heavy use. Oiled worktops (which need treating about

once a month) can be used for light cutting, but lacquered worktops cannot.

▨ Worktops should be made from hardwood like beech, maple, birch or rubberwood. End-grain worktops are the most hard-wearing but can stain.

▨ Clean the top after use with hot, soapy water and dry with absorbent kitchen paper. If the top gets too wet, it may warp or split.

▨ Test the trolley for manoeuvrability – at least two castors should lock for stability. Rubber wheels are more durable than plastic ones.

WORKTOPS

A worktop that doubles as a chopping board is not possible. Depending on the material used, a work surface can be scorched, stained or scratched, although with a little care it will last up to 25 years. So, use trivets for hot pans and chopping boards for cutting food to maintain your kitchen's good looks.

Man-made materials

Laminate worktops score top marks for heat and stain resistance and are a good, all-round choice. Made from layers of paper and plastic bonded to a chipboard, medium-density fibreboard (MDF) or plywood core, most will withstand temperatures up to 180°C (355°F), and high-pressure laminates can resist 230°C (450°F).

Solid man-made materials like Corian can be moulded seamlessly into almost any shape, including sinks and drainers. Made to fit and installed by experts, they may cost up to four times more than laminate. A cheaper option is the thinner 'solid surface veneer' (SSV). Although less versatile, it is around half the price of a solid surface worktop.

Stone and tiles

Joins may show, but cool and heavy granite is the perfect surface for making pastry. So is marble, which stains easily and is not really practicable for continuous lengths of work-top, but looks splendid set into a tiled or timber surface. Lava rock is another good surface for food preparation, but is expensive and liable to chip. Quarry and ceramic tiles are still used for worktops but have been widely superseded by stone, which does not need the grout that can be difficult to keep clean. If you want to use tiles, check that they are suitable for worktops – they need not be any thicker than wall tiles but they should have a stronger glaze.

Metal

Stainless steel first became fashionable on vast fridges and cookers; then came the brushed stainless steel worktops originally found in restaurant kitchens. The surface marks easily, but the scratches blend together over time to give a uniform patina. Textured stainless steel, however, disguises marks.

Wood

A hardwood worktop is a modern classic, but it is also high maintenance. Susceptible to damp, wood is best not used next to a butler's sink, where it is difficult to form a watertight seal. To protect wood above a washing machine or dishwasher from condensation, use special moisture-resistant paper on the underside of the work surface. Wood needs oiling regularly and can usually be sanded if any scratches become obvious.

Above A wooden worktop contrasts beautifully with cool stainless steel and chrome, adding warmth to the kitchen. It needs regular oiling to keep it in top condition.
Below Stainless steel is elegant and hard-wearing but caring for it can be time-consuming. Using a specialist cleaner and buffing it well will help.

Right Although hardwood makes a wonderful worktop, it is not ideal for wet areas. Here, it is reserved for the island unit while granite is used around the deep butler's sink.

---

worktop checklist

▨ Most worktops are between 30mm and 40mm (1¼–1½in) thick (hardwood and granite may be thinner) and 600mm (24in) deep. It is often possible to buy deeper worktops to make a breakfast bar or peninsula unit.

▨ Standard worktop lengths are 3m (10ft) but you can order longer ones.

▨ Post-formed (rounded) edges are less likely to chip but are difficult to join at corners.

▨ If you want more work space, fit the units away from the wall and use a deeper worktop.

▨ Materials can be mixed and matched: combine hardwood with granite or marble for a cool area for pastry-making, or use stainless steel or stone around a sink and wood where food is prepared.

▨ A chopping board inserted in the worktop or one that fits over it helps to protect the surface.

▨ Unwrap and check the condition of a worktop as soon as it is delivered – it may have been knocked or scratched in transit.

▨ For the best results, have your worktops professionally fitted.

A place to eat

Squeeze a breakfast bar into the kitchen and put an end to meals eaten on the run. All you need is a wide shelf at just below worktop height with room for a couple of stools underneath. If you hate feeling isolated while you are cooking, a kitchen–dining room is the answer, while in between there is a range of flexible solutions, from 'casual dining' furniture to extending tables and peninsula units.

Making it work

Knowing from the outset that you want to incorporate an eating area into the kitchen is the best way to make sure it is a success. If you can plan it at an early stage, it is possible to provide fittings that can make all the difference to your comfort. Efficient ventilation is a priority, so install a ducted cooker hood, that will extract fumes.

Lighting is another consideration. Although direct working light is essential in the kitchen, you do need to provide softer lighting for relaxed dining. A pendant light over the table, uplighters or wall lights can all help to create an entirely different atmosphere in the eating area.

Choose appliances that are quiet and well insulated and think about fitting some form of screen, if this is where guests as well as family will eat. Cooks do not always want to be on show and, even if your cooking methods are above reproach, it is best to stack dirty dishes out of sight so you don't have to stare at them after a meal. For a simple screen, adding an upstand to a row of kitchen units is an easy way to form a room divider; it also provides useful extra storage. Alternatively, a peninsula unit that is used as a bar rather than for intensive food preparation will put a clear expanse between the guests and any kitchen muddle.

Selecting a style

If the room is large enough, a separate table gives you the opportunity to introduce a different note into the kitchen. You could use a circular table to offset the straight lines of the units, choose an old style of kitchen or refectory table to contrast with minimalist modern units, or add moulded ply chairs for a more traditional setting. Since see-through furniture increases the sense of space, glass tables and perforated metal chairs are often a successful choice.

Sometimes, extending the kitchen or combining it with another room is the best way to make a comfortable place to eat. Adding a conservatory is a popular form of extension that works particularly well as a dining area, increasing the amount of light and air in the kitchen and bringing a touch of the garden indoors. Knocking two rooms into one can be a good move and gives you the chance to vary the decorative pace, perhaps choosing a bold colour for the kitchen working area and a more tranquil shade for the dining room – or indeed vice versa if you prefer.

Top Modern rush chairs introduce natural texture here, picking up the tones of the natural wood and the honey-coloured stone floor.

Above This simple but effective breakfast bar is made from a wide hardwood worktop projecting beyond the island unit.

Right A small table by the window makes the most of the garden outlook in this seaside cottage. The wooden stool can be tucked underneath out of the way when not in use.

Kitchen flooring

Contrary to popular opinion, there are very few floors that cannot be used in the kitchen, provided they are watertight and resistant to wear. If your kitchen is a thoroughfare, it is well worth opting for a floor that won't show every trace of dirt. For example, pale ceramic tiles look glorious but are perhaps a better choice for a self-contained kitchen than one that is the main route to the garden.

HARD FLOORING

It may be unyielding underfoot, but flooring made from stone, slate, quarry or ceramic tiles is about as hard-wearing as you can get. It is common, when renovating an old house, to come across original quarry tiles or even stone flagstones buried beneath the floor, and they may well be worth restoring. Many can cope with a certain degree of damp, which makes them the ideal choice for period homes where the damp course is not as effective as it might be. Whatever the age of the property, all hard floors need a strong, rigid sub-floor, so most are suitable only for ground-floor use.

Ceramic floor tiles are highly glazed (although they don't have the polished look of wall tiles, which would make them too slippery), so even if they show the dirt, all they need is a quick wash-down with detergent and the occasional wash with diluted bleach, which removes bacteria and can help refresh grubby grouting, too.

Quarry tiles are naturals for a traditional kitchen. They can be sealed and wax polished if you like, but all that is really required to keep them clean is a good mop with detergent. However, Mediterranean-style terracotta tiles are probably worth sealing, because they are often highly porous and likely to stain. Use a specialist stain resister first, followed by wax polish or floor seal. Slate and stone can be given the same stain-resistant treatment, then finished with a coat of special floor sealer or rubbed with a blend of linseed oil and turpentine.

Naturally flexible

Cork, wood and linoleum tiles or sheeting have a warmth and resilience that is welcome in a room where you spend much of the time on your feet. Cork and wood need thorough sealing for kitchen use, which in effect turns them into plastic-coated flooring. The easiest route is to buy high-quality vinyl or acrylic-coated cork tiles or wood laminate flooring (look for kitchen grade), although you can seal natural cork and wood with several coats of waterproof floor varnish. Cork can be fragile and will need sanding and resealing in areas of wear, choose the thickest tiles you can find – 6mm ($^1/_4$in) if they are laid on a solid floor.

Linoleum is made from a blend of natural materials, including wood, flour, cork and linseed oil. Available as both tiles and sheeting (which should be professionally laid), it is springy underfoot and hard-wearing, as long as it is not allowed to get too wet, when it may rot.

Above A classic black and white chequerboard design can be created with ceramic or vinyl tiles to form the decorative focus of the room. All it needs is strong, simple shapes to show it off.
Left Stone floors are unrivalled for both durability and style. Flowing from the hall into the kitchen, these flagstones help extend the sense of space.
Below Glossy white ceramic floor tiles are perfect in this purist kitchen. They will need cleaning at least once a day, but their natural resistance to wear means they will come up shining time and time again.

MAN-MADE FLOORING MATERIALS

One of the most popular smooth floorings for kitchens is sheet vinyl, which ranges in quality from simple printed versions with a vinyl overlay to thickly cushioned vinyls offering increased comfort underfoot and resistance to wear. Vinyl tiles are also widely available but it is worth being selective when you buy. A thin surface layer is not really sufficient to withstand hard wear and, once the surface has been scratched, you will be left with a high-maintenance floor that needs repeated polishing.

Most vinyl floorings are cheerfully budget priced, with the exception of solid vinyl flooring. This pure vinyl has a tremendous depth of colour and is available in a range of sophisticated effects including marble and glass. The density of the material means that it is extremely tough; however, you will find that it can be as expensive as the most costly ceramic tiles.

Design ideas

Practical considerations aside, design is often the deciding factor when choosing flooring. It is a good idea to put together an ideas board of paint samples, fabric cuttings, colour reference and photographs, so that you can see at a glance if your preferred flooring will fit in with the furnishings you have already chosen for your kitchen.

Colour is a major consideration but texture and pattern are important, too. A certain amount of texture is needed for safety, in order to give a good grip on smooth floors, but some floors make a feature of texture, using it to create stud or brick effects for example.

Patterned floors can be practical because they disguise wear and dirt, but at the same time they can make a room look smaller and will restrict the number and type of designs that can be used on other surfaces. That said, the uncluttered layout of most kitchens means that a bold patterned floor can make a dramatic statement. Pattern need not be used all over, of course; it is particularly effective restricted to borders or used for panels that define a dining area or the cook's territory, or to improve the shape of an irregular room. At the other extreme, a completely plain floor makes a room look larger and yet it shows every speck of dirt. As a compromise, consider the many marble and stone effects that are available in both ceramic and vinyl tiles.

There is a similar dilemma when it comes to choosing colour. Pale floors emphasize space and light but can be a challenge to keep clean, while practical, muddy colours can make the kitchen look dark. One answer is to choose neutrals with a touch of honey or terracotta that fit the design ethos but are also easy to care for.

Above A wood laminate floor is a practical choice for a kitchen. This one picks up the colour of the honey-coloured units so as to make the room look larger.
Left This stunning floor is not tiled but cleverly painted – admittedly by a professional.

A similar look could be created using ceramic or vinyl tiles.
Below Marble-effect vinyl tiles make the most of a small kitchen. The grey veining reflects the colour of the stainless steel fittings and makes the tiles a practical alternative to plain white.

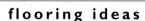

flooring ideas

● For a completely seamless finish, consider a flooring like a stone carpet, made from tiny round pebbles, or terrazzo, which consists of marble chips. Be warned – both are in the luxury class.

● If you have an island unit, create a feature floor panel around it to turn it into a focal point.

● You can create a soft, chalky tile pattern or frieze by colourwashing your floorboards. Top with several coats of heavy-duty floor varnish to protect the surface.

● Cool, strong shades of deep blue or green add colour interest to the floor and are versatile enough to adapt to a variety of schemes and styles in the kitchen.

● Linoleum is available in muted colours and a range of stylish patterns, including clever three-dimensional designs.

● Mix boxes of ceramic, quarry and terracotta tiles before laying them because the colour may vary from batch to batch.

Family kitchen

Knocking down internal walls and adding several windows opened up the space and allowed light to flood into this extended kitchen, creating a cheerful family room in which meals are taken together. The bold use of colour on the walls gives it a contemporary feel.

The original kitchen in Mark and Angela's house eventually proved too small and too dark for the needs of a growing family: their two sons are four and eight. They decided to extend the room into the space provided by a badly built extension, that had been added to the house in the 1970s, and an adjacent veranda.

Luckily, Mark is an architect so he was able to do the design work for the new kitchen himself: the designing and planning stages took four months. The couple juggled their budget very carefully, making savings where they could in order to have the stylish work surfaces that they particularly wanted in the new kitchen. Their choice of birch plywood for both the units and the floor was practical and at the same time economical. The addition of hand-made doors to the ready-made kitchen units was an inspired touch which, together with the modern-looking stainless steel linear handles, adds class to the finished kitchen.

Not wanting the kitchen to look too sterile, Angela and Mark chose a bold aubergine-coloured paint for the walls and striking Italian blue tiles to go around the cast-iron stove (not pictured). This multi-fuel stove is situated next to an existing structural pillar in the middle of the room and gives the kitchen a cosy and welcoming appearance. At one end of the room, a low-level radiator provides additional heating, and is cleverly concealed by a useful bench. An excellent lighting system ensures all the work areas are well lit.

Positioning the cupboards, main work surface and the fridge and cooker along the internal wall of the kitchen has freed up the centre of the room. The dining table now stands here, receiving plenty of light from a nearby window. All that remains to finish off the room is for Angela and Mark to design the perfect kitchen table; it needs to complement the elegant Scandinavian 1950s-style wishbone chairs in beechwood, which were a housewarming gift from Mark's mother.

So, the overall effect of this undertaking has been to create a cheerful and spacious room that looks utterly modern and that suits all members of the family.

Left A bench provides extra seating for a busy household, as well as being a clever cover-up for the low-level radiator. And good use is made of a recess for storage shelves.

Above The dining table is situated in the heart of the kitchen, close enough to the cooking area, but benefiting from natural daylight via new windows. The eye-level grill is convenient to use and safely beyond the reach of young children.

Right The addition of hand-made doors has personalized these standard beech-ply kitchen units. The strong, aubergine-coloured wall and the use of stainless steel for the oven, the cooker hood and the door handles echo the contemporary look of this kitchen.

Country style

Freestanding cupboards and 'distressed' paint finishes have given this country kitchen an individuality that is often lacking where more streamlined fitted units are used. It is spot-on for a 400-year-old farmhouse, while meeting the needs of a lively, modern-day family.

Right *These sturdy, freestanding units bring a traditional feel to the kitchen but the paint colours are contemporary. Baskets sit above the ceiling unit, where everything, from colanders to baskets of eggs, is suspended by butcher's hooks, all within easy reach of the work surface.*

Below *A 'distressed' pale blue spice cupboard hangs on the wall above the bow-fronted pine corner unit, that is topped with black granite to match the Aga.*

Updating a kitchen yet keeping it in style with a 16th-century farmhouse was quite a challenge for Robert and Sue. The kitchen opens onto an original cobbled courtyard and this became an important factor in the planning stages.

'We wanted to find something in keeping with the style of the house,' Sue recalls, 'and I didn't like the repetitive effect that most kitchen companies seemed to offer.' This led them to choose an unfitted kitchen and they turned to a company whose freestanding furniture in different woods and colours really appealed to them.

The majority of the units are painted petroleum blue or earthy green, with a slightly 'distressed' effect to give a comfortable impression of age; their turned wooden handles match the natural timber of one or two smaller pieces. Robert and Sue opted for warm-looking pine work surfaces

throughout the kitchen, which are sealed to make them more practical. Robert and Sue painted the walls off-white, which provides a good foil for all the existing colours and textures in this cheerful family kitchen.

With dogs, cats and three young children constantly in and out, they needed a floor that was hard-wearing and practical. They chose terracotta tiles, which have a warm, natural look and are easy to wash down. Windows on two walls fill the kitchen with light and Sue chose the clean lines of Roman blinds to cover them. 'I was lucky with the fabric for the blinds,' she said. 'I was looking for something fresh that complemented the colour of the units and I found this simple gingham daisy check.'

The farmhouse kitchen is the centre of activity in the house for the family of five, and it has a welcoming, lived-in feel. The Aga is an appropriate hub and ensures that the room is always warm. The room has nothing of the stark, clinical look of some modern, streamlined, fitted kitchens – instead, it is full of texture and detail, without being cluttered. Shelving units and a dresser are used to display much of Sue and Robert's china, while the walls are embellished with decorative plates; window sills hold jugs of flowers and cooking implements, jugs and strings of garlic hang from the ceiling. They have succeeded in producing a stylish kitchen that is entirely right for a farmhouse, without looking old-fashioned and rustic in any way.

The high-tech kitchen

A clever combination of the natural and the high-tech makes the most of this spacious family kitchen in which a multitude of activities take place. The room is as practical as it is stylish, and the quality of the materials used will ensure long-lasting good looks.

Planning a new house gave Andrew and Gilda the perfect opportunity to design the dream kitchen they had always wanted. Andrew, a building technician, and Gilda, a keep-fit trainer, each had slightly different priorities but they both knew, above all, that they wanted a large family room that was light and airy.

'The kitchen is where we cook and chat in the evening while our children do their homework at the kitchen table or watch television,' explains Andrew. 'We spend more time here than anywhere else in the house.'

They decided to banish nostalgia and go instead for a modern, streamlined look, using 'high-tech' materials such as stainless steel, as well as natural ones like the pale wooden units that maintain the room's airy feel. Gilda chose the appliances since she does most of the cooking. Although she doesn't have the time to make elaborate meals, she insists on healthy eating. 'As we both work long hours, we cook quick and simple dishes that need little preparation,' she says. The wall-mounted steam oven, adjacent to the conventional built-in oven, was a luxury that Gilda could not resist and it is in constant use.

Tracking down the right kitchen units for the room was no easy task, but eventually Andrew and Gilda settled on a new fitted range made of sycamore. The retro-style handles were inspired by the sturdy handles on fridges of the 1950s, while the units' exposed hinges are another unusual detail. Two small hobs are set into the central island unit, which is topped with a massive granite worktop that was chosen for its looks and practicality. It was far from simple to install, however – six men were needed to bring the monolithic piece indoors and holes for the hobs had to be cut on site. Andrew himself designed the efficient, futuristic-looking extractor fan that hangs above it, cleverly suspended by lengths of yachting wire.

At the far end of the kitchen is a wall of windows that gives glorious views over the garden. This is where the dining area is situated, which is all sunshine and light wood. To provide the cooking area with more light, skylights were installed in the long sloping roof. White was the colour chosen to paint the walls and this, together with the pale limestone flooring, ensures that the kitchen looks as bright and airy as possible, all day long.

Above *Andrew and Gilda share a cup of tea in the kitchen of their dreams.*
Left *For the stream-lined doors on the 'working' side of the island unit, a more economical material has been used to great effect, in marked contrast with the light wood used elsewhere in the kitchen.*

Right *The pale blond colours of the sycamore units and the limestone flooring soften the look of the stainless steel oven and granite worktop, while keeping the kitchen light and airy. Bar stools allow the family to sit and chat to the cook.*

The home chef

This streamlined yet hard-working kitchen is a comfortable blend of old and new. While it provides every convenience a professional cook might need, it still has the feel of a family room and a colour scheme that gives it a warm and cheerful atmosphere.

Fay and Roger liked the style of the modern kitchen and its L-shaped layout that they inherited when they moved house, but were far from enthusiastic about the colour scheme – a cold, clinical slate grey. 'It reminded me of an operating theatre!' says Fay. Roger runs a fabric company and the couple are both very colour conscious, so they knew that something had to change.

Fay came up with the idea of replacing the unit doors and, luckily, the kitchen manufacturers were happy to supply them. She sent the company a swatch of her favourite fabric to be colour-matched. The soft terracotta colour has transformed the kitchen into a warm, cheerful room that is ideal for family meals. They decided on a fresh spring-green colourwash for the walls, while the terracotta colour of the units is echoed throughout the room in different accessories.

Passionate about cooking, Fay runs her own delicatessen in the local neighbourhood, so she has chosen the maximum amount of storage, catering-size appliances and a practical, easy-to-clean granite work surface. Hanging above the work areas are stylish halogen lights: 'Good lighting is essential – I want to be able to see what I'm cooking,' says Fay. Centre-stage in the kitchen is the large extractor fan over the hob, surrounded by an unusual and practical glass shelf, which keeps utensils close to hand.

One definite advantage of the kitchen wall cupboard Roger and Fay chose is the wide concertina-style doors that roll down to the worktop. They quickly conceal shelves filled with food items and kitchen appliances, thereby banishing clutter from sight once the cook's work is finished. The room is thus restored to a haven of calm in which to sit or eat meals. Roger and Fay love combining different looks, so not everything in their kitchen is modern and streamlined, and their eclectic collection of period glass and ceramics looks completely at home here.

Above *Fay and Roger at work in the kitchen. Pictured is the eye-level glass shelf that surrounds the extractor hood. Behind the vase of flowers, the stainless steel cupboard front has been pulled down for an uncluttered look.*

Left *The stainless steel double oven has mirror fronts that are easily wiped clean. Next to it, the chrome shelving unit houses a collection of glassware.*

Right *The kitchen's L-shaped layout is perfect for a working cook, with everything conveniently to hand. Electrical sockets on the shelf fronts are a practical touch.*

Storage solutions

A kitchen with too much storage is almost a contradiction in terms. However many cupboards it contains, there is constant pressure on space from an increasing collection of gadgets, pans, utensils and crockery – not to mention food. So what can you do if the kitchen is already crammed with cupboards and you want storage to supplement existing units? The solution may be easier than you imagine – and could contribute to the look of the kitchen, too.

START WITH A SHELF

Shelving is the easy answer to many storage problems and helps counteract the clinical look that a fitted kitchen can sometimes have. Even if you have wall cupboards, there is often a space above a radiator or a gap by a wall that can be pressed into service and add decorative interest at the same time.

Shelves above the worktop can be a good alternative to wall units as long as the objects on them are worth displaying – think of shelving stacked with gleaming glasses, chunky white mugs and stylish steel containers. The downside is that shelves get greasy if they are close to the cooker so be prepared to clean them – and their contents – regularly. Another useful place is just below a row of wall units, where a box shelf could be the ideal place to store mugs, the pepper mill and the other bits and pieces that tend to clutter up the worktop. A book-shelf – or even a whole bookcase if you have room – is another useful addition. It is often omitted from kitchen plans, but where else do you keep your favourite recipes? New cookery books are often too attractive to hide away so if you have room, have them facing outwards so the jackets become a foodie art display.

Add boxes or baskets

If you like the look of kitchen units that have wicker baskets in place of drawers, use hampers for additional storage or hang rush baskets from hooks and fill them with kitchen supplies. Crates are always useful, whether they are made of colourful plastic or wood, particularly if they have castors. Use them for items that are awkward to carry – cleaning materials, root vegetables or jars and cans – and keep them under a work surface or in a larder or utility room.

Fit racks and hooks

A good way of storing a *batterie de cuisine*, such as saucepans, ladles and colanders, close at hand is to hang them up. Stainless steel racks and hooks are a perfect match for shiny appliances, while wooden rails provide a warm contrast with the metal. A wall-mounted metal grid with S-hooks is an effective and stylish way of storing utensils other than knives, which can be safely clamped to a magnetic knife rack. In addition, place cup hooks beneath shelves or wall units for a neat and decorative way to store mugs and cups. A wine rack can also add visual interest if it is incorporated within a row of units.

Above Kilner and screw-top glass jars are an unbeatable way of storing dried food and preserves, and their contents can be seen at a glance.

Below A simple box on wheels has a pull handle so that it can be rolled out when needed and stored neatly beneath the table at other times.

Right A lime green wine rack brings an additional colour into this vibrant kitchen and provides the curves often lacking in a kitchen.

Above A laundry carousel comes in handy for airing dusters and rubber gloves, keeping them – and the odd memo – close at hand but clear of the worktop.

Below A vegetable rack on wheels allows air to circulate so the contents remain fresh, and can be hidden under a worktop when not required.

Right Raid offices, shops and storerooms for possible kitchen storage solutions. Steel racks and plastic baskets take care of cleaning equipment and laundry, while a lockable filing cabinet keeps harmful chemicals out of reach.

STORAGE FURNITURE

Quirky cabinets, high-tech storage racks, dressers and trolleys not only add to the look of a kitchen, they also provide valuable storage. Take the kitchen dresser, a hard-to-beat combination of shelving and cupboard space, available in simple modern styles as well as antique and carved versions. If you want a narrow cupboard for a galley kitchen or a shallow recess, look for a dresser base.

Sometimes it is an idea to take a piece of furniture out of its usual context. A chest of drawers, for instance, is ideal for storing cleaning utensils or the ironing, as well as table linen, while an old wardrobe, fitted with shelves and painted, makes an eye-catching pantry. It is often better to choose furniture to contrast with kitchen units – think of a dark oak piece with a bank of cream-painted cupboards or a 'distressed' white finish against pale wood. For a more adventurous look, consider shop fittings or office furniture and partner steel racks with lockers or filing cabinets whose drawers are the perfect size for casseroles or pans.

Inside kitchen units

Planning what goes inside your kitchen units at the outset can pay dividends. There is a bewildering variety of fittings available; two that are well worth considering are deep pull-out drawers for saucepans and a carousel for utilizing space in a corner cupboard. The value of others depends on your circumstances – a pull-out table, for example, is a godsend in a tiny kitchen. Beneficial ideas in any situation are extra shelves inside base units, grids and hooks behind cupboard doors and wire trays clipped on to shelves, all of which can be added after the kitchen is installed to supplement existing storage.

Cold storage

Big fridges are back: the modern version of the larder is the huge American-style fridge with zoned temperatures for cheese, wine, meat, fruit and vegetables – and often a drinks dispenser, too. If style is the main consideration, you can opt for sinuous shapes in aqua, stainless steel designs or jumbo-size retro models. Again, it is worth setting aside space at the planning stage. Refrigeration is now recommended for an increasing number of foods, from eggs to bottled sauces, so it could be worth cutting back on dry storage space to accommodate a larger fridge. If space is limited, there is a wide range of under-counter fridges and freezers, including integrated versions hidden by unit doors. The fridge-freezer is still popular and many kitchen manufacturers make housing units that fit over the top of it, bringing it visually into line with the wall units.

checklist for fridges and freezers

▧ Climate class labelling on fridges and freezers shows where to site the fridge. N (normal) is for rooms with temperatures of 16–32°C (61–90°F); SN (sub-normal) is for cooler places, 10–32°C (50–90°F), such as garages or some kitchens on winter nights; ST (subtropical) is for locations with temperatures of 18–38°C (64–100°F).

▧ Energy labels are a guide to electricity consumption: A is best, C is worst.

▧ Frost-free freezers do not need defrosting but they can be noisier and more expensive to run.

▧ Look for separate thermostats on each compartment of a fridge-freezer. Try to minimize the number of times you open any fridge or freezer door to keep the temperature constant.

▧ Fridges should be at a temperature of 0–5°C (32–41°F) – 0–3°C (32–37°F) for the chiller compartment – and freezers should be -18°C (-0.4°F). Four stars on a freezer show that it is capable of freezing food from fresh.

▧ Doors can usually be hung either side of a fridge or freezer to make the best use of space.

Kitchen dressers

The dresser has never really fallen out of favour, probably because it offers an ideal form of storage, combining shelves, on which to display attractive china, with cupboard space where less visually pleasing items can be kept, behind closed doors.

Many kitchen dressers are still made on traditional lines, helping to recreate the look of a farmhouse kitchen, while more contemporary versions have pared-down styling that suits the minimalist modernity of some kitchens. The shelves may be open or concealed behind glazed doors and their height is often adjustable; the dresser may come in two sections. Choose a style that either matches your kitchen units or contrasts with them to form a distinctive freestanding piece of furniture.

Materials

Wooden dressers are usually made in pine, oak, beech or cherry wood and may be solid or veneered. The wood may be left natural, or it may be stained, painted or given an antique 'distressed' or crackle finish. At the budget end of the scale are dressers made of painted MDF or white lacquered fibreboard and particleboard.

Dresser checklist

▨ Check the precise dimensions before buying a dresser to ensure that it will fit into the space you have in mind. Consider its depth as well as the height and width.

▨ Study the details carefully. The knobs or handles can make a difference to the overall look, although these are easily changed if you do not like them.

▨ Ensure that the lower half of the dresser offers adequate storage space for your needs, otherwise its use will be decorative rather than practical.

A spacious pine dresser with central glass door is painted in an ivory finish. Three drawers offer the only non-display storage.

Pine dresser with two open shelves above a cupboard with lattice-embossed doors and cast-iron handles.

Tall American oak bookcase with one fixed and three adjustable shelves serves equally well as a display dresser in the kitchen.

French-style armoire, attractively shaped at the top, has three shelves behind a toughened glass panel, below which is a cupboard.

Contemporary-style dresser with glazed fronts and shelves; beneath are drawers made from white-lacquered solid wood with simple wooden knobs.

Capacious traditional dresser is made from reclaimed pine with a waxed top; it has been given a modern look with its grey paint wash.

Traditional dark-stained hardwood dresser has three leaded glass panels with carved wooden doors below.

Traditional country-style pine dresser offers maximum storage, with display shelves, three drawers and three cupboards below.

Classic design glass-fronted dresser made from solid wood and cherry wood veneer; it would suit a formal dining room.

'Housekeeper's cupboard' with tall display shelves has a dark wax finish and rounded corners; it would suit a more formal kitchen.

Ovens and hobs

If you find it hard to decide between electricity and gas, why not have both? Whether freestanding or built-in, dual-fuel cookers that combine an electric oven with a gas hob are becoming ever more popular. As for design, there is a wide choice – from the sleek single or double built-in oven with a hob either immediately above or separated by worktop, to vast freestanding range cookers in catering-style stainless steel or deep shades of blue and green that take their inspiration from the Aga.

Above The rural dream … a shiny black Aga that not only cooks but also heats water. Ranges like this traditionally run on solid fuel but gas- and oil-fuelled versions are also available.

Below A freestanding cooker with a large oven and ample gas burners for entertaining. The stylish cooker hood makes it the focal point of the kitchen.

Right A stainless steel built-under single oven and a ceramic glass hob add to the streamlined look of this small kitchen and make the most of the limited space.

Together or apart?

The three main types of cooker are freestanding, slot-in and built-in or built-under. Freestanding cookers are an economy buy, apart from the huge cooking ranges at the top end of the scale. Slot-in cookers, which look built-in but are not, are mid-price although, surprisingly perhaps, they can be more expensive than basic built-in models. Built-under designs with a single oven containing the grill and a hob above are a popular choice, and the built-in double oven with two capacious compartments at mid-height is a good idea if you have the space.

Ovens

Most electric ovens incorporate a fan to speed up cooking and spread the heat. (For the best results, reduce the heat by 10°C/50°F and cooking time by around 10 minutes.) The fan means that you can forget about preheating the oven or swapping trays of food around for browning evenly; however, you do lose some of the colour and crispness given by the traditional 'hot at the top' static electric oven. If you want this feature, look for multi-function ovens that provide both types of heat. Single built-under ovens have an element at the top that

is used for grilling with oven door propped open. If you grill food frequently, it might be better to opt for a double oven with a small top compartment that houses the grill.

Gas ovens create a different form of heat, so food is glossy on the outside and moist on the inside. Temperature distribution varies: most have zoned heat (hotter at the top than the base) but continental cookers often have burners beneath the oven floor so the heat circulates more evenly. The grill may be separate or within the oven cavity.

Hobs

Electric hobs offer the greatest choice. Sealed plates are fast replacing the traditional radiant ring (now restricted to freestanding cookers), but can be slow to heat up and cool down. Ceramic hobs, which conceal the heating elements beneath toughened glass, are often quicker, especially if one of the 'rings' uses powerful halogen light. Instant heat is the reason why gas hobs are so popular although they are more difficult to clean than ceramic ones. If you want the style of a ceramic hob but the speed of gas, choose a gas hob with a toughened glass lid, which acts as a splashback during cooking and can be closed when not in use.

Ovens and hobs

Besides choosing between gas, electric or dual-fuel energy, do you want a freestanding or range-style cooker, or a built-in oven and separate hob? Do you want a single or double oven, the grill at eye or waist level, the hob surround of stainless steel, enamel or ceramic? So many choices …

A freestanding cooker (gas or electric) with eye-level grill, large main oven and a warming or storage drawer beneath is usually the most practical design, with everything at a convenient height. Yet built-in, streamlined appliances are more popular. Cookers with double ovens offer more cooking options, but the main oven is often hard to reach.

You are somewhat restricted if the grill is in the main oven, because oven and grill cannot be used simultaneously.

Range-style cookers have side-by-side ovens or one extra-wide oven with an integral grill, plus a storage or warming drawer and a large, substantial hob. Although styled like traditional solid-fuel ranges, they do not heat the water or run central heating. At the professional end are range cookers in stainless steel or cast iron, but these are quite fierce for cooking and you may have to adapt times and temperatures. Some of the less expensive models are quite flimsy.

Hobs

Gas hobs cook the quickest, although they can be more difficult to clean. Models with lids have a safety device that cuts off the gas supply to the burner if accidentally closed. Electric hobs have heating elements beneath either sealed plates or a ceramic glass top. Sealed-plate hobs, found on less expensive models, are slower, less responsive and awkward to clean. Glass-topped hobs can cover radiant rings or halogen bulbs; halogen is more responsive. Whatever the hob type, you need a variety of burner sizes to cater for different size pans.

Cooker functions

Built-in electric ovens now offer different functions so you can select the best method for the type of food being cooked:

▨ 'Fan-only' means that the heat is evenly distributed throughout. Space the oven shelves evenly so hot air can circulate more easily.

▨ 'Conventional-only' produces moist results, so use for long, slow cooking of roasts or fruit cakes.

▨ 'Lower element-only' can be used to crisp the bases of pizzas and quiches.

▨ 'Upper element-only' is ideal for finishing off dishes, such as browning gratins.

▨ 'Roasting' uses the grill and fan settings together.

This built-in ceramic hob *with steel trim has touch controls and sealed surface for easy cleaning.*

Stylish built-in oven in stainless steel has a single shelf and easy-to-clean enamel interior and grill. This one has a choice of five cooking options.

Built-in gas hob in red enamel finish has sturdy, removable pan supports and four burners, one high speed and one simmer.

Dual-fuel sturdily constructed range cooker is built to last, but it has no grill and the smaller oven is narrow.

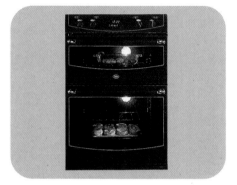

Built-in double electric oven has a high-speed grill and a choice of two cooking options.

Streamlined range-style cooker in stainless steel has a large single oven, which produces excellent roasting results and is easy to clean.

Dual-fuel range-style cooker is a good choice for a large family, with equal-sized fan ovens and an easy-to-clean ceramic gas hob.

Built-in double oven has a fan-only main oven; its smaller top oven is best used for grilling.

Single oven is built into the top of this purpose-made unit simply designed in white resin with modern-looking stainless steel handles.

Stainless steel freestanding electric cooker has a good-sized oven and grill and a stainless steel splashback.

Sinks and splashbacks

Thanks to the dishwasher, the hours once spent washing up can now be put to better use, and so can the space taken up by the sink. In place of a standard sink unit, you can now opt for a deep china sink (ideal for scrubbing all those organic vegetables) or an inset bowl if all you want to do is rinse out the odd mug. Simply protect the wall behind with a tiled or stainless steel splashback.

What are the options?

Inset sinks give a streamlined look to the kitchen and leave more worktop available for other tasks. They vary from small round basins about 375mm (15in) across to one and a half sinks, which include a small basin for draining or for peeling vegetables, and rectangular twin bowls. Be realistic about size – if you want to wash pans in the sink, a standard 450mm (18in) wide by 150mm (6in) deep is the minimum bowl you will need. If you opt for a single sink, think carefully before you decide to do without a drainer. Dishes can only be left to dry if there is some way of collecting the water or directing it into the sink, or it will pool on the worktop and spill on to the floor.

Sinks need to be hard-wearing to resist the odd knock; new enamel, for example, looks smart but is easily chipped. Suitable materials include stylish 18/10 grade stainless steel, a composite made from acrylic and minerals, and ceramic, which is enjoying renewed popularity – especially butler's sinks. However, do bear in mind that china sinks often need extra support and water may seep through the worktop at the sides.

Choosing a splashback

The splashback above the worktop not only protects the walls, it is also one of the most striking decorative surfaces in the kitchen. Ceramic tiles are a favourite because they are water-, heat- and grease-resistant. They are also expensive and, since they last for years, it is worth choosing wisely. Most wall tiles are 150mm (6in) square but smaller tiles may look better if space is restricted. Chunky hand-made tiles can add a sense of luxury to the kitchen. For a fashionable look, choose plain hand-made tiles in three or four blending or contrasting colours, or use tiles in a single plain colour. An alternative finish is stainless steel – the perfect partner for high-tech appliances.

Above The bricks supporting this deep butler's sink have been left bare for emphasis. Plain and patterned tiles in the splashback pick up the main colours in the room.
Far left Old meets new … a white china sink and hardwood worktop are given a fresh look with a stainless steel splash-back, perforated to take hooks for utensils.
Left A tiny stainless steel round sink in the corner of the room is all that is needed in this small kitchen. Simple, plain cream tiles merge with the painted walls to increase the sense of space in the room.

The kitchen collection

Clear out the kitchen cupboards and you might uncover a pile of baking trays that should have been pensioned off years ago and at least one electrical gadget that seemed a good idea at the time. Yet, as every chef knows, the right tools can make all the difference to your cooking. The main thing is to sort the good ones from the gimmicks.

Left A food mixer is the ultimate kitchen gadget because it makes light work of mixing and whisking. Polished steel turns it into a style statement, too – worth its place on the kitchen worktop.

Below Curves and pastel colours add a light-hearted note to the kitchen and help offset the usual rows of rectangular units. Restrict the scheme to one colour and style for the maximum effect.

Right Soft pink gives a frivolous look to a traditional-style chrome toaster. Mix it with other soft pastel colours and 1950s-style prints for the complete retro experience.

ELECTRICAL APPLIANCES

Anything that needs to be plugged in should be kept as close as possible to an electrical socket. Since that usually means a position on the worktop, it is a good idea to choose appliances that are worth looking at. A retro-style chrome toaster and kettle suit the vogue for stainless steel, and a polished steel food mixer is far too attractive to put away – an added bonus, as this is one of the heaviest kitchen gadgets.

Jelly plastics are a more colourful choice: match a bright blue or lime green kettle with non-electrical items such as a bread bin, mixing bowls, utensils and frosted glasses to brighten up the room. Nineteen-fifties-style pastels in sinuous shapes have had a contemporary revival. Baby pink, aqua and primrose are often mixed with chrome for a sophisticated look.

Toasters

It is quicker and more economical to use a toaster than to brown bread under the grill. Two- and four-slot models are available; test them for sturdiness before you buy and check that the slots are wide enough for what you will be toasting, be it muffins or bread that you cut yourself. Electronic sensors that adjust browning time to suit the type of bread give a more even result and allow you to toast bread from frozen.

Food processor or mixer?

Although in theory you can choose between a food processor and a freestanding mixer, keen cooks may find they need both. Food processors are an excellent choice for day-to-day cooking. They are unbeatable for chopping but less good for mixing and whisking, and poor at liquidizing unless there is a separate attachment. A standard food processor does not mince or sieve either – these more specialized functions need separate gadgets, or attachments to a freestanding food mixer. Food mixers are the better choice if you like baking and often incorporate a powerful liquidizer, too. Optional slicing and chopping discs are available but they are expensive and not as effective as a food processor's action. If you don't want to clutter up the kitchen, it is worth analysing your cooking style to decide whether you are essentially a baker or a commis-chef. If you need a machine to make light work of chopping, buy a food processor and a hand-held electric mixer for whisking the occasional cake or meringue.

Above *Too pretty to hide away, these clear, candy-coloured jars are perfect containers for a range of goods and look effective against the summer blue walls and window frame.*

Below *Everyday kitchen items make attractive containers. Piled high with fruit and*

vegetables, they create an edible still life – the culinary equivalent of a flower arrangement.

Right *This futuristic chrome egg rack shows the contribution that basic equipment can make to the kitchen. And yes, despite its asymmetrical style, it takes a dozen eggs.*

ADDITIONAL EQUIPMENT

Whatever you decide is indispensable in your kitchen, make sure it is in good condition if it is on display and tuck other items, like that well-worn comfortable vegetable peeler, in a convenient drawer out of sight.

Kettles and coffee makers

Despite the range of features, the difference between electric kettles really comes down to a choice of shape. Tall jug kettles are economical because they can heat a single cup of water, while the traditional squat shape is more stable. Cordless models have a separate power base for safety: the kettle lifts off when the water has boiled so there is no trailing flex, and some kettles have an integral filter that stops scale pouring out with the water. (It doesn't stop scale building up, however, so the kettle still needs descaling.) Although electric kettles are the norm, an old-fashioned whistling kettle that sits on the hob will heat up just as quickly. Look for an insulated handle and a design that allows you to fill it through the spout for safety.

A kettle may be all you need if you make coffee in a cafetière. You do not have to have a special machine for filter coffee, which can be made in a jug, or for cappuccino – simply invest in an espresso maker to go on the hob and a simple milk foamer. That said, there is nothing to beat a pump-action espresso machine for the full coffee experience, although it is both bulky and expensive.

Microwave ovens

A microwave oven is useful when it comes to providing a variety of meals for different people at different times. The choice ranges from simple microwaves, which are basically for defrosting and reheating (although also excellent for cooking vegetables and fish), to microwaves with grills for browning food and combination cookers, which use microwave action plus convection heat and a grill. These will cook a chicken in less than half an hour and can replace a conventional oven in a small household. Combination and microwave ovens are best built-in to keep the work surface clear. Depending on their size, they can be mounted on a bracket or shelf at shoulder or eye level for convenience.

Batterie de cuisine

Most kitchens contain a welter of utensils and cookware but you may actually need less than you think. The essentials include mixing bowls, storage jars, a measuring jug and a juicer; a colander and sieve; a set of knives, a grater and two chopping boards; a whisk, spatula, wooden spoons, rolling pin and ladle; saucepans, a frying pan and a hob-proof casserole; a few baking trays and oven-proof dishes; scissors, can opener, corkscrew, garlic press and potato peeler. Some you may need more of (baking trays, chopping boards or wooden spoons), but it is down to individual preference, be it a spaghetti spoon or sauté pan that you find indispensable.

equipment checklist

■ Deep pull-out drawers are useful for storing appliances you use only occasionally, such as a bread maker or ice-cream machine.

■ Look for a food processor with storage devices for its attachments, for the sake of both safety and convenience.

■ Glass jars are more versatile than tins for food storage – and they don't need labelling since you can easily determine their contents.

■ If you want an electric juicer, decide between an inexpensive and compact, but limited, citrus press and a juice extractor that uses centrifugal force to squeeze juice from hard fruit and vegetables as well as citrus fruit.

■ Store knives in a separate knife block or on a magnetic knife rack, not in a drawer.

■ Site the microwave or food mixer on a trolley or shelf so that it does not occupy worktop space.

Fridges and freezers

Besides wanting them to keep our food cool, we can now expect these appliances to look 'cool', too. There is a wider range of models than ever before, including tall fridges and fridge/freezers, under-counter models, both curvaceous and box styles, and stainless steel and coloured finishes to suit any kitchen scheme.

Since most people have a freezer as well as a fridge, the majority of fridges are larder fridges, without an icebox, to maximize the storage space for food. Both fridges and freezers now have to be more energy-efficient, which makes them slightly cheaper to run. The only drawback is that energy-conscious models take longer to return to the correct operating temperature after the door has been opened – up to an hour for tall fridges and 25 minutes for under-counter models.

Most fridges now have an automatic defrost and a concealed evaporator plate for easier cleaning. In addition, look for a selection of shelf positions in both fridge and door; some have a flip-up section for tall items. Glass rather than slatted shelves prevent items from tipping over and maintain the temperature better when the door is open. On tall fridges, fans that recirculate the air ensure that the fridge stays at a more even temperature.

Pastel blue 1950s-style *fridge/freezer has adjustable glass shelves in the fridge and two fruit and vegetable containers.*

Freezers

Many people now find that a freezer is indispensable to their lifestyle, freeing them from the rigours of daily food shopping. Because of restricted floor space, upright styles are far more popular than chest freezers; these may be under-counter models or taller freezers, which have three or four extra drawers.

Freezer checklist

▨ Drawers are easier than fixed shelves because they pull right out. Solid drawers maintain temperature more effectively than open mesh.

▨ A separate ice-tray shelf makes it easier to locate ice and allows it to be stored level.

▨ In frost-free models a heater keeps the sides from freezing and a fan circulates dry air, so no defrosting is needed. These can cost more to run than standard freezers and may be noisier.

▨ In standard freezers, look for a drainage tube, which guides defrosting water into a container.

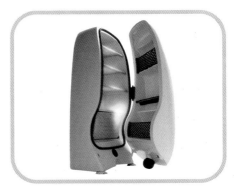

Curvy lines *make a strong design statement, but give this fridge limited storage space. The icebox is at the bottom and the salad basket is in the door.*

Tall circular fridge *has glass shelves that revolve for easy access; the bottom shelf pulls out. There are spacious salad drawers but no shelves in the door.*

Plain freezer *contains four baskets with solid fronts and two shelves with drop-down doors. An audible warning sounds when the door is left open.*

Bright colours *can be used effectively as part of a kitchen decorating scheme. There is plenty of shelf space in this fridge/freezer.*

Neat, uncluttered fridge *design comes in four colours. It has a large salad drawer and separate icebox. The heavy door has versatile storage.*

Under-counter larder fridge *has excellent temperature recovery time. It has a choice of shelf positions – one tilts for easy bottle storage.*

American-style *fridge/freezer fully clad in stainless steel has an ice-dispensing box in the front.*

1950s retro-style fridge *in pastel green. This design classic has a separate ice compartment and three adjustable glass shelves.*

Tall freezer *with an even temperature throughout. It has four smooth-gliding mesh baskets with solid fronts and two shelves with drop-down doors.*

Utility rooms

Once known as the scullery, this room disappeared entirely for a time but now the utility room is back and more important than ever. As kitchens become increasingly like living rooms where cooking takes place, there is a desperate need for a hideaway where you don't need to worry about stacks of ironing left lying about, or where you can feed the pets and scrape mud off your boots. While laundry facilities are an obvious choice, there are many other possibilities for a utility room.

LAUNDRY ROOM

Most utility rooms contain plumbing for a washing machine and often a vent for a tumble dryer but you will also need somewhere to sort and possibly iron laundry, plus storage for clothes and detergent. A small sink is useful for hand-washing; a boiler makes the laundry room the perfect place for drying clothes but could make it uncomfortably warm as a place to do the ironing.

Washers, dryers and irons

Most washing machines and dryers conform to the same 600mm (24in) module as kitchen units. Nearly all modern washing machines are front loaders, and most take a maximum load of 5kg (11lb). New machines now bear economy ratings ranging from A to G (most to least efficient) and many use an eco-friendly spray system, rather than soaking clothes in water. Because of this, it is best to buy a machine with an extra rinse programme, which ensures the clothes are rinsed of every trace of detergent.

Slimline washing machines are available, but if you want a dryer as well it may be better to buy a full-size washer and stack the dryer on top using a special frame. Alternatively, buy a washer-dryer – effectively two machines in one although the drying programme usually operates on half-load capacity only. The washing programmes may be basic and drying is by condenser action, so moisture drains away rather than dispersing in the air. This is convenient as the plumbing is already in place but the results are slightly slower than with a vented drier.

As for ironing, a steam-generator ironing system will lighten the load. Water heated in a separate reservoir keeps up a constant powerful supply of steam to the iron, ideal for large amounts of ironing or for pressing natural fibres. If you opt for a conventional iron, test it to find one sufficiently heavy to give good results but light enough for comfort. It is best to use demineralized water in hard water areas to avoid a build-up of scale, which can ruin a steam iron.

Above A traditional concertina-style wooden clothes rack that folds flat when not in use dries a full wash load in the minimum amount of floor space.

Left A washboard and posser – a traditional washing dolly that agitates the water – make light work of hand-washing clothes.

Right This four-way laundry store means that clothes can be sorted according to the wash programme, and the chrome rail above is ideal for hanging freshly ironed clothes.

ADDITIONAL USES

Besides dealing with laundry, there are hundreds of uses for a utility room, from a walk-in larder to a home workshop.

Kitchen storeroom

Convert the utility room into a walk-in larder by fitting it with shelves for tins and dried foods, plus a large freezer. If the utility room is some way from the cooker, use it for storing unopened packets and bulk buys that you don't need so often, and buy a fridge with an ice-box or a small freezer for the kitchen to keep frozen food close at hand.

Workroom

If the family's hobbies tend to take over the house, it might be worth converting the utility room into a workroom. The sink is invaluable for clearing up and all you need add is a strong worktop, trestle table or work bench to create an adaptable surface for wood carving, raising seedlings, painting or sewing. Provide shelving, cupboards and hooks for storage, plus a lockable cabinet for hazards like solvents and pesticides.

Cleaning centre

Brushes, mops and buckets fight for space in the average broom cupboard and there is still no room for the vacuum cleaner. Better by far is to spread them out in the utility room and rediscover the virtues of traditional equipment at the same time. Rolls of mutton cloth, heaps of yellow dusters and checked glass cloths, enamel or aluminium buckets, polish-impregnated floor mops, traditional carpet beaters, dolly pegs and corn brooms not only look charming – they really work. Use boxes or baskets for storage and fill a rush basket with core cleaning equipment to carry from room to room.

Home office

Stuck for a space to sort out letters and bills? There are all sorts of space-saving storage units available to hide a PC, some the size of a trolley, others designed to fit into a corner or fold away inside a cupboard. If you want to use the utility room as an office, make sure the temperature and lighting are suitable and check that there is room for files and a connection for a modem or phone.

Selecting a decorating style

Elaborate decor is out of place, but since most utility rooms open off the kitchen the colour scheme should acknowledge this. Use the same flooring in both rooms to increase the sense of space and choose a paint shade that relates in some way, be it a bright colour to pick up an accent in the kitchen or a pale colour to blend with it. If the window needs screening, fit a plain blind or put shelves across it, on which you can stand decorative glass bottles to catch the light, or plants for a living window treatment.

Above Find the right brush for the job in hand – traditional dish mops, bottle and scrubbing brushes are a pleasure to use.
Left Stylish wooden panels screen the utility room from the living space and muffle the sound of the washing machine. The same flooring and timber are used in both rooms for continuity.
Below Wicker baskets are a practical way of separating papers, cans and glass for recycling and are equally useful for storing polishes, brushes and cloths.

---

utility room ideas

● Wall-mounted storage systems designed for garden tools are also useful for keeping brushes, mops and brooms in place.

● A deep counter top is useful for all sorts of work – sorting laundry, household repairs, flower arranging and writing bills.

● A large utility room can be divided to provide a shower cubicle and small washbasin – useful after gardening or sport.

● Tuck a folding chair or stool beneath the worktop so you have somewhere to sit and can iron or clean shoes in comfort.

● Use lengths of string to hang fresh herbs and flowers in bunches from the ceiling, to dry them out and scent the air at the same time.

● If you use the utility room for messy hobbies or heavy cleaning, fit a splashback above the sink and worktop to protect the walls.

Laundry appliances

Doing the washing is a chore that most of us face on a regular basis. Whether you have a purpose-made utility room or your washing 'room' is squashed into a corner of the kitchen, try to equip yourself with good-looking and efficient equipment to make this routine task, if not exactly fun, at least less burdensome.

Whether you have a washing machine and separate tumble dryer or a machine that combines the two functions will depend largely on the space available. You can even buy a kit to enable the tumble dryer to be stacked on top of the washing machine. An efficient washing machine will take more water out of the clothes, so they need less time to dry, while a good dryer reduces the time you spend ironing. A sturdy ironing board and a lightweight but efficient steam iron are still needed to give your clothes a good finish.

Choosing a washing machine

The more you pay for a washing machine, the better constructed it will generally be and the longer it will tend to last. The more expensive models usually have a zinc coating under vitreous enamel that won't rust. They should also have stainless steel drums and a thicker inner drum with a higher number of holes. In terms of performance, however, the less expensive models of washing machine often wash clothes just as well.

Choosing a tumble dryer

The main decision is whether you want a condenser or a vented dryer and this depends on where you will put the machine. Condenser models can be placed anywhere because after the steam is condensed, the water collects in a drawer at the top or bottom of the dryer. Vented tumble dryers, which are more economical to run, pass the steam down a hose to the outside so they need access to an outside wall or a window.

A folding laundry bag with cover hangs from a wooden frame. It folds flat when not in use, and is especially ideal for teenage bedrooms or student accommodation.

Optional extras

■ Bracket door hinges on washing machines allow the door to open further for easy loading.

■ A 'hand wash' programme is a bonus if you have a lot of delicate woollen and silk items.

■ Most washing machines now have an extra-rinse facility.

■ Some tumble dryers have an easy-care or pre-ironing programme, which reduces the creases in dry clothes, or can be used to air clothes that have been stored in a cupboard.

■ Sensor controls monitor the moisture in clothes so the heat can be lowered as they begin to dry and the machine switches off when they are completely dry.

■ Vented dryer models may have a 'clean filter' and condenser models an 'empty water' indicator.

Large-capacity vented tumble dryer *with a very wide door opening. This one is quiet in use, has a pre-ironing programme and a 'clean filter' indicator.*

Condenser tumble dryer *with sophisticated technology: sensor and child-lock controls and an airing programme.*

Ironing boards *come in several sizes; make sure you buy replacement covers that fit. Adjustable legs ensure you can iron at the most comfortable height.*

Front-loading washing machines *with a large 'porthole' make loading and unloading easy. This one has a useful wash-time display.*

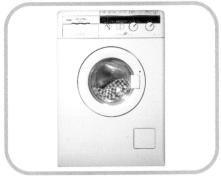

Washer–dryers *save on space; this model has a colour-coded panel for different fabric types.*

Washer-dryer *has a distinctive and large display panel but these machines can have longer washing and drying cycles.*

Lightweight iron *designed to cut ironing time in half: a separate water tank heats the water in two minutes to convert it to a powerful jet of steam.*

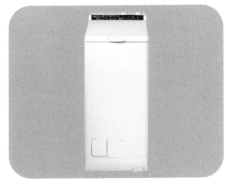

Top-loading slimline *washing machine is a space-saver; it has a rotating drum and extra 'hand wash' and 'quick wash' programmes.*

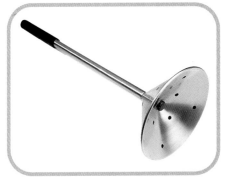

Stainless steel washing 'dolly' *is useful for hand washing; it keeps your hands out of the water and eliminates the need to rub clothes.*

Whatever happened to the hall? The most important, and sometimes the only, room in a medieval manor is now just a passage leading to somewhere else. Yet given a little attention it can, if itis spacious enough, become an art gallery, a dining room, a work space or simply somewhere to curl up in a chair. Above all, a hall should say 'welcome'. As for the stairs, this most prominent architectural feature inside the house deserves a rethink, too.

halls and stairs

Welcoming space

The hall is actually one of the most difficult spaces in the house to adapt. To create a hall that does anything more than get you from the front door to the kitchen or living room demands meticulous planning and plenty of imagination.

Above The owners of this Victorian home were delighted to find the original hall floor beneath the carpet and chose a runner for the stairs to complement it.

Right This distinctive open-plan staircase is left to speak for itself in a minimalist setting. The pictures are hung so as to bring interest to the ascent.

Measuring up

The hall, stairs and landing are the arteries of the house, linking one area with the next; any other function is secondary. Start by making a plan of the area, marking the doorways and windows, radiators and cupboards. Consider the possibility of expanding outwards by adding a porch to trap draughts so you can use the hall in comfort, or creating more space internally by knocking out an understairs cupboard or turning the hall, stairs and living room, for example, into one large open-plan area.

Small halls

There is still a lot you can do with a small hall if you decide against the open-plan option. Keep the floor clear to make walking through easier and remove any coat pegs. (Steal space somewhere for a coat cupboard

if you can, or you will find coats piling up on the newel post.) What is left is a very bare space, just waiting for a touch of decorative magic – richly painted walls to offset a huge painting, a mirror, a set of prints or hanging plates (as long as there is no risk of them being knocked when you brush past).

Square halls

This is the easiest type of hall to use. You could turn the area into a grand dining hall, placing the table in the centre if there is room, or using an extending table that can be pushed against the wall when not in use. Chairs flanking the walls look stylish and can be supplemented by folding chairs when you are entertaining. Alternatively, you could use the hall for pieces of furniture that are too bulky to be accommodated elsewhere – a huge armoire for linen, a glass-fronted cupboard for china or perhaps a piano.

Large halls

A hall that is larger than average but too small or too awkward a shape to be used as a living room need not be a challenge. From a practical point of view, it is the perfect place to add extra storage, for games kit, books or cleaning equipment. Put the telephone in the hall next to a comfortable chair, or take advantage of the fact that this is where the bills arrive and install a narrow desk to deal with correspondence on the spot.

creating a welcome

- In a tiny hall, concentrate interest on the floor, using tiles or painting boards in a faux-tile effect, and keep the walls simple.

- A purpose-built coat cupboard keeps the hall tidy – under the stairs is one possible location.

- Lighting is important in halls where windows are limited. Provide task lighting by work tables and soft lighting that is good enough to read by near easy chairs.

- Make sure the hall or landing is warm and inviting if you want to spend any length of time

there. A sofa or writing desk will not get used unless it is a comfortable place in which to be.

- Stunning modern 'chains' or 'curtains' of light can turn the staircase into an impressive focal point.

- If there is enough room for a few shelves, choose an eye-catching design such as ladder-style minimalist shelving or opt for an antique corner cupboard, depending on your preference.

- If you would like to go open plan but don't want the staircase on view, shut it behind a door in traditional cottage style.

Flooring solutions

Hall and stair floors take more punishment than any others in the house. Floorings here have to resist gravel, mud and rainwater brought in from outside, plus the odd splash of tea or coffee as drinks are ferried through the house, so they need to be durable and easy to clean.

IN THE HALL

Fitted carpet helps to exclude draughts and absorbs damp, making footprints less obvious. Grit from outside constantly erodes the fibres so hall carpet should be the best you can afford. An 80 per cent wool–20 per cent nylon twist-pile carpet over high-quality underlay is a hard-to-beat classic, unless you choose cord. Synthetic-fibre carpets are strongest of all and resist rot, but their pile can soon flatten and become soiled. Density is as important as fibre so bend a sample in half to see if the pile 'grins', revealing too much backing. Look for a carpet recommended for heavy use and consider a soil-retardant finish (which lasts longer if applied during manufacture rather than afterwards).

Seagrass and sisal

Natural fibres like these are popular and hard-wearing, if sometimes expensive. Coir (also called medieval matting) is available in lengths that can be sewn together, but seagrass or sisal, which can be woven into herringbone and plaid designs, are smoother, softer and wear better. On the down side

however, fitted grass floorings can be difficult to clean and the fibres stain easily. They may also be too slippery for use on stairs.

Smooth floorings

Stone, slate, quarry and ceramic tiles are long-lasting. They rarely show wear and are easy to clean but all need a strong subfloor to support their weight. Because they are naturally cool, the hall decor and temperature need to compensate. Vinyl or sealed cork are warmer options but look for the best possible resistance to wear because the flooring soon begins to look shabby once the clear surface is scratched.

Which wood?

Wood is a traditional material for hall floors. Wax polish is not really an option here because it makes the floor slippery as well as hard to maintain; although more oiled wood products are becoming available for areas of heavy traffic, solid or laminated sealed wood is the usual choice. The quality varies widely so it is essential to buy the best and check that it is suitable for use in a hall.

Above Cane furniture and leafy houseplants add a palm-court look to classic black and white floor tiles, while stripped doors and banisters and a dark wood cabinet emphasize the Victorian setting.

Far left A runner can add warmth to a stone floor or help protect carpet. Here it adds an element of pattern, too. The space-saving but decorative hall table creates a focal point.

Below left Traditional wood parquet gains a rich patina over time. It can be sealed with several coats of clear polyurethane varnish for a permanent sheen.

Above *This polished wooden stairway is simple to imitate. Top the treads with hardwood boards, stain the risers to match and complete with an eye-catching new handrail.*
Below *A gold-coloured carpet runner on white-painted stairs draws attention to the graceful design of this sweeping staircase. Brass stair rods complete the look.*

Right *Concrete stairways can take the weight of these ceramic tiles, but if you are stuck with wood, why not use paint instead to continue the pattern of the floor below?*

UP THE STAIRS

Safety is the most important consideration where stairs are concerned. The flooring needs to offer a certain amount of grip, which rules out some loop-pile carpets and several types of rush matting, although sea-grass can be used if it is laid with its weave running across the treads rather than up the staircase. Floorings need to be flexible enough to stretch over the nose of the stairs, so foam-backed carpet and sheet vinyl are unsuitable. So, what are the choices?

Barely there

First of all, consider whether you need a stair covering at all. An open-tread staircase, for example, is designed to be seen that way and anything that is put on the treads will look makeshift. Whether the staircase is made from wood or metal, it is better to renovate it if it has seen better days, rather than to try to cover it up. Even a conventional staircase may be better painted or stained instead of carpeted if it rises from a hard hall floor. You could take a colour from a patterned mosaic or tiled hall flooring for the stairway – a bright colour for fun or muted for a sophisticated look – and coat it with floor-grade varnish for durability. Because of the wear that stairs receive, you will need to renew paintwork regularly, so opt for wood stain if time for maintenance is limited.

The halfway house

A compromise solution currently enjoying a revival is the carpet runner, which sits in the centre of the stairs and is held in place by stair rods. The runner can simply be a strip of plain carpet (although the edges should be whipped or bound), but carpet with a border each side or an oriental carpet has more impact. A runner doubles the cleaning process because the stairs either side of the runner are usually painted or stained and need different attention, but there is one big advantage. The area of stair carpet most subject to wear is the nose of each stair and an extra allowance can be left so that a runner can be moved slightly from time to time to help equalize the wear and tear.

Wall to wall

Fitted carpet is an easy-care choice, although only the best quality will stand up to the wear that stair carpet receives. In a small house, a plain neutral carpet used for stairs, hall and landing – and possibly the living room, too – immediately increases the feeling of space. Opt for a crush-resistant twist pile that doesn't show footsteps in the same way that velvet does, and consider a shade that contains small flecks of colour to disguise the dirt. It is wise to avoid strong plain colours like deep red and blue, which are notorious for showing every thread.

floor covering guidelines

● Rugs and runners can add interest to the hall floor and disguise areas of wear but for safety reasons they need to be held firmly in place with anti-creep backing.

● Rubber stud-effect flooring is perfect for a high-tech hall. Choose industrial grey or bright green and paint the staircase to match.

● If the hall flooring is a different material to the staircase – stone, perhaps, or wood – it is a good idea to carpet the stairs in a discreet neutral colour to avoid drawing attention to the change.

● Changes in level should always be obvious in the interests of safety, so don't choose a floor covering design that obscures the nose of the stairs.

● Flamboyant patterned carpets are rarely suitable for narrow hall floors since cuts and joins will fall in awkward places. If you want pattern, a carpet with a border, a runner, or a disciplined geometric design may be a better choice.

● Pale colours are obviously impractical for any carpet that receives a lot of traffic, but do avoid very dark or solid shades, too.

Hallway decorating

Since you don't generally stop in the hall for long, you can be adventurous when choosing a decorating scheme – consider brilliant colours, over-the-top accessories and odd pieces of furniture. Just remember that the hall provides visitors with their first glimpse of your home.

TRADITIONAL TREATMENTS

Traditional styles tend to be defined by the size of the house as much as by its age. Small cottages rarely have a hall. Even if an extension has created a small porch or lobby, there won't be much room for manoeuvre, but that need not hold you back. Traditional distemper in a range of chalky colours or a simple colourwash technique can turn a utilitarian area into a welcoming one. Shades that can look harsh in modern vinyl paints look much softer made from natural materials, so think of golden yellow, russet, burnt orange, coral and marine blue. If there's room, put up a simple coat rail and perhaps a receptacle for umbrellas and walking sticks.

Grand illusions

With larger houses, which often have a substantial hall, let the house be your guide when choosing a scheme. A farmhouse or Arts and Crafts villa with a stone floor would look attractive distempered in a pastel or neutral shade, offset by plain furniture like a chest or settle. A sophisticated Georgian terrace needs a lighter touch, perhaps panelling or a dado separating two colours or two types of wall covering. For an eclectic look, combine 20th-century classics like a Le Corbusier chaise longue with Victorian cabinets, or mix modern metal with Regency-style pieces and add an ornate mirror or piece of statuary as a witty focal point.

Victorian passages

Over time the hall has shrunk to the familiar passageway most people now recognize as a hall. Even if there is no room for furniture, there is still plenty of scope. To emphasize the period look, choose colours from a historic paint range and restore picture rails, dado rails and ornamental plasterwork if these have been removed. A relief wall covering was often used below the dado rail and painted a dark colour to disguise fingermarks – and it still has its uses today.

Above The hall walls show a modern take on Regency stripes, but these are much broader and are hand-painted. An attractive screen and curved hall table help minimize the angles.

Far left Fretwork radiator covers can be extended to provide useful storage space, while a simple mirror becomes the focal point of this hall, thanks to the topiary display and arrangement of contorted willow.

Below left An opulent mirror and rococo side table create an impact in this hall. The oyster colour of the wall covering is repeated in the table, plasterwork mirror frame and statuary.

LOOK MODERN

You don't have to stick to traditional treatments in a period house. A minimalist approach can show off fine proportions better than any other, and rather than remove 'unnecessary' details like architraves and ceiling roses, it is easy to play these features down with clever use of colour.

Minimalism is not the only contemporary look, of course, although most current styles are simple. Organic shapes are the inspiration for many modern furnishings. Styles derived from leaves, branches and twigs occur in light fittings, curtain rails and accessories like mirrors and picture frames, while flowing abstract forms such as drops of water influence pottery, seating, tables and storage. Animal prints apart, patterns take a back seat, secondary to textures such as sheep and goatskin, tarlatan, chenille and velvet. Bold colours – lilac, lime, yellow, fuchsia and red – are offset by black, white and metallics, and used in contrasting blocks on furniture or feature walls.

Fresh looks

All this makes it easy to achieve a powerful, dramatic look in the hall. Update calm neutrals by adding shapes based on branches – a marble-topped table with curved black metal legs, curling metal lamp brackets and an intricate mirror frame, for instance. Use blocks of strong colour to improve the proportions of a long narrow hall, for example paint the end wall (including the door, if there is one) an 'advancing' shade of yellow or bright pink, and keep the side walls a cool lilac or *eau de nil*. In the same way, painting the ceiling a deep, warm colour appears to reduce its height, especially if the paint is continued down to picture rail level. You can 'lose' features like picture rails and cornices by painting them to blend with walls and ceiling. Similarly, minimize the effect of too many doors by painting them and their frames so they merge into the walls. Alternatively, make a feature of the doors by painting them in contrasting shades of yellow, red and blue like a Mondrian painting.

Mirrors

Large mirrors can increase the effect of space and double the impact of ornaments and furnishings. Mirrors also reflect the light, which is useful in a hall as it can be limited – place them at right angles to a window for the maximum effect. Floor-to-ceiling mirrors in an alcove or between two windows are useful architecturally, but beware putting a large mirror on the end wall, at the turn of the stairs or opposite a door, where it can be startling to come face to face with yourself.

Top Walls painted a strong sea green give a natural look to this hall, emphasized by an earthenware pot filled with twigs for a low-maintenance arrangement.

Above Vivid lilac and lemon walls create an impact in this open-plan entrance, with a large mirror to increase the light. Carefully chosen accessories add a splash of orange.

Left This stunningly simple hall relies on contrast for effect, with off-white walls, ceiling and woodwork offset by the dark metal curtain finials, light fitting and table.

---

furnishing ideas

● Make the most of a single window by choosing an original window covering, be it a perforated blind, draped voile or metallic lamé, a panel made from an Indian sari or a curtain of metal or bamboo strips.

● Double the impact of a focal point – perhaps flowers or ornaments – by placing them in front of a large mirror.

● Pick accessories carefully for a minimalist scheme. Only one or two are needed, so they should be able to withstand scrutiny.

● Don't automatically choose white paint for the woodwork as this can break up space. Instead, consider painting the skirting to blend with the walls, or the door frame to match the doors.

● A large earthenware or metallic pot looks attractive filled with contorted willow and can double as an umbrella store.

● Choose similar materials for accessories – a metal shelf and light fittings with gilded picture and mirror frames, or a side table in light wood with simple wooden picture frames, for instance.

Happy landings

In most homes, the hall gets all the attention decoratively speaking, yet the landing is more than simply a continuation of the hall. It is a place full of unexplored potential for working, seating or storage, and one that can make all the difference to the way the house runs.

USING THE SPACE

Fitting a set of slim shelves to the banisters or landing wall could double your existing storage for books and create an instant library for insomniacs. Dividing the shelves vertically provides perfect storage for CDs or stationery. Fit a set of doors and you can stow away spare soaps, tissues, make-up and other toiletries.

If there is room for more than slim shelving, other items can be stored here – bed linen and towels perhaps, or toys. Fitted with a stair gate, a wide landing can be a safe place to play and the empty floor space is ideal for laying out 'roads', tracks and puzzles. Craft materials and sewing things could also be kept in landing cupboards, along with items like cameras and torches – anything, in fact, that you need too often to put away in the loft and too infrequently to keep handy downstairs.

Feature windows

An alcove or half-landing with a window can be the ideal spot for a small table and an armchair, but if the area is too shallow for furniture, turn it into a focal point. Some landing windows are features in their own right, with graceful oriel or bow shapes or stained glass panes. Others benefit from clever window dressing – draped with light voile, covered with a translucent blind or given an 'alternative' treatment with wire

mesh, glass shelves or chain links as a screen. Fit a curved shelf or a tiny table beneath to take flowers, favourite objects or a collection of shells, candles or glasses and perfume bottles that filter the light prettily. Alternatively, fill a huge floor-standing vase or pot with dried grasses for a permanent display, or arrange a selection of rocks and gourds beneath the window as an instant sculpture. You could even turn the whole area into a stage set, painting the walls with a *trompe l'oeil* design to create a virtual garden.

Left *Floor-to-ceiling storage cubes are perfect in this setting where everything has been pared down – from the window with its simple blind to the staircase, where translucent panels substitute for banisters.*

Above *This landing is furnished as carefully as a sitting room, with co-ordinating blue and white wall covering, table and chair cushion that pick out colours in the floral print curtains.*

If you don't want to clear away at the end of the day, consider using a screen to hide the work area or, if the desk is in an alcove, fit curtains or a blind across to close it off.

Home art gallery

Pictures don't have to compete for attention on the landing and can take centre-stage here. Unless a single painting is large enough to dominate the wall, it is best to display pictures in groups. Hang them at eye level if possible – they should follow your eye-line up the stairs – but high enough not to be constantly knocked. Lay them out on the floor first and experiment with different arrangements to fit the space available. On the whole, the largest picture should take up no more than one-third of the area and there should be some consistency in the spacing.

Aligning pictures so they are the same height or depth gives a regular look to the display; if you align the left-hand side of the group, too, it gives the collection room to grow in a controlled way. Constant spacing creates an irregular shape but looks effective because the pictures are the same distance apart – a maximum of 10cm (4in) is recommended. On a stairwell, this arrangement can be in a triangle, with the apex towards the top of the stairs. Most disciplined of all is a totally constant display, which creates a rectangle or square. It requires paintings or prints that are the same size, and looks very effective in formal or minimalist settings.

Above From landing to art gallery: paintings, plants and objets d'art add interest at every turn. The focus is the grandly proportioned painting flanked by the bookshelves and shallow uplighter.

Right In a multi-storey house it is worth making a feature of the landings. Here a carpet runner, tapestry wallhanging and candelabra are offset by casually propped pictures that add an informal air.

DESK OR DISPLAY AREA

A large or square landing can be the ideal site for a home office. Although a writing desk and upright chair look charming by a window, a computer is less attractive so look for a corner uninterrupted by doors. There should be an area at least 2m (6½ft) square for a desk and chair, plus enough space for people to pass by; an electric socket and clear lighting are other essentials. An L-shaped layout is the most efficient, with shelves above for books, drawers for filing and space for a printer. Built-in furniture is probably the neatest solution but a wide variety of purpose-made computer desks is available, including hideaway models that conceal the computer behind closed doors.

decorative touches

● Attractive door furniture – handles, finger plates and escutcheons – is effective on the landing since there are so many doors here. Besides conventional china, brass and chrome, unusual designs include satin finish art deco or branch-effect handles and Celtic knot or coral pattern door knobs.

● Do not hang original paintings in direct sunlight or they may fade. Non-reflective glass is a good idea if pictures are hung on a bright landing.

● Display pictures against a plain painted wall rather than patterned wallpaper for the best effect. Hang the main pictures from a picture rail if there is one, to draw attention to them.

● Picture frames need not be identical but look best if they relate to each other in style or material. For strength, the depth of the frame should measure at least 0.5 per cent of the picture's longest side.

Your bedroom is the first place you see in the morning and the last before you go to sleep at night, so it needs to be a temple of calm. But bedrooms have to be practical, too, often providing storage for a welter of clothes and perhaps a place to read, watch television, or even work. How can you reconcile all of these needs? All you need is a little imagination.

bedrooms

Practicalities and luxuries

It's easy to throw all your decorating energies into the public areas of your home and give this, your most private of spaces, little attention. But this is one room that deserves extra special consideration. It's amazing the impact that overhauling a bedroom can have on your life.

Top A cast-iron bedstead, painted floorboards and warm wooden furniture combine traditional good looks with plenty of practical storage. Scatter cushions reflect the strong flash of colour on one wall.
Above Four-poster opulence is given a strong, clean-lined approach with a black iron bedstead. Crisp white bedding echoes the simplicity of the smooth polished floor.
Right Built-in wardrobes create a spacious, user-friendly bedroom with everything concealed behind one streamlined façade. The smooth lines of the bed and the plump pillows are serene and inviting.

Private lives

Although hotel bedrooms are impersonal, they are user-friendly because they function so efficiently. You can read, work, watch television, eat and sleep in comfort, and with plenty of clothes storage it is easy to maintain order. In addition, the en-suite bathroom facilities generate a wonderful feeling of privacy and luxury.

In your home, even if space is at a premium, a well-designed bedroom will make life easier and more harmonious. The bed must suit your individual style, space and comfort requirements. Lighting must be versatile – subtle enough for rest and romance, but bright enough to enable you to locate essentials with speed. Curtains and blinds must be functional as well as stylish. If your bedroom is multi-purpose – part-study, office, gym and television room – it is important to assess how you can best use the available space. The bed style, shape and size is a crucial starting point since it is usually the largest piece of furniture in the house and must fit its space comfortably. Match the style to that of the room: clean, unobtrusive lines in a loft space, practical prettiness in a cottage bedroom, for example.

Clearing the decks

Efficient storage is the key to success. Clothes, shoes, jewellery, tissues and cosmetics should all have a place out of sight. Well-designed and organized clothes storage makes dressing in the morning much easier. A full-length mirror is essential and can be tucked away behind wardrobe doors.

If space permits, a separate or linked dressing room liberates bedroom space, allowing room for less functional furniture.

bedtime checklist

■ Before buying bedroom furniture, make a scale drawing of the room on graph paper to determine how much space you have after the bed is in position. Try to allow a space of 450mm (18in) around the bed to give room for movement.

■ Bedside units are easiest to use when they are around the same height as your mattress, usually about 500mm (20in).

■ Duvets are an essential modern convenience – use traditional quilts, blankets, throws and cushions to dress them up or to add colour and texture.

■ Pale colours in the bedroom are serene and relaxing, while bright tones guarantee a cheerful start to the day, whatever the weather.

■ Position bedside wall lighting at least 600mm (24in) above mattress height. If possible, the dressing table should be situated close to a source of natural light.

■ Introduce en-suite bathroom facilities only where you have sufficient space, and try to ensure some continuity of decoration between bathroom and bedroom.

Beds and bedding schemes

The bed is the focal point of the bedroom and bears witness to our most intimate moments. The style of bed and the way we 'dress' it must suit our personal taste, as well as the style and scale of our bedroom environment. Above all, it must be comfortable.

Above *A bold mix of stripes, checks and florals on a plain colour base unites a large room and integrates a variety of different styles of furniture.*
Left *This traditional iron bed looks pretty painted white. Pristine white bed linen, furniture and furnishings are offset by gentle touches of pale colour.*

Below *The clean, modern lines of the bed and furnishings are the perfect frame for this room with a view – complementing not competing.*

SLEEPING IN STYLE

A bed is so much more than just something to sleep on and your choice of bed can reveal a great deal about you. Styles range from the blatantly nostalgic to the most contemporary of innovative designs. Whatever look you want, there has never been such a wide choice – from lavishly upholstered half-testers, kitsch divans with padded and quilted headboards and cast-iron Victorian originals to French *lit bateaux*, sleigh beds or sleek wooden platforms on castors.

However, the bedroom environment should in some way dictate your choice of bed. Ultra-modern styles can look out of place in period properties, but this need not limit your options. There are plenty of traditional styles with a modern twist, and vice versa. Look around and explore the market – this is not a purchase to rush.

Once you have selected a bed, the rest of the room can be planned. Colour schemes should harmonize or complement – walls, curtains, bed linen and soft furnishings should all work as a whole. Soft colours and gentle patterns are easy on the eye and relaxing to live with; rich warm colours and dark jewel tones can be comforting at night, but less energizing in the morning.

Dressing up

Although the style of a bed is significant, its mood can be dramatically changed according to its treatment. Cool white bed linen is always popular. It looks fresh and clean and it feels safe and inviting. If you are nervous of colour, you can always introduce it by degrees in the bedroom with a blanket or a few cushions. Be as subtle or bold as you like – even just a touch of colour can have a strong impact on the room as a whole.

Bold patterns, checks and stripes all have a vibrant contemporary feel and can bring warmth and mood to a featureless room. Florals are very pretty but need to be used with a sure hand. Combining a mix of patterns, stripes and florals is especially effective.

BED LINEN

Duvets are hugely popular and a great modern convenience, but their contemporary style can look a little out of place on traditional beds. Linen sheets are certainly wonderful to sleep between and soft blankets simply luxurious, but when it comes to laundry and bed-making, the labour-saving lure of the duvet is understandable. It is easy enough to conceal a duvet under a lightweight quilt or a blanket. 'Tog' values indicate how warm a duvet will be, so choose according to your personal body thermostat.

Throws, blankets and quilts are perfect for dressing up a bed or altering the mood of a room. Valances conceal unsightly bed bases and can also help balance colour schemes. There is still plenty of beautiful old bed linen to be found in second-hand shops and in markets, which can add an individual and distinctive touch to an overall scheme. Go easy on the frills though, especially if the bedroom is to be used by a man.

Bed drapes are the height of luxury and range from filmy romantic mosquito nets to more opulent drapery suspended from a corona, half- or full tester. The look is easily achieved with curtain poles suspended from the ceiling and draped with generous lengths of fabric.

Pillows

Pillows come in various sizes and while you may not wish to sleep on a pile of cushions, you want to be able to read in supported comfort. Large square pillows provide good back support – particularly important with wooden and iron beds. The softest pillows combine duck down and feathers for the ultimate in luxury, and there are special pillows available for people with allergies.

practical ideas

● The principles of *feng shui* suggest that the bed should be positioned so that its occupant can see anyone entering the room. The bed should rest against the wall, not float in space.

● Sleeping in a room that gets the early morning sun allows you to wake more naturally.

● Blanket boxes, chests, sofas or chairs have a strong impact placed at the foot of the bed. They are also a useful place to store folded-up blankets, bed covers and cushions overnight.

● Tables draped in fabric look pretty in bedrooms but attract dust. A sheet of glass cut to size preserves the look and is easier to keep clean.

● Dust is a common allergen, so keep bedrooms as clean as possible for a healthy environment.

● If the bedroom is a multi-purpose room keep colours and furnishings neutral, with clean lines.

Above *The traditional dark wooden bed looks solid and secure, and bright white and neutral colourways for walls and furnishings make the room look fresh and inviting.*
Left *Plain walls and furniture are offset by a skilful mix of texture, colour, pattern and print.*
Right *A colourwashed sleigh bed is given a pink, feminine touch with a gentle mix of traditional florals and soft stripes on walls, furnishings and bed linen.*

Mattresses

No matter how beautiful the bed, if you don't pay attention to your choice of mattress your sleep will suffer. High-quality bedding really makes a difference, so take the trouble to try out as many mattresses as you can and buy the very best that you can afford.

Above Mix-and-match bed linen for a gentle but individual look. Combine delicate pastels with washed-out florals and offset them with white.

Left An uncompromisingly modern box bed conceals spring support for the ultimate in comfort. The stark white bedding emphasizes the purity of the line.

Right The contemporary design of an iron bed frame forms a focal point in a large space. A mix of bed linen combines warm colours, prints and tactile quilting.

Firm but gentle

The best mattresses can be expensive, but they do last longer, so regard this purchase as an investment. The foundation, or base, that the mattress sits on is important – the stronger the base, the longer the mattress will last. Box-spring bases are generally regarded as the most comfortable option; they support the mattress, and the mattress supports you. The choice of base is dictated by your style of bed.

The mattress core provides the support for the body. A mattress should be firm enough to support the spine, while allowing shoulders and hips to follow their normal curvature. There are many different varieties of mattress available but inner-sprung ones are the most comfortable and, within this group, pocketed springs are the most highly rated. The number of springs in a mattress indicates the level of support – the more springs, the greater the support. In addition, the gauge of the spring is a further indicator – the heavier the gauge, the firmer the mattress.

Two mattresses of the same construction will feel quite different depending on how they are upholstered. The upholstery on top of the mattress is what you feel next to your body; it's what comes between you and the coils and is most important for your basic comfort. It will give you the sensation of lying on a feather bed or a firm board, even though both styles support the body in precisely the same way.

Mattress care

A mattress will last longer and give you better rest if it is turned on a regular basis, ideally once a week. It should be turned end to end one week, then turned and flipped over the next week. This process ensures the mattress wears evenly all over. You cannot clean a mattress – a light sponge is as far as you can go in stain removal – but it should be vacuumed thoroughly and regularly. Ensure that the area under the bed is well ventilated, to help moisture escape from bedding and mattress.

Window treatments

Curtains and blinds add the finishing touch to a room, framing the windows but not necessarily serving much of a practical role. In the bedroom, however, more than in any other room, there is a need to control light levels and enjoy complete privacy, so window dressing must be ultra-efficient as well as good looking.

Above Fine, plain gauze curtains create a soft, romantic style – and not a frill in sight.
Below The Venetian blinds show off, rather than conceal, beautifully proportioned windows, as well as producing dramatic light and *shadow effects. At night they successfully block out the light.*
Right A simple light gingham curtain is hard to beat. A scalloped wooden pelmet conceals the curtain track and makes an attractive focal point.

Drawn to perfection

Bedrooms may contain a number of demanding design elements: large, attention-grabbing pieces of furniture, assorted colours, prints and textures on walls and bedding, blankets and upholstery. In this area of the house, window dressings should blend and co-ordinate with your main colour palette. Curtains that scream for attention do not hang comfortably in a haven of peace. Similarly, poles and finials should be in harmony with the room.

Current thinking promotes the introduction of natural daylight to a bedroom. The principle is that if you sleep in a room facing sunrise you will wake naturally with the sun. This gentle awakening should make you feel more refreshed and alert in the mornings.

Light and dark

If you prefer complete darkness, then bedroom curtains should be lined and sometimes interlined to reduce light levels. If you want flowing, diaphanous drapes, you could hang a blind behind them to help minimize the light. Pelmets are useful since they efficiently conceal blackout blinds and ugly curtain tracks, but as most daylight comes in at the top of the window use them with caution if the room is already dark. Wooden shutters always look stylish and are effective. Scour second-hand shops and salvage centres for originals or have your own shutters made to measure.

Blinds are wonderfully flexible and suit many home environments. Even if you are on a tight budget it is possible to create some beautiful blinds at little cost. You could use plain fabrics and keep the look ultra-simple, or tie them up with co-ordinating ribbons and trim them with braids and glass beads. You can even mix together different prints and patterns in stripes, patches and pennants.

When it comes to curtains for the bed, the modern style is for less costume drama and more clean-lined luxury. But bear in mind that four-poster curtains should complement and not precisely match the curtains at the windows.

If you long for luxuriously curtained windows but are cautious of making an expensive mistake, keep things simple and don't scrimp on fabric. Full curtains should be at least twice as wide as the space they are to cover.

Bedroom lights

Lighting is one of the most powerful ways in which you can influence the mood of the bedroom, transforming it into a relaxing haven. Subtle background lighting should be supplemented by clear task lighting for reading and applying make-up. Take time to work out what combination of lights will best suit your needs.

Soft background lighting in a bedroom was traditionally supplied by a ceiling-mounted fixture, usually a pendant light, but it can equally be provided by wall lights or by downlighters. You will probably need task lighting in the bedroom, usually for dressing or for applying make-up (ensure that lighting is even on both sides of a mirror), as well as clear, easily controlled bedside lighting for reading in bed. This could take the form of small, wall-mounted spotlights or a lamp on a bedside table.

It is a good idea to have the insides of deep wardrobes or cupboards well lit, too, so that you can see clearly to the back of them at night. If you fix the switch to the door jamb, the light will conveniently come on automatically whenever you open the wardrobe or cupboard door.

Lighting checklist

▧ Use an enclosed shade for ceiling lights in bedrooms to prevent glare and so that you do not have to look up at a bare bulb when in bed.

▧ Try to ensure that bedside lamps are well shaded so they do not disturb a sleeping partner on the other side of the bed.

▧ An on–off switch on the flex makes it easier to turn the light on or off, rather than a switch just below the bulb, which entails groping around under the shade.

An individual table lamp on a 1950s ball-foot base throws a subtle light through the scalloped-edge parchment shade.

Simple steel wall light with adjustable arm and soft pleated shade is ideal above a bed; a pull cord enables it to be turned off from the bed.

Stylish modern table lamp is a good height for a bedside table, casting sufficient light for reading.

Metallic 'sunburst' ceiling light suits a contemporary bedroom, but should not be fixed directly above the bed or you would be looking at a bare bulb.

Floor lamp with opaque glass shade can be angled to wash light over the walls or to highlight decorative features of the room.

Textured oval lamp base and matching shade are made of Japanese textured paper rolled with leaves and bark.

Hand-made hooped paper shade with its 'Chinese lantern' look would suit an oriental-inspired bedroom scheme; the metal base has a pull switch.

1950s-style lamps have a tapering base in lacquered or stained birch and conical paper shades; their neutral colours work with any scheme.

Sculptural plastic lamp casts a wash of light and would make an interesting focal point in a modern-style bedroom.

Simple spotlight on a flexible metal stand and with a blue glass shade is ideal for reading in bed.

Individual style

Here, a simple, uncluttered setting forms an effective backdrop for some quirky, whimsical and unpredictable touches that transform this bedroom into a relaxing, very personal space.

Above *The labels on these old, glass-stoppered dispensary bottles echo the glint of gold from a decorative Venetian mask.*

Right *Sun streams through the voile-covered window on to the Edwardian day bed, its mattress upholstered in ticking to match the bedding scheme. The delicate antique French dressing table with a triple mirror is effectively positioned against the backdrop of the wall's broad painted stripes.*

Far right *The modern, metal-framed 'campaign' bed has been given the surprising addition of silk and leopard-skin cushions, which embellish it by day. The traditional bedding scheme is simple black and white: white sheets and pillows with the ticking bolster, the valance and the bed quilt in a black and white toile fabric. The circular bedside table is a Biedermeier-style 'pot cupboard' in satinwood, with a marble top.*

Behind the frontage of a stone-built Georgian town house in a leafy street, the rooms are surprising icons of contemporary design. The period of the building is rarely allowed to influence the decorating and furnishing treatment imposed by Julia, an interior designer. Wherever she lives, in whatever style of house, she likes to stamp on it her own distinctive style.

Throughout the rooms of her house, Julia has tended to keep colour schemes neutral but she likes to introduce accessories with splashes of more unexpected hues. Her own bedroom is no exception. The walls are painted in broad stripes of cream and pale lavender distemper, which she likes for its soft, chalky effect. She plans to add narrow silver lines later for definition. The subtle painted stripes form a happy background for some dramatic individual pieces of furniture, old and new, some of which were brought from her previous home, a large house in the country. These include a modern iron 'campaign' bed, an Edwardian day bed, a painted French chair, a delicate Louis XV dressing table and a Georgian mahogany chest of drawers.

Nowhere are Julia's quirky decorative touches more evident than on the bed itself, where luxurious lilac silk cushions are combined with large, square, tasselled bed cushions covered in a leopard-skin fabric, and juxtaposed with a bolster covered in black and white ticking to match the bed valance. The Edwardian day bed has been

upholstered in the same ticking to link it with the overall furnishing scheme, and shows a witty play on mattress ticking that appeals to Julia. At the window is a simple Roman blind in sheer white voile, which lets natural light stream into the bedroom but screens the room's interior from the view of anyone in the street.

Julia has already decorated this large bedroom twice. 'And it's not finished yet,' she says. 'I like change and I think one should continually move on. It's so easy to get set in one look and, especially if you work in interior design, it's important to keep experimenting with new things.'

Under the eaves

A loft conversion gave Linda and Mike the luxury of an open-plan bedroom and en-suite bathroom, a peaceful and spacious retreat from their busy family life. Its modern ethnic treatment gives it an individual style, unique in this Victorian town house.

In forsaking the peace of the countryside for a large family house in a busy street on the edge of a city, Linda and Mike felt it was important to create a home environment that felt absolutely right. Although their Victorian house had five bedrooms, it had only one small bathroom and some of the downstairs rooms needed replanning, too. So the couple embarked on a series of structural alterations in order to achieve a light, more modern space and comfortable rooms that they knew they would really enjoy using.

A decision was taken to convert the loft, making a wonderful through room that Linda and Mike decided to have as their bedroom. With the bed at one end of the room and an open-plan bathroom at the other, the new staircase comes up in the middle, 'dividing' one space from another.

The building work took much longer than expected and, having spent much more time and money on it than anticipated, Linda's budget for decorating and for furnishings was greatly reduced.

'My aim was to offset the traditional features of the house and our old or antique furniture with a clean, modern look,' says Linda. In the loft bedroom, however, nearly everything is new and Linda, an interior designer, chose to give the room an 'African/ modern' look. Wooden flooring was laid throughout and the window walls at either end of the room left unplastered. These natural finishes offset the opulent but ethnic look of the gold velvet and purple silk cushions and the African-inspired quilt for the bed. The rest of the room has been left plain and uncluttered, with the plastered walls painted an off-white colour, the simple curtain and blind made of white cotton and no rugs on the floor.

The steep pitch of the roof gives the bedroom a drama of its own. At the bathroom end, the bath sits in a surround that spans the entire width of the room. Candle-style wall lights on either side of the window give a diffuse, subtle lighting that is utterly conducive to relaxing baths. A resin drinking fountain makes a stylish washbasin, and was much cheaper than its porcelain equivalent. It is mounted on an inexpensive wooden table and fed by a pedestal 'mixer' tap fixed to the floor. A full-length cheval mirror and an antique cane stool are the only other pieces of furniture in the loft. With good reason, Linda describes this and the enlarged family bathroom one floor down as her 'real pride and joy' in the whole house.

Top left At one end of the bath, a group of burning candles create a soothing ambience for a relaxing soak.

Below The bath is tucked cosily under the eaves, while the freestanding basin makes an unusual feature at the bathroom end of this spacious loft room.

Right The sloping roof reinforces the sense of a retreat in this loft bedroom. The warm wooden floor, the unplastered brick wall and the simple white tab-top curtains offset the richness and colour of the African-inspired bedding scheme.

Transformed by colour

Colour will always transform a living space but when the proportions of a room are as generous as this bedroom it can be used to even more dramatic effect. The inventive colour combinations deployed here create a look that is as fresh and welcoming as it is eye-catching.

Above *White-painted furniture and woodwork shine out against the royal blue walls, the freshness accentuated by the lime green furnishing details. The bedside lamp and even the flowers echo the colour scheme.*

Right *. Windows on two walls let the light flood into this bedroom, with its imposing proportions. The tall fitted wardrobe with its carved pediment banishes all clutter. The antique wing chair, a gift from Maggie's mother, has been re-covered in cream to give it a stylish and more contemporary look. A well-chosen rug covering part of the beech floor has all the room's colours.*

Far right *The ornate pine bed head has been painted matt white to contrast with the deep blue walls. Waffle bed covers in lime and mauve are folded on top of a snowy white bedspread, while the cushion fabrics pull this original colour scheme together very effectively.*

James and Maggie's search for their first home brought them to this flat on the first floor of an elegant Victorian villa. Although it had only one bedroom, they were immediately attracted by the large, sunny spaces and the generous proportions of the main rooms. The kitchen and bathroom were compact, but the bedroom was virtually the same size as the living room, with tall ceilings and long, elegant windows.

The only drawback was that although the major rooms were large, the flat had virtually no storage space. In the bedroom, there were no cupboards or shelves and no obvious alcoves or any nooks and crannies where storage could be inconspicuously built. Maggie's first priority, therefore, was to organize the construction of a large, made-to-measure wardrobe along one wall that would hold all their clothes. Based on the design of a French armoire, the wardrobe was made inexpensively of MDF, and painted white. It has a dramatic pediment and the door panels are made of mesh and lined with fabric for a look that is less austere than solid doors.

Maggie wanted to 'mix contemporary and traditional, to create something

sophisticated but comfortable, with a bit of character'. In terms of a colour scheme, the couple wanted a Mediterranean look. The real drama of the bedroom is derived from the deep royal blue walls; everything else is painted white, in stark relief – the doors, window frames and ceiling, the built-in wardrobe and inexpensive reproduction pine bedside tables and a chest of drawers. With bed covers and cushion fabrics in zingy mauves and limes, the scheme looks young, fresh and imaginative. Since the tall windows still have their original shutters, James and Maggie didn't want to cover up the elegant Victorian frames with curtains. Instead, they fixed simple white roller blinds, which can be pulled half-way down when necessary to screen out the sun.

The en-suite bathroom was a tasteful pale green but looked bland and insipid when viewed from the highly coloured bedroom. It was therefore redecorated in lime green, with a Roman blind in lime and purple to pick up the shades of the bedroom. The use of colour similarly imbues the rest of the flat; everything is wonderfully light and bright, clear and uncluttered.

Sea view

Born and brought up within a few miles of the sea, Clare had always longed to return to it. Her dream became a reality when she spotted a 'For Sale' sign outside a pretty cottage along the front in a small seaside town. Her favourite room in the house is her bedroom, where triple windows frame a wonderful view of the beach and the sea.

Living in her pretty, pastel-painted house on the sea front, Clare makes the most of the views, the sea air and the sound of the sea washing over the pebbled beach. Initially, the rooms all had cottage proportions, so Clare knocked down some walls on the ground floor to create a more spacious feel and made the largest of the three upstairs rooms, facing the sea, her bedroom. This is her favourite retreat. The blue decorative theme, used throughout the cottage, is perfect for the seaside setting and fortunately many of the items Clare has collected over the years, such as shelves, wall cupboards and china, also fit into this colour scheme.

Clare's bedroom is a peaceful haven, its harmonious, sea-inspired tones providing a tranquil effect. Simple Roman blinds at the three windows allow superb views of the beach with its groynes running out to sea.

'I love spending time in here; I think of it as my castaway island. The windows look straight out over the sea – so much so that you could forget you're actually on dry land,' Clare says. 'It's a wonderful place to curl up and escape from the world, especially with the open log fire, my vast collection of crime novels and, of course, my bed!'

The poles supporting the bed 'frame', bolted on to the bed base, are a dramatic feature; they are made from the branches of a monkey puzzle tree that broke off during a storm. 'I've used fishermen's tarred rope to decorate the poles, and sometimes I like to drape blue and green muslin over them to match the walls,' says Clare.

Clare is the author of several craft books. She also designs greetings cards and her creative streak has made its mark on her home. 'I'm always scouring the beach for interesting bits and pieces. I have vast collections of shells, stones, feathers and worn pieces of coloured glass.' She turns her beachcombing finds into decorative items for the house, such as mirrors, picture frames and candleholders. Her treasures are lined up along the windows of her bedroom and add personality to this room. The furniture is kept simple – a stripped wooden dressing table and a couple of individual chairs – while good-quality fitted carpet makes the room comfortable in winter as well as summer.

Above *Candles fit perfectly into naturally holed stones found on the beach nearby and make appropriate table decorations.*

Left *Ammonites, fish and starfish, threaded on to leather thongs, are hung in the window for decorative effect.*

Right *Simplicity is the key in this light, blue-painted seaside bedroom, allowing the spectacular view to take centre stage. The unusual bed frame is made from storm-damaged tree branches.*

Clothes storage

One of the great secrets behind having a calm, organized life is fabulous clothes storage. No one but you may ever see it, but that does not mean that it's not important. Reorganize this functional area and dressing in the morning will become a simple and efficient procedure.

NEAT AS A PIN

It is horribly easy to wreak havoc in a bedroom with just a few pieces of casually discarded clothing. The calm, ordered environment that you took such trouble to create suddenly acquires all the allure of a second-hand clothes shop. Many of us expend a lot of energy, time and money purchasing clothes to make us look good, then all too often we take them home and treat them with complete contempt. We squash them crumpled into drawers, we trap them in the doors of overstuffed closets and generally abuse them. Yet dressing and undressing is a daily chore and it makes sense to render the whole operation as painless as possible. If you can never find what you want to wear in the morning, or perhaps your clothes always seem crushed and spoiled, it is probably time to overhaul your clothes storage space.

Be realistic

The first step is to be completely ruthless with your clothes. Make a realistic assessment of those clothes that you actually wear. If you haven't worn anything for over a year it's time to think about either storing it

elsewhere or getting rid of it altogether. If you don't wear something because it never looks right, or because it's uncomfortable, get rid of it. You can recoup money by taking good items to a specialist second-hand shop, which will give you a percentage of the sale price. Alternatively, you could give things away to a charity shop. Precious clothing should be wrapped carefully in tissue paper (not plastic as this can damage fabric in the long term) and stored somewhere out of the way.

The storage options

The next step is to assess the clothes you are left with and decide how best to store them. Drawers are always useful for small items such as underwear, hosiery and accessories, but often they are not very user-friendly as you have to rummage to find what you are searching for. Larger items such as T-shirts and sweaters are much easier to locate when they are folded on shelves. Underwear and socks can be stored on shelves too, contained in large open boxes. Don't overfill drawers – if they start becoming hard to close, reassess the value of their contents.

Above *Wicker boxes tucked into a shelving system contain bedside clutter, while brightly coloured boxes utilize the dead space under the bed.*

Left *Keep lines clean with individual pieces of furniture customized to suit specific storage requirements.*

Right *A contemporary solution to clothes storage turns an open-plan 'wardrobe' and chest of drawers into a design statement.*

VANISHING TRICKS

Floor-to-ceiling built-in wardrobes offer the best storage facilities and the doors can be designed to blend in with the style of the room. For a whimsical approach, hunt out interesting old doors and have your storage space built around them. However, built-in wardrobes need not be expensive. A budget approach is to utilize an alcove space, put up some shelves and a rail, then hang a curtain in front. Inaccessible shelves are useful for storing bulky, infrequently used items such as hats or suitcases.

Good hanging space is essential, but be aware that you don't have to allow a full-length drop – 1.5m (5ft) – for all your clothes. Shirts and jackets need a fall of only 1m (3ft), which means that you can have either a double layer of hanging space or some additional shelves. If you organize your clothing into sections and group colours together, you will be able to identify quickly what you want to find or locate a suitable alternative. Good-quality contoured hangers are worth investing in for good clothes care.

Think, too, about how you want to store all your accessories. Shoes can be tucked into boxes like pigeonholes, and scarves and ties can be folded over ribbons strung across the backs of doors.

Trunks, chests and boxes are brilliant for storing bedding or towels. If you are short of space, utilize the area under the bed. Seasonal clothing can be folded into boxes and stored out of the way when not in use. Make sure the boxes have lids to protect clothing from dust. If you use boxes with castors, it will make them easy to move for cleaning purposes.

A full-length mirror will ensure you can quickly check on how you look as you dress. Climbing on to a chair to check on your bottom half is not a good idea. Study yourself in different mirrors before you buy one – some mirrors make you look better than others, and if you think you look good, you will look good.

User-friendly furniture

Make sure that all your pieces of storage furniture are easy to use and well maintained. Wardrobe doors should close tightly and drawers should run smoothly. If you have to tug at a drawer to get it open and then fight to shut it again afterwards, you will find that you don't bother to use it – or the items inside it – half the time. The problem may be solved with a well-placed tack, some sandpaper and some beeswax or something similar to ease the runners.

Below A streamlined dressing table is inviting and user-friendly. With these facilities you can take pleasure in applying make-up and in selecting the right jewellery and accessories.

Bottom and right If space is at a premium, utilize every inch of storage available. Stylish and attractive-looking boxes are available in all sizes in wood, metal, cardboard and wicker to suit all budgets.

---

bedroom storage checklist

▧ Lighting up your wardrobe makes selecting clothes so much easier. Use an internal strip light that is activated by an automatic switch on the door jamb.

▧ Store shoes away in their boxes and stick a Polaroid snap on the end of each box to make each pair easy to locate; alternatively, use transparent plastic boxes. so you can see the shoes.

▧ Keep a sealed box of shoe polishes and a sewing kit in the wardrobe so that everything you need for clothes maintenance is close at hand.

▧ Coat hangers require a space of about 60cm (24in) deep. The hanging rail should be positioned

high enough to allow your longest item of clothing to clear the base of the wardrobe.

▧ Wooden or pretty cardboard boxes tucked under the bed or beneath bedside tables offer superb storage and keep those bedside essentials accessible but out of sight.

▧ Castors on the bottom of storage boxes make them easier to move. Either buy storage boxes with wheels or buy castors, which come in various sizes and are easily available from do-it-yourself stores, so you can put them on existing boxes.

▧ Scour hardware shops for storage ideas to suit your special requirements.

Wardrobes

Built-in wardrobes and bedroom cupboards have been a more popular choice recently, but not all bedrooms have a suitable alcove or wall space to make this possible. Freestanding wardrobes may be a better solution in a large bedroom and the advantage is that you can take them with you when you move.

In addition to storing clothes, wardrobes may have to house shoes, luggage and possibly sports equipment – in short, everything that needs to be concealed. Depending on the type of clothes storage needed, you may look for full-length hanging space (if you have long dresses or coats) or prefer to have some shorter-length space, with shelves at top and bottom.

Where a bedroom doubles as a workroom by day, the wardrobe could be fitted with shelves and used to keep work-related clutter behind closed doors. In a shared bedroom, for example, one accommodating two children, a full-length wardrobe can be used to demarcate and divide the space, or even to make a separate dressing area in a large bedroom.

Wardrobe checklist

▧ Check the dimensions of a freestanding wardrobe carefully before buying it if you want it to fit into an alcove.

▧ A minimum interior depth of 53cm (21in) is needed to hang clothes sideways.

▧ Use the area beneath long hanging space for shoe racks and the space beneath short hanging space for pull-out wire baskets or shelves for sweaters or accessories such as belts.

A portable extending clothes rail *made of steel and fitted with castors is fully mobile; it is as useful in the utility room as it is in the bedroom.*

Double wardrobe in cherry wood would blend with a period or modern interior; this one has a single drawer below.

Solid pine wardrobes suit country-style bedrooms; this one has an interior shelf, hanging rail and a half-length mirror inside.

High-tech metal wardrobe has a frame finished in natural anodized aluminium with acid-etched, sand-blasted, glass door panels.

French-style armoire comprises two large cupboards top and bottom and a central drawer, and is painted pale grey with an aged finish.

Plain and simple contemporary wardrobe in maple veneer has two shelves and a hanging rail.

Single panelled-door wardrobe with a drawer is painted white with an antiqued finish.

Budget 'safari' wardrobe has a pine frame and a natural canvas cover, with a door-like opening in the middle.

Generously proportioned painted armoire with panelled doors has hanging space and a single shelf, with a deep drawer at its base.

Colonial-style tall chest of drawers made of cherry wood is hand-finished for an authentic-looking antique effect.

Chests of drawers

While its design has become more streamlined over the years, there is no real alternative to the chest of drawers. In the bedroom, drawers are the perfect solution for separating and storing small items of clothing, such as underclothes, socks and belts, enabling you instantly to pick out whatever you need.

Antique chests of drawers, usually in a rich, polished wood, have pleasing proportions and make an aesthetic contribution to the decor of any period-style bedroom, while contemporary chests may offer more versatile storage. There are many permutations on the chests of drawers now available in terms of dimensions, and number and width of drawers, as well as finishes. These range from natural wood to special paint effects and even metal, so it should be possible to find a chest to suit any style of bedroom.

You can often pick up chests of drawers in junk shops. Provided the frame is sound and the drawers intact, a chest is often worth renovating. Strip off all the old paint or polish, sand and prime it, then repaint the wood to suit your colour scheme. Replacing the handles, too, will give the chest a completely new lease of life.

Chest checklist

▧ Ensure that all drawers run smoothly and are securely fixed so that they will not pull right out and tip over.

▧ You can buy dividers for full-width drawers, enabling you to separate items – for example, socks and tights, necklaces and bracelets – and find what you want more readily.

▧ If you acquire a second-hand chest of drawers, lining the drawers with scented drawer lining paper will banish any musty smell.

This Italian-designed and craftsman-made *'chest on chest' in brown-painted ash and polished pear wood is a modern classic.*

Colonial-style, metal-framed rattan chest of drawers would look just as at home in a conservatory as in a bedroom.

Replica of a plan chest, traditionally used by architects to store drawings, makes ideal storage in a bedroom that doubles as a workroom.

Minimalist-looking versatile chest in maple veneer combines a wide five-drawer unit with a narrow four-drawer unit.

Contemporary-style chest with slots in place of handles has a beech-veneered carcass and resin board drawers, with silver-coated steel legs.

Compact, multi-drawer chest painted in pale grey is based on a French mercerie; it is ideal for all kinds of storage.

Traditional white-painted chest with brass drop handles has two narrow drawers at the top and three full-width ones below.

Tall, Shaker-style chest in beech has five drawers and is ideal for a narrow space or alcove.

Solid pine chest with five drawers has ball feet and turned wooden handles.

Low, three-drawer dark wooden chest with metal slot handles has simple lines that would suit a modern interior.

Beds and bedside

Beds come in all styles and the table that sits alongside can be chosen to match, in materials and period, or to contrast, so that it stands alone as an individual piece. The most important thing is to ensure that the table is the correct height for when you are in bed.

At their simplest, there are divan beds that comprise a low base, a mattress and a plain bed head. At the other extreme are fancy four-posters or brass and cast-iron beds with ornate head and footboards. With these types of bed, the mattress is often raised on separate box springs, which bring it higher off the floor. These variations are why you need to take care choosing a bedside table of the right height for your bed, especially if you intend to stand a reading lamp on it.

The bed is often the focal point of a bedroom and can also take up most of the space in the room. Dress it up or down to suit your style: it may be festooned with pillows, cushions and throws or covered with a simple quilt or duvet. The most important part is the mattress and this must be the best you can afford; it should be firm enough to support your spine but not so hard that it throws your hips and shoulder out of their normal curvature.

Choosing a bed

▨ Before opting for the luxury of a king-size bed, make sure the bedroom is large enough and bear in mind that you will need appropriately sized sheets, duvet covers and quilts.

▨ Test a mattress for comfort and firmness before you buy, lying on it for a few minutes with your partner. Beds can be ordered with a different firmness of spring on each side.

▨ If storage space in your bedroom is restricted, buy a bed with pull-out drawers in the base or use drawers on castors beneath the bed frame, concealed by a valance.

A contemporary-style bedside cabinet in rich cherry wood has one drawer and an enclosed shelf.

Ornate cast-iron bedstead decorated with gold leaf motifs and tassels, which would suit an opulent bedroom setting.

Three-drawer bedside chest in beech has the advantage of providing concealed storage.

Low bed with solid pine frame and panelled ends, which would look good in a country-style bedroom.

Three-drawer 'plan chest' would provide useful storage at the side of a bed, provided there is enough wall space for it.

Waxed French pine low bed has solid sides and a curved headboard and footboard.

Hardwood bedside 'trunk' has an innovative drawer design that allows access from both sides.

Plainly styled low divan with padded headboard and footboard would look right in a minimally styled bedroom; these covers are removable.

Simple wooden table with antique wax finish is the perfect bedside place for a book and a lamp.

Retro-style wooden divan in solid maple has a veneered headboard; its look is reminiscent of wartime utility furniture.

Guest bedrooms

With space at a premium in most homes, few households can afford to reserve a spare room exclusively for visitors who come to stay. Most guest bedrooms have a dual function and it is perfectly possible to create a room that is flexible enough to fulfil its varied roles.

Flexible space

The first rule is to ensure that the main function of the part-time guest bedroom is clearly defined – whether it is principally a study, storeroom or dressing room. At the same time, it should be possible to swiftly change the emphasis when required, since you do not want to have to drag furniture around whenever friends and family come to stay.

A bed can be concealed in many different ways. A sofa bed is an obvious solution and need not be expensive although, as with anything else, you get what you pay for. Built-in foldaway beds that pull out of a cupboard are easy to use and increasingly popular. A day bed is a stylish solution, offering wonderful seating when decorated with cushions but ready for guests at a moment's notice. Similarly, a plain divan can easily be dressed up for day or night time use, while a futon that folds up into a seat is another solution.

Children are easy to accommodate and they like nothing better than the notion of camping for a couple of nights. Modern air beds are comfortable enough for short-term use; alternatively, cover some foam squares with durable fabric and arrange them together to make a bed when children come to stay. Sew strips of touch-and-close tape where they meet to prevent the cushions taking off in different directions.

Guest room extras

Lighting needs special consideration. As well as lights for general purposes, the room should contain a bedside lamp so that guests can read in comfort, and don't have to fumble across a strange room in the pitch dark. It is also helpful if the room contains such items as a mirror, a radio, a clock and even a hair dryer. If cupboards and drawers are already full of your own bits and pieces, put some hooks and pretty, padded coat hangers on the back of the door. Boxes tucked under the bed can also provide your guest with storage for their clothes.

If the guest bedroom is also your office invest in a simple, fabric-covered screen, so that computer, filing cabinets and office equipment can be concealed in a moment.

Above The smallest space can allow you to accommodate a guest in comfort., but keep fixtures and fittings plain. It's important to find space for a mirror and a few pegs.

Left Play down the impact of a bed by keeping coverings in dark or neutral tones. Steer away from fussy details and avoid obvious bedroom furnishings.

Right Maximize your space with a purpose-built work station on a wooden platform; guest beds slot in below.

Occasional beds

If you don't have a spare room but you love to have guests to stay, the answer lies in choosing a bed in disguise. Whether it's a sofa bed, a futon or a stowaway bed that tucks underneath another, there are stylish designs to suit all circumstances.

Sofa beds may be three- or two-seater sofas, with sprung or foam upholstery that converts to a mattress. Frames are usually metal and the mechanism either pivots and opens out, or, with cushions removed, unfolds from the body of the sofa. For a sofa bed in regular use as both a double bed and a sofa, you will need a three-seater with a sprung mattress; feather cushions add a touch of luxury. For a compact spare room or a study, a smaller, two-seater sofa bed will provide comfortable seating and an extra bed for a weekend guest.

The futon, a Japanese invention, is basically a thin, firm tufted mattress, which can be used on the floor or on a simple slatted base; when the base is folded, it becomes a sofa. Simple yet stylish, futons are good value and make a perfect spare bed for a teenager's or a student's room.

Stowaway beds, in which a compact single bed folds out when two beds are needed, are a versatile solution for children's rooms. The lower bed is on castors and has legs that can be raised when pulled out, to make it the same height as the top bed.

The comfort factor

▧ Test a sofa bed by both sitting and lying on it. The bed should be stable and you should not be able to feel the frame through the mattress.

▧ Check the seat depth of the sofa. Some models are quite deep so as to accommodate the opening mechanism, making them uncomfortable for shorter people to sit on.

▧ Feather cushions can be plumped up over and over again, whereas a foam filling has less give and will compress over time.

▧ Make sure the bed does not fold up or lift off the floor when you sit in the middle. Sofa beds with castors are easier to move but won't keep still when being opened out.

▧ If the sofa bed is used mainly as a sofa but the covers are not removable for cleaning, choose darker, patterned designs that will not readily show the dirt.

In this contemporary interpretation of the chaise longue with a tubular stainless steel frame, the multi-density foam base becomes a mattress when needed.

Basic futon mattress, *without frame, stashes away into a neat roll with handles – a portable, budget solution for teenagers and students.*

Stowaway bed *pulls out from beneath the mattress of the top bed; each bed has a slatted base and a sprung mattress for comfort.*

Double futon *has a birch wood frame and slats that are close together to make a firm bed base. Unlike most futons, this one is standard bed height.*

Double futon *on a rubber wood base converts into a three-seater sofa.*

Simple tufted futon *mattress sits on a wooden frame low to the ground.*

Simply styled, *cotton-covered, metal-framed sofa opens up to become a comfortable single bed with a spring coil mattress.*

Two-seater sofa *with tailored fixed covers and a spring mattress converts into a comfortable bed for overnight guests.*

Stylish day bed *on stainless steel legs has a beech frame with multi-density foam filling.*

Compact and versatile *single French pine bed has a second bed stored underneath. The legs are automatically released when the bed is pulled out.*

Children introduce you to a whole new way of decorating. For the first time, you appreciate the merits of washable walls and realize how much storage one small person requires, whether it's for nappies and toys or homework and CDs. You will need to take children's own preferences into account, so involve them as much as you can. They may feel so proud of their room, they might even keep it tidy.

children's rooms

Being flexible

Do you need a room for one or two, or even three? Should it be a nursery, or a bedroom that doubles as a playroom or a study? And what about space for all those pre-teen sleepovers? If these are your questions, here are some answers.

Above *The iron bedstead and traditional chest provide an old-fashioned touch in this room under the eaves, and are practical as well as pretty.*

Below *Purpose-built bunks not only look impressive, but also incorporate useful extra storage – from the drawers beneath each bed to the desk and shelf unit squeezed in at the end.*

Moving on

You will find that your child outgrows that charmingly decorated nursery in surprisingly few years, so it makes sense to choose flexible furnishings right from the start. Since wardrobes, chests or any other furniture with nursery motifs are likely to be spurned as soon as a child starts school, a better choice might be plain or painted wood. A light, natural finish blends with almost any setting, while a painted one can become red, orange or black as your child's tastes change. It's the same with size: apart from very small chairs and tables, the general rule is the bigger the better. Tiny children often have more clothes and larger toys than older ones, so it might be a good idea to invest in a tall chest of drawers and a toy cupboard. About the only thing that you will not need until later is a full-length wardrobe, so it's worth seeing if unwanted hanging space can be filled with shelves or storage crates for the time being.

Two's company

Despite the trend towards separate rooms, in reality many children still have to share. They might even choose to do so, so that one bedroom can become their playroom – a new spin on the old-fashioned day nursery and night nursery idea. Bunk beds are an obvious space-saving idea, but they do need to be sturdy if they are to be safe and to last a long time. You should consider length and head-room if you want them to cater for teenagers, and for safety reasons avoid putting young children in the top bunk – six years is about the right age.

Children who share a bedroom do still like to have a certain amount of private space, even if it is just a shelf next to each child's bunk. You might also want to make special provision for an older child, so that his or her playthings and homework are not accessible to the younger one – for everyone's sake.

Making the most of space

A cabin bunk with desk or sofa and storage underneath is a particularly good way of saving floor space in a small bedroom. Wall-hung storage is always useful, too, whether it takes the form of bookshelves, cupboards or CD racks. Equally convenient are items of furniture in multi-purpose and space-saving designs, for example pull-out desks, folding chairs and cupboards with drawers as well as hanging space, all of which free up the room available for children to play in.

child checklist

▨ Children spend much of their time on the floor, so flooring needs to be warm but easy to clean, especially if the bedroom is a playroom, too. Sealed cork or wood, linoleum or cushioned vinyl are all options.

▨ Desks that fit into corners make use of what is often dead space.

▨ Washable, solvent-free paints are a good choice for walls. Wallpaper can be a mistake since toddlers love tearing and drawing on it.

▨ Make sure that pegs, doors and drawers are within a child's reach so they can learn to find their clothes and put them away. But fit locks or high bolts to any cupboards that you don't want them to access.

▨ A toy cupboard is easier to use than a toy box and you can put games with fiddly pieces, like jigsaws and Lego, out of reach.

▨ If the room gets the morning sun, blackout blinds are an idea to prevent children waking early.

Above *Learning about colours and shapes is easy in this bright bedroom. There is plenty of storage and the dense carpet won't stop the progress of wheeled toys.*

The nursery

Since you have no idea of the baby's personality, or often of the sex, the nursery is a blank canvas for decorating. Preparing for your new baby is room is exciting, take a romantic approach with white lace, a traditional one with soft pastels, or adhere to the child psychologists' belief that babies are most likely to react to red, black and white.

Above Take away the border and this room suits any age. The fitted cupboards and storage hamper with cushion will be just as useful when this baby has become a teenager.

Right It's simple: a cot, a child's chair, warm yellow walls and plenty of wood. All the room needs is a cupboard and a wooden chest for storage, and an easy chair for you.

Sleep, baby, sleep

Although most parents like to have their baby's room finished ahead of time, it probably won't be used for a while. The latest advice on preventing cot death is that babies should sleep in the same room as their parents for the first six months and sometimes longer. By the time your baby sleeps alone, he or she will be on the verge of crawling. It's worth getting down on all fours to see the world from a baby's eye-view so you can minimize any obvious hazards.

Your baby will probably have outgrown the cradle or Moses basket and be ready for a big cot by the time he or she moves into the nursery. If you are tempted by a second-hand one, make sure that any old paint is completely stripped away in case it contains lead (which could be several layers down) and check that the bars, mechanism and mattress all comply with current safety recommendations. You won't need cot bumpers, duvets or pillows until after your baby's first birthday.

Baby care

A stable surface is essential if you plan to change your baby's nappies in the bedroom. You can buy a purpose-made unit, perhaps to match the cot, or use the top of a chest of drawers. Keep nappies and wipes in a drawer underneath or on a shelf close by if you can – turn your back for an instant, and that's when your baby rolls off. A washbasin is well worth installing for convenience and it's surprising how soon you will need storage for toys. It is also worth providing a comfortable chair for you for feeding and cuddling baby before bed. An old-fashioned nursing chair with a low seat and minimal arms gives you an idea of what is best.

Little extras

Changing mats, bedding and curtains are perfect for adding pattern to a room. The big stores bring out new ranges every season so there is plenty to choose from, but it's worth buying all the items you think you might need at the same time in case the design is discontinued. If you don't want nursery patterns, you can create any number of original effects using stencils or fashionable blocks of colour. Colour is also an effective way of uniting odd pieces of furniture. Simply paint each piece the same shade and add distinctive handles to turn a random assortment into a designer collection.

A room for little ones

This is a time of first steps, first words, the first bed and the first determined bid for independence. It involves the need to provide safe and stimulating surroundings for children, who love exploring everything they can get their hands on or into.

Above Pink packs more of a punch when freed from Barbie-style frills. The high wooden bed provides a useful hiding place underneath for storage crates full of toys.

Left There really is a monster under this bed ... but he's quite friendly. The jungle theme is emphasized by animal motifs on walls and bedding, as well as the bright colour scheme.

The big bed

Children usually love moving into a bed from a cot as it shows they are really grown up. Although it's often not worth buying a child's bed, a full-size single can seem enormous to a toddler and it may be worth adding a safety rail to prevent falls. A small table or shelf within reach is useful for a drink or possibly a night light.

A joint effort

It is sometimes better to wait to redecorate the nursery rather than rushing a lot of changes through all at once. However, if there's another baby on the way, it's wise to get your first child settled well before or some time after the birth. When you're moving children to another room, it's a good idea to consult them and incorporate their ideas if you can, however young they are. One joint enterprise could be to have a go at a mural or painting pictures on the walls. It's not as difficult as you might think if you keep the outline simple. Just draw a grid over a design on paper that you like and pencil a larger grid on the wall. Copy the outline that appears in each paper square on to the wall and paint it in. Alternatively, create a simple landscape – blue on the ceiling and the top half of the wall for sky, and green below for fields – and stick on images cut from card, such as clouds or sun, farm animals, Thomas the Tank Engine or your child's own artistic efforts.

Flooring and furniture

Whether you are painting or potty training, a washable floor gives peace of mind. Add rugs for comfort if you like, but they must be firmly anchored. For a soft flooring, consider needlepunch 'office' carpet, or cord; too much pile will make Lego towers wobble and wheeled toys run slowly.

A nursery-size chair and table make pastimes such as puzzles easier. Create a quiet corner if there's space, with a rug, cushions or a bean bag for comfort and a bookcase close by to encourage reading.

Below Pint-size furniture can be appropriate as this trio shows. A vividly coloured low stool and chair are accompanied by the junior equivalent of a plan chest, perfect for storing crayons and jigsaw puzzles.

Playrooms

It's every parent's dream: a room where the children will play, if not quietly, then at least out of earshot. A playroom needs careful planning, though, if it is to be a place where children want to stay and enjoy creative play rather than be used just as a depot for toys.

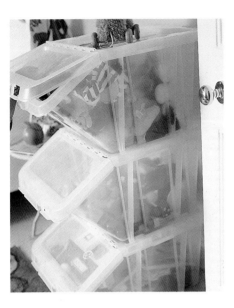

Places for everything

Some toys have to be kept out because they are simply too large to put away, and it is often a good idea to organize space around them. A play kitchen can become part of a home corner with a small table and chairs, soft toys and doll's pushchair, while an easel is a focal point for crafts, with a waterproof floor covering beneath and painting overalls hung on pegs nearby. Ride-ons need as much space as you can give them. Although

they don't usually cause problems when used by toddlers, as soon as children get boisterous, it's better to keep them outside.

Ideas for storage

Varying the toys you make available to children, and keeping the others out of sight, helps them enjoy their play more. It's easier to keep all the bits and pieces together and old toys are treated like new ones once they have been rested for a while. Invest in a series of matching containers – plastic crates, hampers or toughened cardboard boxes – in different sizes, so you can separate Lego from Barbie accessories, for example. Keep them in a cupboard, under a work surface or on shelves and put anything you don't want the children to play with unsupervised, such as paints, play-dough or intricate puzzles, out of reach.

Walls and floors

Painted walls and warm but easy-clean flooring can be design conscious as well as practical. The playroom is the perfect place to try a feature wall, or paint one wall scarlet, bright yellow or deep blue and the others in paler, contrasting tones. Include a blackboard to give children's creativity free rein, and a large pinboard or a whole wall of hessian or cork to display their artwork. If you opt for soft flooring, have a splashmat available for painting or pasting activities.

Above *Clear plastic storage boxes like these have one compelling advantage – you can see exactly what's inside. Here, they are arranged as a space-saving tower.*

Far left *Ready to play: jungle masks and mural set the scene while miniature toys, like the doll's house and Noah's ark animals, form an attractive display.*

Below left *A playroom decorated with a fishy theme for a Little Mermaid. The fish appear on the wallpaper, co-ordinating border and stencilled toy box, while the mirror frame is decorated with shells.*

School-age rooms

According to retailers, children have outgrown toys by the time they are nine. Of course there will always be a place for one or two favourites, but, on the whole, children at school are more interested in electronic games and music, so this is the perfect time to update their rooms.

Above *A compact desk doubles as a bedside table in this small bedroom. The two lamps help compensate for the restricted natural light provided by the small window.*

Right *Built-in cupboards turn awkward space into efficient storage, keeping everything ship-shape in this loft conversion. Pale blue walls and flooring offset by natural wood create a sophisticated colour scheme.*

Far right *Twin beds fit snugly under the eaves, leaving plenty of room for play in this attic bedroom. The traditional look is emphasized by the rag rug and embroidered cloth.*

THE LOOK

Peer pressure, pester power – whatever you call it, it comes to the same thing. School-children are quick to catch on to a trend and vociferous about demanding the latest craze. If it happens to be a character wallpaper, try compromising. Suggest a sophisticated colour scheme: light walls with plenty of space for posters. Add a few splashes of bold colour on furniture or woodwork and keep window and floor coverings relatively neutral. It is far better to indulge their wishes by having character or football club colours on bed linen, for example, than on wallpaper.

Work space

Children need a quiet and comfortable place for homework. A wide work surface with adequate lighting, plenty of space for artwork and drawers to one side for pencils and paper is fine, although later you may want to invest in some form of computer desk. There are plenty of compact designs around, with a raised platform to bring the monitor to the correct height, a slide-out surface for the keyboard and storage for a printer.

Space-saving sleepers

If the room is small, look at a space-saving bed. Cabin bunks, with a desk or sofa, chest and wardrobe beneath, are a solution if your child enjoys sleeping up high. A midi-sleeper, which incorporates drawers, a bookshelf and perhaps a pull-out desk, is best if the ceiling is low. Even if you don't need a bed complete with furniture, one with a long drawer where a road or railway layout can be kept is useful, or opt for a pull-out bed for when friends stay over.

Living together

While two school-age children sharing a room usually just need separate storage for their things, children of very different ages may need more complex arrangements. It might, for example, be an idea to frame a cabin bunk with brightly painted MDF and partition the room, so the older child can play or work in peace, and playthings with small pieces are kept safely away from a toddler. If a teenager and school-age child share, try to give the older one the bed close to the door or the bottom bunk to minimize the disruption caused by a later bedtime.

TEENAGE DENS

Tread lightly when approaching the subject of teenage rooms. You are dealing not only with volatile hormones but with a fierce desire for independence that can turn the mildest suggestion into a declaration of war. You may see nothing wrong with a room that was furnished and decorated at some expense only two years ago, but to teenage eyes, it's a reminder of how childish they were at 12. So why not negotiate – you supply the paint, they do the work; the frilly curtains can go but the flooring stays … or something similar. Otherwise, close your eyes to terminal untidiness and provocative posters and save your strength for something worth fighting about …

The age of electronics

Once most of the toys have gone, the bedroom fills up with a host of electronic gadgets – from a computer to games console, stereo system and television. These need plenty of power points and, if you want to link the computer to the Internet, a phone point for the modem too. This equipment also makes demands on space. If your teenager insists on a full-size stereo system, rather than a smaller one, it is worth considering a purpose-made storage unit that can also take a games machine or television. CD racks will be needed, so buy

them in different colours to keep music separate from games disks and CD-ROMs. And, if you are concerned about what your teenager might be accessing in his or her room, it is probably better to resist pleas to have equipment there in the first place.

Creating the look

Most teenagers want a room that is more of a bedsit than a bedroom. A makeshift look is all part of its charm and you're likely to find that friends prefer to sleep on the floor when they stay over, rather than use the spare bed you've so thoughtfully provided. That said, your teenager will probably be grateful for the use of a sofa. There is no need to buy new; an old one covered with an ethnic or animal-print throw and a mix of furry and inflatable cushions will be appreciated just as much. Add a chair and some floor cushions, a simple bedspread or graphic bed linen and furniture in black or light wood to complete the look. If you are buying a new bed at this stage, think about a futon that doubles as a sofa or a low slatted bed close to the floor.

Teenagers usually have definite ideas about colour. Acid brights, burgundy, deep blue, black, white and grey often meet with approval but pastels and primary colours, with the exception of red, may well be given a cooler reception.

Above Brightly coloured plastic tubing and brick-effect wallpaper just waiting for graffiti give this bedroom a touch of urban chic. The dustbin beneath the bed continues the theme.

Below left Walls painted lime green with contrasting dark blue accessories turn a straightforward bedroom into a teenage den. Stretchers are a simple way to make posters look impressive.

Right Oriental simplicity: a minimalist scheme in grey, white and black with an asymmetric shelving unit and adjustable black lamp creates a room with an unmistakably grown-up style.

teenage ideas

● Industrial shelving with black or brightly coloured metal brackets can serve as bookshelves and storage for stereo and CDs. Add plastic or painted wooden crates the same depth as the shelves for keeping stationery and other bits and pieces together.

● An oriental look in lacquered red and black, with a futon, a bamboo screen and a blind could be ideal for a teenager's bedroom.

● Washable throws, bed covers and rugs in deep colours make practical and trendy cover-ups.

● Keep lighting subdued, big paper lanterns and a lava lamp are ideal, but provide a good adjustable desk lamp or a spotlight above the desk to prevent eye strain when studying.

● A hanging rail can often substitute for a wardrobe and may prompt teenagers to tidy away their clothes. Add a canvas laundry bag for dirty washing.

● A swivelling office chair with good back support is well worth investing in for long hours spent at the desk.

A well-planned space and the right decor in the bathroom can make all the difference to how you start or end the day, whether you opt for a refreshing wake-up shower or a self-indulgent soak, a beauty salon for one or a family bathroom for four. Simply decide what you want, look for inspiration in the following pages and we'll help you to make it happen.

bathrooms

Decision time

Today's bathrooms are places to pamper and indulge yourself and even the smallest space can become a comfortable retreat. All it takes to turn a bathroom into a sanctuary and create your own private oasis is a little imagination and a lot of careful planning.

What do you want in your bathroom?

Starting from scratch gives you the chance to create a bathroom with great impact. A roll-top tub, for example, looks splendid set in the centre of a room with a traditional shower above and drapes on each side to stop splashes, or you could build a sleek, modern design into a platform to give the effect of a sunken bath. You might decide that you want a bidet, a separate shower cabinet, a washstand, or two washbasins to beat the morning rush.

However big or small your bathroom (the average size is less than 3 x 2m/10 x 6½ft), it is a good idea to make a wish list of what you would like to include in the room and sketch out a plan on graph paper to make sure you have allowed enough space. You will need 700mm (28in) standing space in front of a washbasin and 1m (3ft) for elbow room, an area of at least 600mm (24in) square in front of a WC or bidet, 700mm (28in) alongside a bath for ease of climbing in and out, and 1m (3ft) square for a shower cabinet.

Plumbing essentials

The choice of layout is often restricted because there is only one possible place for the bath, and that can dictate where the basin and WC go, too. Although plumbing can certainly be moved, hot-water pipe runs should be kept as short as possible for economy, and waste water outlets need to be close to exterior walls. Alter the position of the soil stack only if it is essential, because this is difficult and costly, and you may need special permission to make sure that it complies with building regulations. Simply turning the WC through 90 degrees can often solve the problem.

The right shower

Matching the shower to the water supply will ensure that showering is a satisfying experience. Mixer showers need a cold tank at least 1m (3ft) above the shower head for sufficient water pressure. Controls can be manual or thermostatic; the latter cost more but prevent you from being scalded if cold water is drawn off elsewhere in the house. Power showers add a booster pump to a mixer to give a strong spray. They can also be installed where there is insufficient pressure because the water tank is low, but they do use a lot of water. A shower cabinet or fully tiled walls are essential to prevent water damage. Instant electric showers can be installed almost anywhere because they heat water on demand. They are economical, but look for a wattage of at least 8kW for an adequate flow and don't expect the full power shower experience.

Above White shower curtains hung from screens provide a stylish solution to splashes from the overhead shower. Tongue-and-groove panelling neatly conceals pipework to the basin and WC.

Below Modern clean lines and bright colours, contrast with the timber beams in this comfortable bathroom under the eaves of a barn conversion. Large tiled areas are essential in a family bathroom.

bathroom checklist

■ If you are setting a washbasin against an internal wall, choose a pedestal-mounted one or a washstand rather than one that is hung on the wall, unless you are sure the wall can take the strain.

■ The pipes will be on show if you site the bath in the centre of the room, so you may want to choose chrome rather than standard copper.

■ If you opt for taps made in another country, make sure that they are compatible with your local water pressure.

■ Enamelled baths can be resurfaced *in situ*, which lasts about seven years. Off-site renovation gives better wear because the surface can be kiln-dried but it is costlier and more disruptive.

■ If you buy a renovated bathroom suite, the tap and waste connections may need adapting. Ensure your floor is strong enough to bear a heavy load.

■ Many countries have registers of qualified plumbers governed by a national code of standards and offering complaints procedures.

Above *This colourful children's bathroom has been designed on a nautical theme that can be adapted as the children grow older. The two sea-green cupboard doors are grooved so that they look like six doors.*

Walls

Think about who uses the bathroom before choosing a treatment for the walls. Singles and couples may be able to get away with wallpaper, especially in a large, well-ventilated room, but if you have children or you like particularly hot showers or baths, opt for a surface that shrugs off splashes and condensation. Most robust of all is a fully tiled bathroom but, for a softer look, you can use tiles for a practical splashback, with paint to emphasize or contrast.

TILES

Sleek and glossy, wall tiles are as good-looking as they are practical. However, because they are expensive to buy and renew, it is worth choosing tiles in colours and designs that will adapt to different schemes. This does not mean restricting yourself only to white, because a rich colour can be just as flexible. You may choose spectacular tiles to form a focal point in your bathroom or pick a blend of related shades, which gives you the option of emphasizing light or dark colours, warm or cool ones.

Narrowing the choice

Wall tiles are shinier, thinner and less robust than floor tiles, although for bathrooms it is sometimes possible to find tiles that are suitable for both wall and floor.

Most are universal tiles that can be used anywhere on the wall. Field or spacer tiles have unglazed edges for wall-to-wall tiling or the centre of a tiled area, while edge tiles are curved on one or two sides, to finish off a panel or a splashback. Although most tiles are based on the 100mm (4in), 150mm (6in) or 200mm (8in) square module, there are smaller tiles available, 75mm (3in) square, and also some rectangular tiles in a

variety of sizes. Narrow printed or moulded border tiles, ideal for finishing off a partly tiled wall, can also be bought.

Designs with a difference

Mosaic tiles on a peel-off backing sheet are easy for do-it-yourself use for tiling around intricate areas. Better left to professionals, however, are tiles that build into a large mosaic and also hand-made tiles. These are much chunkier and often smaller than mass-produced tiles and sometimes have elaborate raised designs and an irregular surface, which is part of their charm.

If you don't want pattern, white tiles like mini-bricks have a bevelled edge that is brilliant for reflecting light. Glass bricks can create an interesting shower screen or try an old favourite, contrasting coloured grout, to add interest to a wall of plain tiles. If you are feeling creative, you could use odd or old salvaged tiles to liven up a plain wall (make sure they are of a similar thickness for the best effect) or bits of broken tile to create a mosaic in the centre of a panel or on a window sill. Whatever you choose, you will need waterproof adhesive and grout, especially if you are tiling around a bath or shower.

Above A huge circular mirror and warm-coloured wood offset the glossy green tiles in this small bathroom. Positioning the mirror so as to reflect the opposite wall increases the light and the sense of space in the room.
Below A curved wall of semi-opaque glass bricks creates a distinctive shower area in this spacious bathroom.
Right Sea-green mosaic tiles on the bath panel and surround as well as the splashback give an architectural look to this small bathroom. A slatted blind provides a perfect screen at the large window.

Above Wine-coloured paint, metallic accents and natural wood are perfect partners for an Edwardian-style bathroom suite. Sparkling white on the skirting and plain white towels keep it fresh and bright looking.

Below A panel installed under the dado looks like tongue-and-groove boarding,

but, in fact, it is sheets of MDF, cleverly scored to look like planks of timber, and painted in neutral tones.

Right These walls, colourwashed in a soft sand to tone with the mosaic tiled panel and offset by filmy blue drapes and accessories, create a seaside atmosphere in this simple bathroom.

PAINTS

Because it is rare to spend very long in the bathroom, it is the perfect place to indulge in an eye-catching colour scheme. The beauty of using paint is that it is relatively easy to apply and inexpensive to change when you tire of the colour. Although coloured bathroom furniture inevitably limits your choice, the current popularity of white bathroom fittings will give you the opportunity to indulge your creativity.

So what will you choose? For an opulent look, deep shades of burgundy, forest green or midnight blue are rich and relaxing. Frame the walls with glossy white skirting and door and window surrounds, or use a matching colour for the woodwork to continue the effect. If you prefer a vibrant contemporary scheme, go for jazzy lime, citrus yellow or orange, Mediterranean blue, hot pink or one of the many shades of lilac on the market. Paint effects are easy to create with the ranges of do-it-yourself products now commercially available. The more muted looks have become decorating classics and where better than a bathroom to try a colourwash? Or you might introduce the idea of texture, using suede-like honey, velvety grey or one of the new water-based metallic paints in verdigris, silver or burnished gold for the ultimate in luxury.

Lasting good looks

Most modern emulsion paints contain vinyl for durability. Silk and sheen finishes have a slight edge on matt here, although they do tend to reflect irregularities in the plaster. Paints specially intended for kitchens and bathrooms are designed to be more resistant to moisture. They have a slightly higher shine than many emulsion paints and a more limited range of colours, but are well worth considering if the bathroom is in constant use or humidity levels are high.

Colour options

Bathrooms are often small and, since the space is already broken up if the walls are half or three-quarter tiled, consider painting the upper part of the walls and the ceiling in the same colour. (If you opt for a dark shade, make sure you provide adequate lighting that creates pools of light, so the effect is rich rather than gloomy.) Painting the bath panel or side of a roll-top tub in a colour to blend or contrast with the scheme creates an eye-catching feature, as does using specialist paints to liven up dull tiles. For a stylish and budget-price floor, simply stain the floorboards a soft colour and top with a few protective coats of floor-grade varnish. Lastly, paint the mirror, picture frames and shelves to blend or contrast with larger areas.

---

decorating ideas

● Woodwork looks attractive in a mid-sheen or eggshell finish to complement vinyl sheen walls. In addition to the traditional oil-based type, this finish is now available in a low-solvent, water-based version, which makes painting large areas more pleasant.

● Paint effects are easier to achieve if you use a slow-drying, semi-transparent product over a sheen finish – available in most mainstream paint ranges. Use with specialist applicators to create a dragged, rag-rolled, grained or stippled look.

● To colourwash in the traditional way, apply two coats of diluted emulsion paint over a plain painted background with a wide brush, cross-hatching in different directions to create the effect.

● Try a paint effect over a pale toning background to increase the sense of space, over white for freshness, or with a contrasting pastel to add a colour accent.

● Conceal damp patches with a special barrier paint, which can be overpainted in any colour. Treat the damp at source first or the problem will recur.

Flooring

Finding a floor that is stylish as well as being waterproof and kind to bare feet used to be quite a challenge. Luckily, it is no longer necessary to sacrifice good looks for practicality in the bathroom because an increasing range of materials, from cork and carpet to wood, are available in finishes that can withstand the odd puddle. Add to this the ever-popular ceramic or vinyl tiles and cushioned flooring and you have a wide choice of floorings to suit every setting.

Above *Pebble flooring is best kept for small areas. The stones are selected for size and shape, set in cement then carefully cleaned to remove excess grout.* *Left* *Glass-effect solid vinyl tiles in lilac open up a small bathroom. The flooring is warm yet robust and the small grid design makes the most of limited space.* *Below* *White is a practical choice for ceramic floor tiles, which are easily washed clean. They look crisp and light against this sea-green paintwork.*

Twenty-first century style

The best bathroom floorings are a triumph of technology. Even those that look traditional are carefully treated to withstand both warmth and damp; although this quality is not inexpensive, it ensures that the floor stays looking as good as the day it was laid.

This is particularly important for materials not naturally moisture resistant, like cork and wood. For durability, look for cork tiles coated in vinyl or acrylic. Tiles dipped in vinyl resist any water that finds its way between the tiles and protects the edges from rot. Wood strip floors also need special treatment before they are suitable for bathroom use. You may have to shop around: do not assume that a brand recommended for heavy domestic use or even kitchens will measure up. Water-resistant yacht varnish can provide a good finish for untreated cork or wooden floorboards, but watch for areas of wear and revarnish regularly.

Man-made options

Fitted carpet may not be a style leader but if you love softness underfoot, a carpet that combines a synthetic pile with a waffle backing that allows the air to circulate is a good choice. You can use conventional bedroom carpet in an en-suite bathroom if it is treated with respect. Wool carpet, for instance, may discolour and rot if allowed to get wet. If you have an en-suite shower, it is probably better to opt for smooth flooring.

Cushioned vinyl flooring is a practical choice in family bathrooms and it is warmer than vinyl tiles. Tiles, however, give you the opportunity to exercise your creativity by creating panels and borders, and they are easier to lay around bathrooms fittings. They range in quality from cheap printed tiles with just a skim of vinyl for protection to stylish solid vinyl with a superb depth of colour. These may cost as much as ceramic tiles but should last just as long.

Inside out

Ceramic tiles need a rigid sub-floor so are often best suited to ground-floor rooms. Floor tiles are usually thicker and more matt than wall tiles. Although resistance to wear is less important in bathrooms than it is in kitchens or halls, the tiles must be non-slip. You can also have fun by using garden materials like decking or pebbles set in cement for a seaside look, although these are possibly better as accents rather than an entire floor if comfort is a consideration.

Heating

The difference between a luxurious bathroom and one that is just somewhere you use to keep clean may be nothing to do with the decoration and everything to do with the temperature. If the room is comfortably warm, there is less of a temptation to slip into a hot bath (which is bad for you) rather than a tepid one (which is good). Combined with good ventilation, consistent heat can also help combat that bugbear of all too many bathrooms – condensation.

Safe and warm

The bathroom is the one part of the house that most central heating does not reach. When the heating is switched off, the bathroom stays cold and even in summer many bathrooms need something to take the chill off the air. If the bathroom is relatively close to the hot water cylinder, the answer is to provide a heated towel rail, multi-rail or towel rail/radiator combination, connected to the hot water system. These come in a variety of designs from solid Edwardian to sculptural modern, and they are usually adequate for space heating. Large bathrooms, however, may benefit from a radiator as well in winter – an aluminium alloy one conducts heat more efficiently than a radiator made of pressed steel. For a streamlined look, conceal the radiator behind panelling or plasterboard, with vents to allow the heat to pass through. Panelling can be used to disguise pipework and the cistern as well, although you will still need to leave access to the plumbing.

The electric option

If a towel rail connected to the water supply is not a possibility in your bathroom, an oil-filled heated towel rail wired to an isolated electric switch outside the bathroom may be enough in a small room and it will at least warm the towels. Otherwise, a wall- or ceiling-mounted heater may be the best option, although, since warm air rises, these are not exactly ideal. Many are not in fact powerful enough to heat the average bathroom – look for a capacity of 3kW, which gives you the option of several levels of heat. Do remember that all electric appliances must be approved for bathroom use and operated by a cord pull or external switch for safety.

Drying the air

Heating is only half the equation, because good ventilation is essential to prevent condensation. Allow for six to eight changes of air per hour for a bathroom, 15–20 if there is a shower in the room. Ventilation should not be a problem in modern bathrooms, but in older ones it is often necessary to fit an extractor fan, which is mandatory in windowless bathrooms. Some fans are activated when you pull the light cord, other types switch on automatically as humidity rises. There may also be a manual boost you can use if the atmosphere gets steamy.

Above A thermostatically controlled multi-rail on the outside of a shower enclosure keeps towels conveniently close at hand. The simple chrome effect suits the style of this modern bathroom.

Right The towel ladder in this contemporary bathroom is more versatile than a heated towel rail. The clean lines of this stunning radiator contrast effectively with the ragged tiled edges.

Lighting

The message that a single light in the centre of the ceiling is not enough is getting through. Almost every room of the house, from the kitchen to the living room, is now equipped with uplighters, downlighters, spotlights and lamps – every room, that is, except the bathroom. This is a shame because here, more than anywhere else, there is a need for lighting to flatter and relax, as well as for fittings that provide clear light.

Mood lighting

All lights used here should be approved for bathroom use and there is quite a wide choice available. Uplighters give a soft light that is best bounced back by a pale ceiling. They can be set on the wall, in a countertop, or even the floor, although if you go for this option it is best to separate them from the traffic area – one novel idea is to surround them with pebbles to give the impression of shingle. There is usually sufficient space in the loft above first-floor bathrooms to make downlighters relatively easy to install. These create pools of light, although the effect is not quite as soft as that given by uplighters. Wall lights are another way of providing the gentle light that is so important for a relaxing atmosphere. You can increase the effect of a lighting scheme substantially by using mirrors to reflect both daylight and artificial light. Another trick is to fit lights behind a sheet of safety glass attached to the ceiling or wall for a diffuse daylight effect.

Architectural lighting, where the light source is barely noticeable, is often the best choice for a bathroom, particularly if it is small. But an ornate fitting that contributes to the decor can give the room character. Just check with the supplier that it is suitable for a bathroom before you go ahead.

Task lighting

Mirrors used for make-up and shaving need more focused light. Bathroom cupboards often incorporate a small fluorescent tube, or alternatively, buy a strip light with a shaving socket. You can also fit light bulbs around a mirror, Hollywood-style, for extra light. Just as effective are spotlights, angled to prevent glare, so that light is reflected from the ceiling or wall. Carefully positioned, these can provide general lighting too.

Safety concerns

It is of vital importance to be protected from electric shock in the bathroom. There should be no risk of touching the light directly when you switch it on and off, which is why external switches or cord pulls are essential for main lighting. But electricity is not the only hazard. Steps and changes of level are often overlooked so do make sure these are well lit to prevent falls.

Candlelight

Bathing by candlelight is a good way to relax, and scented candles make it even more pleasurable. Choose scents to complement aromatherapy bath essential oils – rosemary to revive you, geranium and rose to unwind, lavender and sandalwood to relieve stress.

Left Barely discernible against the cream ceiling, downlighters bathe this spectacular bathtub in soft light. Carefully positioned mirrors increase the impression of both light and space.
Below This stylish washbasin has been placed on a table creating a very individual unit.
Right An art deco wall light provides a focus of interest as well as light in this chic bathroom. The arrangement of light, shelf, bottles and picture creates a virtual still life.

Window dressings

Privacy, light and decoration often conflict when you are choosing a treatment for the bathroom window. A deep sash window has wonderful proportions and admits plenty of light, but it might also give the neighbours a clear view of your daily routine. A tiny window may cry out to be left uncovered but looks dark and dismal at night. What is the answer if curtains are too formal but a blind is too bare?

Above Frosted glass means there is no need to draw the curtains during the day so these light 'dress' curtains are swept behind metal hold-backs, leaving the radiator clear for warming towels.
***Below** With small windows, and where* *there isn't much room to spare on either side, blinds are the solution.*
***Right** A sheer blind covers the base of this large sash window for privacy but allows plenty of light through at the top. It can be looped up out of the way when necessary.*

Sheer poetry

One popular solution is sheer fabric, which can be draped over a pole, used for tab-top or café curtains, or made into a simple blind. Whether sheers are of voile, light cotton or lace, they filter rather than exclude the light, but protect your privacy and look effective at the same time. White or cream are favourites but rich colours that allow the sun to shine through can look spectacular. If this appeals, consider using saris, the jewel-like colours of which are intensified by light.

The advice about using plenty of an inexpensive fabric rather than being mean with a costlier one is especially relevant in bathrooms, and not only because cheaper cottons are easier to drape. It also makes good sense because a steamy atmosphere is particularly hard on fabric. Reconciling yourself to renewing the window treatment frequently could be a more realistic option than trying to rescue a tired piece of cloth.

Support systems

A static window treatment does away with the need for conventional tracks and poles. The fabric can be looped around metal brackets, suspended from driftwood or a branch, or made into a pelmet and tacked in place. Telescopic poles that fit tightly to the window frame are useful for café curtains, but wooden dowelling, painted and cut to fit, or slim metal rods do the same job and can look more attractive. Window treatments that cover the pane but clear the sill are a practical solution for many bathrooms. Shirred panels of fabric can be fixed inside the top and bottom of the frame on plastic-coated wire, blinds and café curtains may be caught up with ribbons or tapes, and metal hold-backs are stylish and simple if you want to keep curtains out of the way.

Bathroom alternatives

Alternatively, forget about fabric and opt for shutters, blinds or stained or painted glass. Narrow-slat Venetian blinds, wooden pinoleum or fine-pleated blinds can be hung in a window recess or used to cover the entire window wall. Stained glass can be commissioned in modern or traditional designs (your local crafts council should have a database of craftsmen and examples of their work), and there are numerous courses where you can learn to make your own. Painting glass is simple using specialist paints from art shops. Alternatively, plain glass can be obscured with etching paint from do-it-yourself superstores. Use it to create a frosted glass effect.

Bathroom furniture

Replacing the bathroom suite gives you a chance to have the room you really want, rather than one you have inherited. If you hankered for a huge bathtub, a separate shower, a Victorian washstand or a sculptural basin, here is your chance to have it … and new flooring, tiling and decor too. Check the planning guide on page 226 to find out how much space to allow, then draw up a plan before you go shopping.

Above *The wide pedestal-mounted basin is ideal for siting against an internal wall. Its classic rectangular lines suit many styles of bathroom from Edwardian to art deco.* *Below* *A semi-countertop basin is partly recessed into a shelf. The tongue-and-groove panelling below conceals the plumbing.* *Right* *A traditional roll-top bathtub is given theatrical treatment with a silver side, which blends with the floor, and gold claw feet.*

Baths

The standard bath is 1700mm (66in) in length but shorter baths, 1500mm (60in) long, are available. There are plenty of other styles, for example oval and round baths as well as corner baths, which make surprisingly good use of space, especially in square bathrooms. Most baths are made from pressed steel or plastic. Some tubs, especially restored ones, are in hefty cast iron, which imposes a terrific stress on the floor, so take advice before installing one of these for the first time. A sunken bath looks stylish but since you need to have space to sink it into, it is often more practical to build a platform around it. Another luxury is the whirlpool bath, with its invigorating jets of water.

Washbasins

Most washbasins are made from vitreous china and need some support from a work-top, cupboard or pedestal because of their weight. However, small basins can usually be wall-mounted. Some vanity units contain plastic or enamelled basins; these are more likely to scratch or chip than ceramic ones. A circular basin perched on a counter or shelf is a deceptively simple design – a modern version of the Victorian ewer – where the taps are built into the wall.

Bidets and WCs

Both are made from vitreous china and should ideally be sited next to each other for ease of use. Bidets can be wall-hung or floor-mounted. Over-rim bidets fill up like an ordinary basin; in some other types water is flushed into the bidet below the rim.

Most WCs are close-coupled, whereby the cistern sits on top of the pan. You can also buy back-to-wall cisterns, which are hidden behind the wall so that only the lever shows, as well as high-level cisterns and even corner-cistern WCs.

Shower trays

Ceramic shower trays are the most robust and, unlike man-made materials, do not flex, making leaks less likely. They may be rectangular but are usually square. Fully tiled or purpose-designed shower cubicles are the best option, although an alternative is to tile the room and have a sloping floor with a soakaway in place of a shower tray.

Taps

There are dozens of designs – from traditional cross-head taps and telephone-style bath mixers to minimalist levers in chrome, brass or bright colours. Ensure your choice conforms to national water regulations.

Washbasins

As sanitaryware enters a new era, washbasins are more stylish than ever. No longer necessarily made of vitreous china, they come in granite, stainless steel and even glass. And whether they are wall mounted or supported by a stand, they have an elegance hitherto undreamed of.

Bathroom sanitaryware is no longer always bought as suites, with matching bath, basin, WC and bidet. This fact has freed up the design of modern basins, some of which have become almost sculptural in their conception. Most contemporary styles incorporate a single mixer tap, which suits the spare lines of their design.

As the size of modern bathrooms becomes smaller and smaller, these styles take up less room than traditional, built-in, heavy-looking basins. And where the basin is mounted on a stand, the best of these provide underneath storage – something that is often at a premium – in the form of a small cupboard or at least a shelf. An enclosed stand also hides some of the plumbing, which is otherwise on show, although this is integral to the high-tech look of some models. Chrome piping is considered more attractive than the standard copper pipes.

Siting a basin

■ The washbasin must have enough space in front of it to allow you to bend over comfortably to wash, as well as plenty of elbow room on either side. The basin will be difficult to use if it is jammed up against a side wall.

■ For wet shaves and applying make-up, natural light is preferable so the basin is best sited by a window. If this leaves no space for a wall-mounted mirror, you could fix an extending mirror to the window surround.

A pedestal ceramic basin with chrome taps has an aqua-painted wooden cupboard built around it, offering shelf storage as well as a useful surface on which to place things.

Wall-mounted circular basin in polished stainless steel has a clinical look well suited to a minimalist interior.

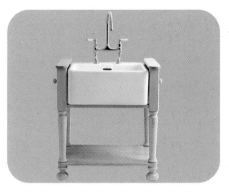

Butler sink on a freestanding unit made of maple could be used in a laundry or utility room, as well as in a country-style bathroom.

Polished granite circular basin has a chrome band around the top, which matches the column-mounted tap fitting.

Ultra-contemporary, wall-mounted glass and chrome basin where even the plumbing fixtures have a stylish look.

Chrome stand for this plain basin with its useful surround incorporates a heated towel rack.

Simple white ceramic basin has a classic monoblock mixer tap in chrome.

Scallop-shell corner basin with polished brass taps has a period feel and would suit a traditional-style bathroom.

Contemporary version of a Victorian washstand – the ceramic basin is supported on a tall, simply designed stand housing a storage cupboard.

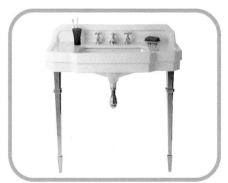

Heavy, art deco-style ceramic basin is supported at the front on tapering metal legs; this style includes both a surround and a splashback.

Showers and taps

To match the innovative designs taking place in bathroom sanitaryware, tap fittings have become more elegant and streamlined than ever before, the big manufacturers are increasingly being led by individual designers, who are producing taps in exciting contemporary styles.

Whether we take an invigorating shower in the morning or a relaxing bath after a day's work, we tend to take for granted the water that comes out of our taps. When it comes to choosing a design of tap fitting, there is a wide choice of shapes, styles and materials.

The style you select should be in keeping with your bath and the bathroom decor. 'Telephone'-style mixer taps, for example, suit a traditional style of bath best, while the cleaner lines of the most up-to-date tap fittings go well with high-tech or minimalist bathroom interiors. In terms of materials, the choice is usually between high-sheen chrome, dull nickel, polished brass and gold plated. Brass and nickel are traditional, while gold plated spells opulence and shiny chrome represents state-of-the-art modernity. Whichever you choose, go for consistency across bath, basin, shower and bidet fittings. There are specially formulated cleaners for all these materials.

Choosing taps

■ Pillar taps are conventional separate hot and cold taps, requiring holes cut into either side of the bath or basin.

■ Mixer taps need a single hole (monoblock mixer) or two holes (twin-hole mixer). In both, hot and cold water mixes in the spout or when it leaves the tap, reducing the risk of scalding.

■ If you have weak or arthritic wrists, choose quarter-turn or single-lever styles of mixer tap.

■ 'Telephone'-style bath/shower mixer taps should have a check valve to prevent back-flow if the shower head drops into the bath water.

Traditional, bath-mounted 'telephone'-style mixer taps with a shower attachment are available in a chrome, brass or nickel finish.

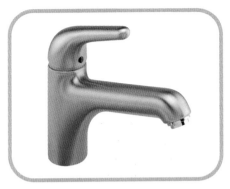

Satin-finish brushed steel mixer tap.

Slim, elegant chrome tap with a slotted lever and elongated spout.

Chrome tap designed by Phillipe Starck has a unique lever and clean, contemporary lines.

Traditional brass mixer tap is surface mounted to sit over a bath or basin.

Elegant chrome mixer tap has a short, angled spout and lever.

Modernistic chrome mixer tap has a slim spout and a T-bar lever.

Stubby mixer tap in satin-finish brushed steel operates with a slotted lever.

Separate hot and cold taps with porcelain levers operate an elegant brass mixer tap for the bath.

Chrome mixer tap operated at the sides has gold-finish detailing.

Spacious luxury

Jill and David's new bathroom has a luxurious feel, which derives as much from the elegance of the fireplace and the matching period basin as from its generous dimensions and warm-looking decorating scheme.

The luxury of a spacious bathroom is one that Jill and David greatly appreciate, with two young children and a baby on the way. Like many bathrooms in period houses, it started life as a bedroom and they have allowed the room's existing features to influence the decorating scheme. The original tiny bathroom had not been used for 20 years, as the house was a series of badly designed bedsits until Jill and David moved in. Although reluctant to forgo the chance of a spare bedroom, they realized that a large bathroom would be a boon for their growing family.

The original bathroom was decrepit and the bath somewhat rusty, but Jill and David really liked its style, so they moved it into the new bathroom and called in specialists.

'We knew what magic they could work on an antique bath, so we asked them to recoat the inside as well as paint the outside and restore the taps,' said David.

A bath coated *in situ* will last from seven to twelve years; it is an economical proposition compared with sending it away to be completely re-enamelled and kiln-fired, which gives the best finish but is almost as expensive as buying a new bath.

The original washbasin was beyond repair but Jill and David managed to find a reproduction casting of an original. The table-mounted basin echoes the style and colouring of the room's original fireplace – even the tiles of the 'splashback' are the same colour as the fireplace tiles.

These tiles in fact dictated the room's colour scheme. An oil-based sunny yellow ochre scumble on the walls can be wiped over and resists condensation. The yellow curtain fabric cheerfully picks up the theme, which reflects the rich colouring of the stripped and sealed old floorboards, as well as the built-in pine cupboard.

Left *With its shapely legs and tiled splashback and mirror, this reproduction washstand was a real find. Tongue-and-groove panels conceal the plumbing behind it and match the panelling below the window and elsewhere in the room. Matching 'globe' wall lights on either side illuminate the mirror.*

Below *The distinctive Arts and Crafts fireplace gives this bathroom an unusual focus. Its period feel is picked up in the burnished steel cistern, mounted on decorative wall brackets. Yellow ochre walls perfectly complement the colour of the fireplace tiles.*

Cool retreat

Combining their creative painting skills and adding a few well-chosen furnishing items has enabled John and Melanie to turn their bathroom into a very individual, tranquil haven.

Melanie and John broke with family tradition when they decorated their bathroom. Deep, rich colours had been their choice for most of the rooms in the house but they decided it was time for a change and that the bathroom was the most suitable candidate for a cooler scheme. 'I wanted a pure, airy look,' said Melanie, 'so we opted for pale blue.'

John has his own painting and decorating business and Melanie is a paint-effects specialist, so they worked as a team on this room. John did the basics, such as painting the floor in a white eggshell finish, while Melanie concentrated on decorating the walls. She used an oil-based scumble glaze for the marbling below the dado rail, then created a colourwashed cloud effect above it. 'The effect came about purely by chance when I started to paint,' she confessed. All the family, including four-year-old daughter Camilla, love it.

Working to a limited budget meant that they kept the green art deco-style pedestal washbasin as it was still in perfectly good condition. But they replaced the rusty old bath with a cast-iron Victorian roll-top bathtub advertised in the local paper. This was the original bath from a nearby terraced house. It had only just been taken out and

its inside was still amazingly intact. Melanie painted the outside of the bathtub white and gilded the feet for fun.

A great fan of car boot sales and auctions, Melanie found both the cupboard with glazed doors and the rack of decorative coat hooks on one of her forays. She renovated both of them with loving care, painting them white and replacing the glass in the cupboard doors. The freestanding cupboard offers valuable new storage space for towels and pretty accessories since previously there were no built-in shelves or fitted cupboards in the bathroom at all.

Everything else in the bathroom, from the laundry basket to a wicker chair, is painted white, together with the dado rail itself. For the finishing touch, Melanie made two white voile curtains for the room. One is a dress curtain pulled to one side of the window above the washbasin and the other is used to back a shower curtain and give it a softer look. These delicate furnishings echo the watery decorative theme and help to create a bathroom that is a restful haven for all the family.

Left *The bargain-buy cupboard has been revamped with coats of white paint and new glazing. Towels match the bathroom's aquatic colour scheme.*

Top *Decorative accessories suspended from ornate coat hooks provide a stylish finishing touch. Apart from the walls, the theme is strictly white.*

Above *A close-up of a shelf in the cupboard reveals a seaside-inspired 'still life' created from shells. The tongue-and-groove back of the cupboard has been left with its original paint.*

Right *The marbled and colourwashed paint effects on the walls are separated by the dado rail, which matches the white floor.*

Maximizing space

Rosalind and Peter wanted more space and a style to suit their Edwardian home so they added a shower and built wooden cupboards and shelves. Tongue-and-groove boards and colourful tiles create a bright and cheerful effect.

Above *Reflected in the simple circular wall mirror are the washbasin, tiles and wall cupboard. Since the lower half of the window is frosted opaque glass, there is no need for a curtain.*

Far right *The honey tones of the wooden panelling and the floor stand out against the vibrant blue wall and the multi-coloured tiles of this compact but cheerful bathroom. The tiles echo the colours of the Edwardian leaded window. Cupboard space enables toys and toiletries to be tidied away so that clutter is banished.*

With two children under the age of five, Rosalind and Peter decided they had to improve the badly designed bathroom in their Edwardian house, to make more of the space.

'As the room is small, our options were limited, but I desperately needed storage space for towels and accessories, so that was our starting point,' said Rosalind.

Reorganizing the space at one end of the bath made room for a cupboard with shelves on top, giving much-needed storage for towels and toiletries. The addition of a cupboard under the washbasin and another above the WC gave extra space for children's bath toys and other items.

There was no room for a freestanding shower, so they added a shower at one end of the bath. As they had only a limited budget, they kept the existing sanitaryware but boxed in the bath with a side panel. They chose tongue-and-groove boards for the bath panel and to hide the plumbing, as well as for the cupboard doors, leaving them unpainted; the light pine matches the bathroom's wooden floorboards and the stripped pine window frame. The rest of their budget was spent on a folding shower screen and tiles for the shower area as well as the lower half of the walls.

When it came to choosing a colour scheme, Rosalind was in favour of soft tones while Peter preferred bold colours. They bought a few tiles in different colours to try out in the room, which convinced Rosalind that the strong colours worked best. For the final combination, they took their inspiration from the Edwardian leaded light at the top of the window. Sticking with the bold theme, they chose a rich blue colour for the top half of the walls, which sets off the pale woodwork extremely well.

Above *The tiled walls of the shower surround are a practical and good-looking waterproof finish; the folding shower screen provides a third 'wall' when in use. Towels are stored on shelves above the cupboard.*

Clean and simple

Converting a cottage bedroom into a minimally styled bathroom gave the Barbara and Stephen the bathroom they wanted. It derives much character from the low-level ceiling, uneven floor and exposed beams, so the best solution was to keep everything else as simple as possible.

When Barbara and Stephen moved to their tiny cottage in the country, the small bathroom was downstairs.

'It was a cramped room, just big enough for a bath, washbasin and toilet,' says Barbara. 'We decided to wait until the children had left home before converting a bedroom into an upstairs bathroom, which we would find much more convenient.'

They did all the work themselves and the room was converted within three months. Because it was an old cottage, there wasn't a straight line in the room, least of all the floor, but the irregularities all add to the room's charm. Having decided to keep everything simple, they sanded and waxed the wooden floorboards, painted the walls a soft white and looked for white sanitary-ware. The couple wanted a freestanding bathtub but did not want to have to reinforce the floor and worried about getting a cast-iron bath up the cottage's narrow staircase. They started investigating the availability of roll-top bathtubs in lightweight acrylic and found their 'Victoria and Albert Warwickshire' bath in a shop in a local town. Here they also ended up buying the pedestal washbasin and

WC. They treated themselves to expensive, stylish 'telephone' taps for the bathtub and matching chrome taps for the washbasin. Because of the uneven floor, Stephen had to make wooden discs of different depths for the bath to stand on. He lined the wall behind the WC and washbasin with wooden panelling to hide the plumbing and to create a narrow display shelf.

They are enjoying the neutral tones of their bathroom. 'As the ceiling is low and the bathroom window is very small, we need to keep the room as light and airy as possible. We don't want any clutter, and I'm sticking to white towels.' The iron curtain rail was made to measure at the local forge and Barbara made the simple white curtains herself from inexpensive natural flax. A soft white flokati woollen rug covers the floor. The only other items in the room are a French iron table and a folding wooden slatted chair, from a local antique market and in keeping with the period feel of the cottage, as well as a white-painted laundry box, which doubles as a useful seat. All Barbara wants now is a heated towel rail, to bring a touch of luxury to her otherwise perfect bathroom.

Above *A narrow shelf either side of the window, below the exposed wooden beam, is just wide enough to hold decorative bottles of bath oil and other accessories.*

Left *White-painted panelling hides the plumbing pipework and provides a mounting for the low-level cistern. Three pots of mind-your-own-business add a fresh green touch to the room.*

Right *Keeping everything white results in an uncluttered, pristine space, which is relieved by the warm wooden floor, the irregular wooden beams and the slightly 'distressed' furniture. The decorative claw feet of the freestanding bathtub are mounted on specially made wooden discs to deal with the uneven floor.*

Storage and display

Cosmetics, shampoos, cotton wool, dry towels, shaving kit, toothpaste … it is rare that a single cabinet will take all the bits and pieces that clutter up the bathroom. Although piles of towels, bottles of bath oil and scented soaps are as lovely to look at as they are to use, many other things are better stashed away out of sight where they are easy to find and won't detract from the style of the room.

Above *A narrow shelving unit provides plenty of storage for bottles and jars, which can be spotted immediately through the glass doors. The shallow shelves prevent jars from drifting towards the back.*

Right *Canvas pockets suspended from a wooden pole keep items together – or apart – and are a good way of using wall space.*

Far right *Open and closed: display units are excellent if the contents are carefully chosen, but things that are less pretty are better hidden away. This laundry bag slips off its stand to be taken away and provides no excuse for leaving clothes lying around. Alternatives for hiding laundry are storage seats, Lloyd loom linen baskets or tables.*

ON DISPLAY

Shelves, cubes, racks and small tables have a place in every bathroom. Even the most compact one has some dead space at the end of the bath or over the cistern; you can buy freestanding shelf units that fit over the WC if you don't want wall-mounted shelves. Several short shelves are often better than a single long one since they make it easier to group objects together for impact and ease of use. Try to keep like with like – groups of bottles or baskets of soap. A pile of freshly dried folded towels looks lovely if the bathroom is dry and well ventilated, especially if they contribute to the colour scheme. Stack them on a high shelf away from the bath and basin if possible so they don't get soggy. Don't put towels on display if there is any condensation.

Hunt around for interesting shelf units and small tables. The bathroom is rarely the place for expensive furniture but pieces like bamboo tables, converted meat cages, plate shelves and wine tables can be restored, stripped, painted or stained to suit the decor.

Hiding places

Cupboards and chests of drawers are not regular bathroom fixtures but are well worth the space they take up. Cupboards under the washbasin are the perfect place for storing toiletries and spare toilet rolls. Glass-fronted cabinets show their contents at a glance and are more practical than shelves for small items because they protect them from dust. Not all bathroom cabinets are suitable for medicines. If you have small children, do invest in a lockable wall-mounted cabinet.

Chests of drawers are good for towels, brushes and cosmetics – put dividers inside the drawers to contain fiddly bits and pieces.

ACCESSORIES

In a space as cramped as the average bathroom everything has to earn its keep, and that applies to accessories too. Essentials include the mirror, a hook for robes, a toilet roll holder, waste-bin and somewhere to put your toothbrush, but there will always be a place for a few purely decorative pieces, too, which provide the perfect finishing touch.

Mirrors

Most bathrooms need a large mirror for general use, plus a smaller magnifying mirror in good light for shaving or make-up. An extending bracket allows the mirror to be pulled up close when needed. Larger mirrored panels can be used on walls or cabinet doors where they increase the effect of light, while a striking frame can make a mirror the focal point of the room.

Shower screens

A shower above the bath needs a screen or curtain to deflect the spray. A water and mildew-resistant curtain is the cheapest option, topped with an outer fabric curtain if liked. Shower screens made from toughened plastic or safety glass that fold or slide away when not in use do a better job of keeping water inside the bath, but can make access difficult if space is tight.

Containers

Jelly plastics, shiny chrome, natural wood or bone china – there is a huge range of co-ordinating bins, soap dishes and tooth mugs available to suit every style of bathroom. Not everything has to match, however; it is sometimes more interesting to use an odd dish or saucer for soap or a decorative jug for flowers or toothbrushes.

Bath mats

Mats of slatted board or cork have a natural warmth and style: check the dimensions because the size of these can be a little on the mean side and look for roll-up designs that can be stowed away. Looped cotton is a popular and practical material but printed dhurries and rag rugs, available in all sorts of sizes and designs, are equally suitable as long as they can be washed.

Artwork and artefacts

The bathroom is not the place for a valuable painting, but framed prints and photographs are often just what the bare walls require. Appropriate decorative accessories could include anything on a watery or a seaside theme, such as shells or pebbles. Or add a sculptural element, perhaps with one beautiful shape: a tall crystal vase, huge soapstone dish or a modern classic chair.

Top *Collections of unusual bottles, in coloured glass, can be used to create interesting bathroom displays.*
Right *This hanging storage pocket in shocking pink is a simple but effective place to keep toiletries – equally useful whether you're at home or on holiday.*

Right *A sheet of mirror above the basin appears to double the size of this bathroom. The red tiled alcove and girder-style storage make stylish use of limited space.*

---

storage ideas

● Use wall-mounted trellis to support climbing plants and create a hanging garden screen or room divider.

● For a mirror frame with a difference, give it a metallic or verdigris finish using paint, or cover it with layers of shells and varnish it.

● Fix a wire grid to the wall and attach wire baskets and racks for storing toiletries.

● Fix weights to the hem of a shower curtain to make sure it stays inside the bath when the shower is in use.

● A storage system can be as simple as a shelf or a cupboard, a canvas pouch or a seat with hidden depths. A corner cupboard, table or linen basket makes excellent use of dead space.

● A net bag is perfect for storing children's bath toys because it lets them drain dry.

● Polish mirrors with a little diluted washing-up liquid to prevent them steaming up.

● Freshen up a shower curtain by treating it with a specialized mould killer, followed by a soak in diluted bleach.

home offices

No commuting, no fixed times, no office politics – working from home is everyone's dream. But the reality of working long hours in the same surroundings makes an inviting workplace essential. An unwelcoming room makes it hard to generate enthusiasm for work, so think about what you would *like* in your home office, as well as what you need. After all, you're the boss.

Practicalities

Technology is what makes working at home a possibility but as the list of must-have equipment grows, so does the pressure on living space. Plan for somewhere to put the computer, a work surface on which to sort papers and write notes, plus storage for documents and other items.

Where will you work?

If you have a study, the problem is solved, but if you have to adapt space elsewhere, consider all the implications. Before you opt for the obvious – a spare bedroom, say – try to visualize yourself working there. Will it be a welcome retreat or will you feel shut off? If so, is there a more central place where you could work – perhaps a conservatory or dining room? Or would you prefer to sit with a laptop and cordless phone wherever the mood takes you, keeping the printer and filing in a cupboard or under the stairs?

The hardware

It's difficult to think of any business that does not need a computer, for accounts and a database if nothing else. Unless you opt for a laptop, which is not ideal for full-time use, you will need a monitor, hard disk and keyboard, a printer (which can double as a fax) and possibly a scanner for sending images electronically. There is an ever-increasing range of clever workstations designed specifically for home use, which can store all the components of your computer. (Try one out before you buy to make sure there really is enough room to use the keyboard and that the computer is at a comfortable height.) Go for the biggest work surface you can fit in so you can spread out when you're working, and make room for the phone. An additional line is a priority if

you e-mail or use the Internet a lot, because if you have only one line your phone will be constantly engaged. You may even want a third phone line for business use, so that you can put on the answerphone in the evenings and at weekends, and take calls from friends and family on your home phone number.

The software

Any old chair will not do: comfort and support are crucial if you intend spending a substantial amount of time at your desk. It's hard to beat a purpose-designed office chair with height adjustment and swivel mechanism, but if you have a favourite chair you want to use, make sure it has lumbar support to protect your back and add a cushion or two if you need extra comfort and height.

Lighting

Efficient lighting is essential to prevent eye-strain. Tempting as it may be to work in front of a window, it is not the best place for a computer screen. See if an L-shape set-up is a possibility, so the computer is against the wall and you can turn to face the window when writing or using the phone. You will almost certainly need extra 'task' lighting after dark to give clear light over the desk without shadows. The light provided by a desk lamp can be too bright and low. Consider an adjustable lamp or fix spotlights or halogen lights to the wall or a shelf instead.

Left *Sheets of music make an inspiring wall-covering for this study under the eaves. An old filing cabinet has been spruced up and topped with a deep worktop to create a practical and stylish desk.*

Above *Stout yet inexpensive wooden desks can still be found and are easy to reno-vate. The budget price window covering, made from a scrap of fabric and a length of dow-elling, filters the sunlight.*

office checklist

■ Look at the position of electric sockets and telephone points and have more fitted if necessary. Assess the ventilation, too, since a lot of electrical equipment in use can cause a build-up of heat.

■ Although glass-topped tables are attractive, non-reflective work surfaces are best if you are using a computer. Make sure the desk or table is high enough for you to work at without bending.

■ Your eyes should be level with the top half of the screen when you are sitting at your desk so alter your chair to suit. (A footrest will help you sit correctly.) The screen may need raising too.

■ A slatted or translucent blind is the best window covering for shading the screen from glare.

■ Fit a long worktop (visit kitchen suppliers) if you use specialist equipment like a sewing machine, or need to spread out documents or pictures.

■ You can never have too many shelves – they are the most flexible form of storage and you can see the contents at glance.

Private study

Nothing can match a room of your own when you need to concentrate. Whether you are running a business or catching up with the bills, a place dedicated to work could be just what you need. Many studies are small, one-person rooms ideal for freelance work, but if business expands you may need more space. In this case a loft extension can be ideal, separate from the living area but with all the advantages of working from home.

A sense of tradition

Even if you don't earn a living at home, you may want a quiet room where you can read, work, revise or listen to music in peace. A study that is used mainly in the evening can look good decorated in a rich, traditional scheme, which creates a warm, enclosing look. Antique or reproduction desks are a natural choice here, and there are period designs available that will conceal the computer effectively. An alternative is to add a simple side table or length of worktop to act as a separate computer table, and keep the leather-topped desk for use when you are writing and making phone calls. Dark wooden filing cabinets will blend with the surroundings but a better solution might be to hide clutter in a slim built-in cupboard painted to match the walls. Traditional bookcases suit this style of decor and a big leather armchair could be an added incentive for deserting the television.

Room at the top

There is usually plenty of floor space in a loft conversion; the feature that is at a premium in most of them is height. Although sloping ceilings can be a disadvantage in a living room or bedroom, the space under the eaves is actually the perfect site for a desk since there is more than enough headroom when you are sitting down. Otherwise, built-in furniture that nudges you towards the centre of the room is the solution here. Line the eaves with filing cabinets and banks of deep cupboards and put any equipment that you stand up to use – such as the printer and photocopier – away from the walls so that you don't bump your head. Put in plenty of roof windows if planning regulations allow, so as to let in the maximum amount of light. Sleek light fittings in graphic shapes and colours are perfect, striking a note of minimalism that is ideal for loft living.

Sit back and relax

Feature walls are back in fashion, so why not try being creative with the wall above your desk and give yourself something interesting to look at when you pause for thought? You could paper it with sheet music or black-and-white prints separated by borders and topped by paper bows as in an 18th-century print room, or paste up a huge enlargement of a favourite view for a *trompe l'oeil* effect. Or simply arrange a collection of paintings at a low height on the wall so that they are at eye level when you are sitting down.

Above left *Black ash gives a professional look to this loft-conversion study. The colour scheme is simple and the strong shapes add decorative interest.*

Below *A curved length of wood in place of a desk creates a focal point in this work-room, which is glazed on two sides, having a glass wall and roof.*

Right *Period piece: glowing red walls and traditional furniture set the scene in this study. The captain's chair looks the part and is comfortable, too, with its swivel base and height adjustment.*

Home office furniture

If you work from home and have a dedicated room or office, it makes sense to equip yourself with the best furniture you can afford. Today's designs combine good looks with comfort and practicality, so there is no excuse for clutter, chaos – or a bad back.

What you sit on is a different matter and if you spend hours sitting at a desk, a dining chair simply will not do. A good office chair is the best bet and there are now many designs that look bright and modern and not at all utilitarian and office-like.

One of the joys of working from home is that you can plan the style and layout of the office to suit yourself. Choose your own colour of filing cabinet – or use boxes and baskets to store papers if you prefer. Give shelf space to objects you enjoy looking at and enliven the walls with favourite paintings and photographs. There is every reason to make your office a place where you enjoy spending time.

The desk

Provided it is stable and the right height, any work surface will serve as a desk. The surface should be high enough for you to work at without bending and deep enough to take a computer and any other equipment you need. The best purpose-made desks incorporate storage as well as computer space – some have a fold- or pull-out keyboard shelf – and are a pleasing design at the same time.

Choosing a chair

■ If you do a lot of work at a computer, your chair needs to be height adjustable, should swivel and have castors.

■ Adjust the seat to a height at which your eyes are level with the top half of your screen; the screen itself may need to be raised.

■ Your knees and elbows should be at right angles when working at a screen – use a footrest if necessary to bring your knees to the right height.

■ Take a break from the screen every 20 minutes or so and try to get up and stretch your legs at least every two hours.

This wooden desk on simple, contemporary lines has shelves for files built into one side.

Plywood storage unit *with castors has poly-propylene semi-transparent drawers, offering mobile storage in a small space.*

Fluidly designed desk *has an organic shape and incorporates three storage drawers on an aluminium swivel mechanism.*

Smooth-lined modern chair *with leather back and seat could blend into many a setting.*

Adjustable-height *beech veneer stool with steel base offers occasional seating; it can be stored under a desk when not in use.*

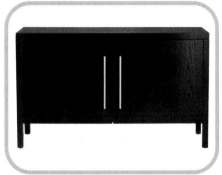

Wooden cupboard *on legs provides low storage, while equipment such as a printer could sit on top.*

Contemporary upholstered armchair *on steel legs offers comfort as well as style.*

Side table on castors *has concealed storage behind louvred steel doors on both sides.*

A design classic, *the Charles Eames aluminium-framed swivel chair is the ultimate office luxury; it has a medium-high backrest and an adjustable seat.*

Classic leather-upholstered, *executive-style swivel armchair, by Charles Eames, provides respite from an upright desk seat.*

Dual-purpose room

Anyone who works from home without the luxury of a dedicated workroom or office knows how difficult it can be to combine working and living space. Artist Ingrid has achieved just that, creating her dual-use space herself, using a limited budget and a lot of imagination. 'It's great to have a room where I can both work and entertain,' she enthuses.

Above With curtains masking the laden shelves, the room is turned effortlessly into a sophisticated dining area in the evening. Colours are kept simple to make the most of the space: white walls and curtains complement the table and chairs that have been painted dove-grey.

Right By day, Ingrid's workroom has the benefit of natural light streaming through the deep sash window. Tied-back curtains reveal the ingenious use of wooden wine crates to store her art materials – paints, brushes and tools – while books and files sit on the shelves of the flexible storage system.

Not everybody whose job is based at home enjoys the use of a sole-purpose room in which to work. In this case, Ingrid, who is a decorative artist, had to find a way of transforming the spare room of her flat into a place to work by day, while still being able to use the room for entertaining in the evening.

'The decision was simple,' she says. 'I needed more space and light for my work so I shifted my office into the spare room, which has to double as a dining room at night. It's the best move I ever made.' Not only has Ingrid gained more space, she now has the benefit of a large sash window, which lets in light from dawn to dusk.

Adequate storage space was a priority for all the paraphernalia that Ingrid needs for her work. She did not want to spend too much, but needed an efficient system that would make the most of the space available. After some research she found a very economical shelving system in a catalogue, which suited perfectly. The shelving is flexible enough for her needs, allowing for extra-deep shelves and height extensions. Ingrid bought enough to cover an entire wall, and recalls that 'apart from the nightmare of carrying it all upstairs to my third-floor flat, the installation went surprisingly smoothly.'

It was not such an easy task to find affordable storage boxes to sit on the shelves, until Ingrid came up with the idea of using wooden wine boxes. She rang round all the local wine merchants until she found one who had plenty of boxes to spare. According to Ingrid: 'They're the perfect size for storing tapes, paints, tools, books and magazines.'

The finishing touch is the floor-to-ceiling curtains that Ingrid made to keep the dust off and conveniently hide all the tools of her trade in the evening, when the room has another use. Made in simple white cotton, the curtains are tied back at intervals, in line with the uprights of the shelving system.

For the room's budget incarnation as a dining area, Ingrid painted a plywood table with a toughened enamel paint and re-covered her old dining chairs, painting them in a colour to match the table.

Now she can simply close the curtains and pull the table into the centre of the room when friends come round – and the transformation from workroom to dining room is complete.

Versatile rooms

If you don't have a separate room in which to work, it *is* possible to integrate work and home, given careful planning and goodwill on all sides. If you live on your own you can please yourself, but if the room is shared you need to mark out your territory so that important papers and equipment are not touched.

TOGETHER ...

From novels to the prints that were the start of Laura Ashley, hundreds of businesses have been launched from the kitchen table. This is more possible than ever now, because instead of clearing away stacks of papers, you may have only a laptop to close down. For professions centred on the kitchen, like catering or recipe testing, it makes sense to set up a permanent workstation there, even if it's just an extra length of worktop with a wall-mounted telephone and a couple of shelves for books. The kitchen may also be a good place to work if you need access to an outside workshop – perhaps for making pottery or restoring furniture – so you can do your paperwork without disruptive walks to check on work in progress.

At the other end of the house, the bedroom or dining room may be ideal if you specialize in soft furnishings or dressmaking, because both have a large clean surface that helps when cutting out fabric. And with Internet access from the television looming, the living room could be the perfect place to set up a mobile communications centre. A disciplined approach to work is important and it's a good idea to clear up at the end of each day – the domestic equivalent of 'hot desking'. Scattered papers and stationery not only look untidy, they are also a constant reminder of work.

... or apart

In large open-plan rooms, it's a good idea to create some kind of visual barrier to define the different areas. A screen of wood, glass, bamboo, or metal and canvas is one of the most obvious, or opt for a blind that can be drawn down from the ceiling. You do not necessarily need a physical barrier. Simply arranging the furniture so that the area for relaxation focuses on the fireplace and the workstation is by the window, for example, can be just as effective. Pin up pieces of work – fabric samples, font sizes, pupils' work and so on – for decorative emphasis.

There will always be things you don't want to have on show. These can be hidden in office storage, or an armoire or cupboard with plenty of shelves for easy access. Some furniture is dual-purpose – a leather office chair can look equally at home in a living room, while storage tables or floor cubes will absorb clutter. Make sure you have a few hideaways in which to stash things when visitors arrive and have at least one lockable drawer if there are children in the house.

Above *Every corner of this designer's house is crammed with work in progress, from the dining table behind the sofa (cleared when friends come to eat) to the shelving and side tables.*

Right *Floor-to-ceiling frosted glass panels screen the work area from the living space in this minimalist home. The 'desk' is simply a long shelf that runs the width of the room, with shelves built into the narrow supports.*

Above *An L-shaped work surface tucked into a corner of this small cottage provides plenty of space for working at home without intruding on the rest of the living room.*

work space checklist

■ If you opt for a separate work area, it makes working life easier if you keep it as self-contained as possible, with reference books and equipment like the printer close to the desk.

■ Do not try to make do with a space that's too cramped – it will be frustrating and uncomfortable.

■ Make sure you can work undisturbed, especially if you choose a space in the living room or hall.

■ Think vertically. A monitor, keyboard, tower hard disk and printer can be stacked to economize on space and files stored on shelves above the work surface rather than each side.

■ Style the work area to suit the room. Paint a desk to match – or contrast with – the sofa, or stain it to blend with other furniture if it's in the living room. If you work in the kitchen, create a desk from surplus worktop and spare cabinets.

STEALING SPACE: UPSTAIRS ...

If you are racking your brains for somewhere to work, start at the top of the house and consider all the spare corners, however unpromising. Is it possible to move the bedroom furniture around to make room for a small desk or work space for instance? It would be relatively quiet, but think twice if you have difficulty sleeping. You may find it hard to switch off if you're faced with a pile of work from the time you wake up until the moment you close your eyes. What about the landing? Older homes and apartments often have unused space here, sometimes by a feature window that gives light without glare – just make sure it's not too cold and draughty for comfort.

... and down

Downstairs, the dining room is a favourite retreat. The table gives you plenty of room to spread out, although you may need to protect the surface from scratches and stains. You can buy a trolley for your computer that swings over the table so the monitor is at the right height; this also means that you can push the computer to one side at the end of

the day. If one room serves as both living and dining room, it's a good idea to conceal the workstation if you can. A deep alcove is the perfect place. Fix a worktop to the wall with shelves above and storage for papers and the printer below, and hide it all behind folding doors, filmy drapes or a blind.

The hall offers plenty of possibilities too, as long as it is well heated. Knocking out an understairs cupboard can create the perfect work space if you plan with care. To find out if there's room to work in comfort, measure it from the back to see if there's space for a desk and add an extra metre of clearance for a chair. However, the hall may well be a thoroughfare, and constantly shifting your chair is not conducive to concentration.

Special requirements

Office space is sometimes a secondary consideration. Craftwork, for example, may be best carried out in a room with washable walls and floor, and access to a sink – in a conservatory, large kitchen or a utility room perhaps. It may also be worthwhile taking over the utility room for catering or cake decorating, relocating the washing machine and dryer near a bathroom and fitting in an extra fridge or freezer instead. This can provide the extra storage and work surface you need, while keeping commercial cooking separate from the family food.

Room outside

Why not consider a summerhouse? Many manufacturers make garden buildings designed for year-round occupation by home-workers and easily adaptable for office use. If there is space in the garden, a wooden summerhouse with a veranda and pitched roof will look attractive and provide what for many people is the ideal solution to the working at home conundrum – somewhere you can leave behind at the end of the day, but which is only seconds away from home.

Below left Don't dismiss the dining room table – it's the obvious place to work, especially if you can manage with a laptop. Provide storage for papers nearby, for hassle-free clearing up.

Above This hideaway under the stairs has an angled worktop to make the most of the limited space. Books line the hall walls; paintings and a pin-board are arranged above the desk since shelves could be oppressive in this confined area.

Storage solutions

Imagine no more panics about locating important papers or computer disks in your office, no more time spent retracing your steps in search of the letter you know you had yesterday. Organization is essential when you are working from home and efficient storage is the place to start.

WHERE TO PUT IT

Logic is the secret of successful storage, so make a list of exactly what you need to store. Most storage systems are designed to cope with paper – bills, receipts, correspondence, work in progress and reference materials. However, as computers become more sophisticated, electronic storage is fast taking over. You may need storage for journals and books, printer paper and cartridges and computer disks. You may also have specialized storage needs – for audio or video tapes, jewellery, photographic equipment or seed catalogues, for example. Look at the size and shape of what you have to store and browse in

hardware stores, shop-fitter outlets and second-hand furniture shops, as well as office suppliers, to see just what is available and how it will suit your needs.

Open or closed storage?

The basic choice is open shelves and grid systems versus closed storage – cupboards, filing cabinets and drawers. A traditional desk, for example, has deep drawers for hanging files, shallow drawers for stationery and a pull-out pencil drawer, so everything you need is close at hand. If most tasks are taken care of by your computer, however, all you might need is a simple table, perhaps with a platform shelf for the monitor containing a few tiny drawers for pens or paper clips. Papers can be kept elsewhere because you won't need constant access to them.

A problem of closed storage is remembering where you put everything. Draughtsmen's plan chests and old-fashioned shop fittings can be useful because they provide lots of shallow drawers, which save frantic rummaging. Storage boxes with small drawers meant for nails and screws are ideal for odds and ends of stationery.

The contents of shelves can help to brighten up a room, for example stacks of colourful stationery – ring binders, box files and cassette boxes. Pick colours to co-ordinate with a blind or cushions, and paint a chair or filing cabinet to match.

Above Tiny drawers, neatly labelled, are perfect for keeping items such as jewellery-making equipment or odds and ends of stationery such as staples and paper clips.
Left Round hat boxes add a light touch to an office and are just as useful as rectangular boxes for storing stationery and notes.

Right See what a lick of paint can do. Floorboards, table and chair, filing cabinet, chest of drawers and walls are all painted in the same shade of creamy white to create a calm retreat.

Above *Room for two: a narrow surface provides useful extra work space under the window to accommodate an extra person or the overspill from the main desk.*

clever storage ideas

● To get rid of clutter, line up steel storage canisters on open shelves and label them so that you can easily identify the contents.

● Try découpage – designs cut from paper, stuck on and varnished – to pretty up files and boxes.

● Cover files and boxes in smart wrapping paper and lacquer them for strength.

● A storage system based on cubes means you can fill each compartment separately, so that you

know just where you've put your dictionaries or magazines or the sewing things.

● Think about archive storage if you are reluctant to get rid of papers but fast running out of space. Look in *Yellow Pages* for companies that will collect boxes of information and transfer it to microfilm for you.

● Metallic paints can turn a collection of containers or a piece of furniture into a focal point – try bronze, old gold or silver.

THE INVISIBLE OFFICE

How much office equipment do you really need? It's worth reducing it to the absolute minimum, especially if you have had to steal work space from the living room or bedroom. Keeping it to the minimum is increasingly possible with the advent of digital television, which promises access to the Internet through the television screen, and WAP phones, which connect to the Internet via your mobile, freeing you from fixed telephone lines. Just curl up on the sofa with your laptop and switch on the television – no one will know whether you're working on a major business deal or watching your favourite television soap! Or you could take your WAP phone outside for a little alfresco communication. We're not quite there yet, but it's a real possibility. As equipment dwindles in size, the main restrictions will be psychological rather than physical ones – negotiating a quiet place to concentrate and convincing friends and family that yes, it may not look like it but this really is work!

Storage with a secret

Until the information technology revolution and the paperless office come entirely of age, there will inevitably be files and papers to be stowed away. If you work and live in one room, choose storage that doesn't scream 'office' when you are trying to relax. Instead of having an obvious and possibly clumsy-looking four-drawer filing cabinet in the living room, opt for furniture with a hidden secret. In place of a straightforward coffee table, for example, you could choose a low chest with drawers, and instead of a stool for casual seating, you might find an ottoman that opens to reveal storage inside, or a side table that does the same thing. Modular systems that form part of a wall of storage tend to contain a variety of compartments with optional shelves and doors, so you

can stack stationery out of sight in the cupboards and keep your china and books on display.

If you cannot find exactly what you want in the stores, the solution might be to have something made specially. Cupboards built into an alcove below bookshelves can be used to conceal filing, or you could build a tall cupboard into a corner; if you paint it to match the walls, it will almost disappear. Traditional pieces of furniture can often be adapted to modern needs. You might be able to convert a sideboard into a stylish filing cabinet or use it to house a printer, with room for paper inside and stationery in the drawers above. An old chest of drawers makes a practical and attractive stationery cupboard. Paint it pale and pretty if it's going in your bedroom or a strong colour for the living room or hall. A wardrobe is another possibility – just fit it with shelves and drawers to keep all evidence of the office behind closed doors.

Boxes and baskets

Simple solutions to the storage problem include everyday containers like boxes, baskets, pots and storage canisters. They can all look equally effective as long as you stick to the same shape and size. You can buy sets of cardboard boxes in a variety of colours and designs, or cover shoe boxes in marbled paper if you want to economize (label them so you know what's inside). Wicker baskets are a favourite for storage. Stack open trays beneath side tables, pile up hampers, or stow large shallow baskets beneath a bed or sofa.

Canisters and pots can hide a whole variety of bits and pieces. Sort these into categories – pencils and pens, sticky tape and string, labels and glue – and allocate a different coloured container to each so that things are easy to retrieve.

Above *Wicker baskets designed for a country kitchen fit comfortably under this little side table and provide useful storage for paperwork.*

Below *Cubes are a flexible form of storage that can expand as your requirements grow. The colourful funnel-shaped baskets are ideal for storing awkward shapes.*

Shelves and bookcases

You can never have too many shelves in a study or a home office. A line of book spines can be decorative in itself and any spare shelf space can be given over to small *objets d'art* or other items you find pleasing. There is a wide range of versatile bookcases and shelving units on the market and the best will grace your work space.

Whether you opt for a floor-standing or wall-mounted shelf unit will depend on the space available and what you need to store. Anything kept on open shelves should be reasonably pleasing visually – use box files and storage boxes, which come in a range of colours and interesting designs. Colourful storage will immediately help to make your work space feel less office-like.

Utilize any natural recesses in the room for a tall bookcase or a low unit with wall-mounted shelves above. A complete storage wall can be a solution in a room with no alcoves, with shelves of varying heights for books, files and display purposes. In a dual-purpose room, such as a bedroom or dining room, storage units make a useful divider, giving a sense of separation from the work area. Bear in mind that shelves need a back if they are not being placed against a wall.

Wall shelves

■ Books are heavy (six average paperbacks weigh over 1kg/2lb), so it is essential that wall-mounted bookshelves are firmly secured to a sound, solid wall, with sturdy fixings.

■ Most shop-bought wall units come with fixings but if you make your own shelves, make sure you use the correct fixtures and screws for the supports and the type of wall.

■ Adjustable systems are more flexible than fixed shelves. The shelves are carried on brackets that slot or clip into vertical support strips, screwed to the wall. Shelves can be moved up or down easily.

■ Choose a bookcase that has shelves of varying heights, to suit paperbacks, encyclopedias and at least one size in between.

This modular shelving system combines natural pulp board tubes, hardboard shelves and plastic joints to tailor storage to your own needs.

'Cell' shelving unit in beech veneer extends or rotates to fit into any space.

Perforated steel shelving unit on steel framework has five shelves and would suit a modern, minimalist work space.

Beech plywood dividers create useful pigeon holes in this wall-mounted shelf unit made of folded aluminium.

Ash storage unit with nine equal compartments is suitable for large files and boxes as well as for displaying items.

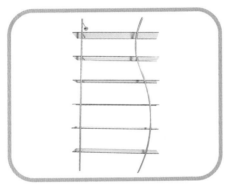

'Long-wave' shelving unit with toughened glass shelves has steel uprights that can be fixed to the wall at different intervals.

Stylish unit in perforated steel and maple veneer comprises drawers and a deep cupboard as well as open shelves.

Budget shelf units are made from recycled pulp board covered in craft paper; supplied flat-packed, they are a lightweight and practical storage solution.

Steel storage unit with canvas pull-out baskets could serve as a mobile stationery cupboard or house computer disks and other small items.

Wider, three-shelf version of the perforated steel shelving shown above (top centre).

Open up your home with glass and revel in the extra light all year round. Today's conservatories are far more than indoor summer-houses – they are one of the best ways of extending your home. Adding a conservatory gives you the opportunity to rearrange your living space. The obvious choice is to use it as a summery sitting room, but if you need more space for relaxing or eating, you could relocate the main living room or dining room to the conservatory, releasing space in a shadier part of the house for a study, a family den or a music room.

conservatories

Think it through

First the good news: there is less red tape involved in building a conservatory than in any other form of home extension. However, it can cost more than you think, which is why careful planning is a must.

Calculating the cost

The price of the structure is only the start because building, heating, flooring, furnishing and blinds can double or even triple the cost of a conservatory. The most expensive conservatories are custom-built to suit your requirements. Some companies insist on erecting the conservatory themselves, others are happy to work with the architect and builder you choose. Less expensive, do-it-yourself conservatories based on a modular design are a popular choice and, despite their name, are often professionally installed, although you need to arrange labour and planning permission yourself. Suppliers usually offer a design service and a five- or 10-year guarantee.

Where will it go?

Do consider the aspect of your conservatory. A south-facing one could be too hot in summer unless there is plenty of shading and ventilation – blinds are a must. An east-facing conservatory could be perfect for a kitchen-dining room, sunny in the morning but cooler in the evening, while a west-facing one has the sun later in the day and is perfect for entertaining. North-facing conservatories will need extra heating in winter.

Is it legal?

If the conservatory is to be a small one and predominantly of glass, building regulations (which monitor safety) and planning permission may not apply. There are exceptions, however, so do check national regulations. These tend to look at by how much a conservatory would increase the volume of the house, the proximity of a conservatory to the road, whether it is above a certain height or within a specified distance of the boundary. It will also depend on whether your house is listed, in a conservation area or covered by a restrictive covenant.

Top A conservatory can be a replacement for, as well as an addition to, a regular sitting room. A large one like this allows for flexible seating in different areas.
Above This conservatory makes a wonderful dining room, which runs virtually the width of the house. The wicker chairs provide appropriate and comfortable seating.

Right A kitchen is not the first room you think of when planning a conservatory but this room, complete with breakfast bar, shows how successful it can be. On fine days there is plenty of space to eat outside, too.

conservatory checklist

■ If you opt for a custom-made conservatory, get at least three quotes. At this end of the market, most conservatory companies will apply for building regulations and planning permission and even listed-building consent if required.

■ All conservatory companies should offer an insurance-backed guarantee.

■ Make sure you have clear plans of the conservatory and its surroundings.

■ Ask for written details of the work to be carried out, specifying who is doing what. Agree a time and date for completion in writing.

■ Never pay in advance or on delivery unless you are simply buying the components – even then, have your builder inspect them thoroughly as soon as they arrive. If the conservatory company is arranging installation, it's usual to pay a deposit, a second instalment when the base and brickwork are in place and the rest on completion.

Garden rooms

While modern conservatories do not necessarily contain plants, conservatory windows have a view of an ever-changing garden. What is more important than keeping greenery inside, is that the conservatory should create a stylish link between home and garden, inside and out.

For looks that last

Hardwood or red cedar – white-painted or left natural – are the traditional choice for conservatory frames, but you can now find green and blue-stained versions or you can paint or stain natural wood yourself for the finish you want. Wood is inevitably a high-maintenance material, which explains the popularity of low-cost, easy-care uPVC; you can also buy composite frames that are hardwood inside and uPVC outside for a combination of good looks and durability. Aluminium is the strongest material for frames and, like uPVC, is available in a range of colours.

Home comfort

Conservatories need both double glazing and heating for year-round use. You need toughened safety glass in windows, doors, low panels and the roof. Polycarbonate is an alternative material for roofs – it is light but must be ridged or tinted because it transmits heat too effectively. Other options are treated low-emissivity glass, which gives increased insulation in winter and reflects heat in summer, and anti-glare finishes.

For heating, you could add extra radiators if the central heating boiler can cope; or install underfloor heating, which is efficient but expensive, or electric heaters. Ventilation is critical in such a hot spot, so the area covered by opening windows and doors should be equivalent to about one-fifth of the floor space. Even so, you may need a roof vent (some open automatically as the heat rises) or an extractor fan. Ceiling fans help the air circulate but do not reduce the temperature.

Green and pleasant

Shelves or staging are effective for grouping plants in the conservatory, or you can have integral troughs installed at the outset to create permanent beds if you don't mind the earthy smell. If the plants are to be the focal point, choose luxuriant and showy palms, climbers and citrus trees. Be more restrained if you are planning a playroom or study, and avoid heavily scented plants in a dining area.

Above A dark frame adds an architectural air to this large conservatory, used traditionally as a peaceful retreat and a haven for plants.

Far left Small can be stylish: the white frame and pale walls stretch space in this tiny conservatory, while flamboyant chair and table covers create the atmosphere, aided by a single dramatic palm.

Below left Efficient heating and ventilation are a must if you want to keep books or upholstered furniture in the conservatory. This elegantly designed conservatory has room for both.

Flooring and windows

Simple is often best when it comes to choosing conservatory floor and window treatments. This is your chance to bring a touch of continental sunshine into your home with Mediterranean-style tiles and plain calico or canvas blinds. Or look East and take your cue from the rattan and bamboo of Malaysia and Singapore, complete with swaying palms, or look West for the California beach-house style.

Above Partnered by café chairs and a mosaic-top table, a terracotta-tiled floor creates a cheerful Mediterranean look and brings warmth to this conservatory.

Right Fresh and simple: white floor tiles and plain white blinds make for an airy atmosphere and increase the sense of space. The contrast of textures – shiny tiles and soft blinds – brings added interest.

Far right Pinoleum roof blinds comprising fine, natural-finish wooden slats shade this conservatory-dining room. (Pinoleum blinds are also available in a painted finish.) The hard-wearing stone floor links the conservatory with the terrace, providing a sense of continuity.

Choosing the floor

Hard-wearing and water-resistant, terracotta and ceramic tiles are unaffected by humidity and relatively easy to clean – a requirement for a room that leads straight on to the garden. Plain tiles make the most of the space but you could make the floor the focal point, with a tiled border or panels of tiles in a dazzling colour or intricate design if you don't want pattern over the entire floor.

Stone is even more hard-wearing than tiles but, if the conservatory doubles as a playroom, choose a softer surface such as cushioned vinyl, linoleum, carpet tiles that can be taken up and washed, or resilient needlepunch 'office' carpet. Sisal and coir are not comfortable to crawl on but are attractively rustic forms of soft flooring. They can be difficult to clean so a better option might be loose-lay squares or strips of medieval matting. Natural wood always looks beautiful but needs proper sealing and conditioning to stand up to the micro-climate of the conservatory.

In the shade

Blinds are essential unless the conservatory has reflective glass. If ordinary blinds are used in a conservatory they will need replacing regularly, being decorative rather than insulating. Special conservatory blinds are expensive so, if funds are limited, concentrate on providing blinds for the roof. Materials specially designed for conservatory use include densely woven polyester, metal-coated acrylic and glass fibre finished with PVC, all of which withstand extremes of temperature and humidity without rotting or distorting. Blinds can be made to measure in a variety of styles, from rigid Venetian blinds to pliable Roman, roller or pleated versions. More advanced, thermal-coated blinds block the sun completely, while blinds with a honeycomb weave offer extra insulation. If appearance is your main concern, opt for pinoleum or plain calico or canvas blinds. Other ingenious and stylish ways of shading the light are to use screens, tall plants or even a display of Chinese umbrellas.

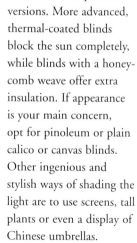

Furnishings and accessories

Decide whether your conservatory is extended indoor living space or whether it really belongs to the garden to determine its style. If the conservatory is a continuation of another room, the furniture needs to blend with existing decor; if it is self-contained, metal or cane garden furniture might work well.

Style...

Unless there is complete climate control via air conditioning, heating and ventilation, a conservatory is not the place for treasured antiques or paintings. The sun will cause fabrics to fade and humidity can cause rot so it is best to steer clear of expensive upholstery, too. However, a favourite armchair with a washable loose cover could be the perfect place to curl up and admire the garden, while a storage unit for the odd piece of china is always useful. More ambitiously, combine cast-aluminium or wicker garden seating with a conventional dining table or add an ornate side table or cabinet for a unique personalized look.

...and substance

Unlike garden furniture, conservatory furniture does not have to be weather-resistant or easily stacked away. Classics like wicker and cane will resist heat and humidity and their curves can complement sometimes stark surroundings. Metal is a fashionable favourite, and is especially effective in dining rooms with a glass- or wood-topped table. Neat, delicate designs help increase the sense of space in small rooms. Ornate traditional furniture is usually cast from aluminium, but weighty cast-iron pieces are an option if they do not need moving too often. Whatever the seating, comfortable seat cushions are very worthwhile.

Accessories

Decide on the position of any large plant containers before you furnish the room as they will be too heavy to move regularly. Introduce colour, or turn an assortment of terracotta pots into a matching set by painting them with colourful emulsion paint, or use a silver, dull gold or verdigris paint and mix with metallic containers. Paintings are problematic in most conservatories but framed prints or plates look just as effective.

Add interest by varying the height of ornaments and plants using shelves or an *étagère*, by hanging plants from the ceiling, or by introducing the odd piece of 'sculpture' – a piece of driftwood, obelisk-shaped candles or a dish of attractive pebbles.

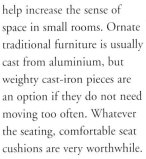

Above The striking Arts and Crafts-style bench is the focal point of this conservatory, balanced by the tall palms at the other end of the room.

Far left Wicker is a conservatory classic and the eye-catching touches of aqua on these chairs add decorative interest. Plant pots could be painted to match for a simple but effective colour scheme.

Below left This modern-looking chair is less weighty than the traditional style of cast-iron furniture. The small matching table is perfect for work, reading or a light lunch.

Taking the inside outside

When the weather is beautiful it's a shame to be indoors, even in a conservatory. However lovely the setting, it just cannot compete with the glory of the garden on a still summer's day. So when you're buying furniture to use inside, look for styles you can take outside too, be it an easy chair that's light enough to move or a table that looks as good in the garden as it does in the kitchen.

Above Pile a wicker sofa high with cushions covered with remnants of fabric linked by colour or theme – in this case, roses – and push it outside to make the most of the sun.

Setting the scene

Like the conservatory, a terrace, patio or deck links house and garden so it, too, needs styling. To make full use of it you will need lights (for safety and emphasizing changes of level, as well as background light), shelter in the form of shrubs or walls, furniture and a focal point – perhaps a specimen plant or tree, an arbour or a water feature. As well as these permanent fixtures, it's easy to introduce temporary scene-setters for entertaining. A pavilion offers shelter from both sun and rain, while outdoor fairy lights, garden torches, candles in pots or storm lanterns all look pretty and supplement existing lighting – citronella candles help repel insects, too.

Give the garden a facelift by painting fencing and trellis with vibrant colours (best kept for short runs) or the now classic green, lilac or blue. Rejuvenate a worn-looking terrace by lifting broken paving and replacing it with alpines, low-growing herbs, pebbles or decorative aggregate, or sow thyme in the gaps between stones.

Dual-purpose furniture

Café chairs and tables with wood or translucent plastic slats and the lighter metal furniture made from cast aluminium or tubular steel look as good indoors, especially in a conservatory or dining room, as they do in the garden. They can certainly be left out all summer, although it's wise to check before leaving garden furniture out all year. Generally speaking, only treated wood or hardwood, painted metal and stone can survive temperatures below freezing. Because most garden furniture is not frost-proof, many pieces fold or stack for storage. If you choose chairs and tables that blend with the furniture indoors you can use them for extra seating at Christmas and other celebrations.

Right A swirling voile canopy hung from the branch of a tree makes a feature of this simple wicker chair, adding an element of shelter and helping to filter the sun.

Below left A brilliantly colourful setting for an outdoor feast relies on the careful arrangement of light ply chairs and a clever table setting to create the mood.

Extending in period style

Sarah knew that adding a conservatory to her Victorian terraced cottage would give the kitchen area more light and space, but she feared that making structural alterations would spoil the authentic feel of her lovingly restored house. Her only regret now is that she didn't do it earlier.

Although Sarah was reluctant to alter her unspoiled cottage, with all its period detail, she felt awkward when friends stayed because the only bathroom was accessed through the guest bedroom. Also, the poky kitchen was dark and small with little storage or worktop space. She eventually decided, after 15 years, to add a conservatory in the backyard area, opening on to the kitchen and adjoining dining room, and at the same time to build a single-storey extension out from the kitchen to house a utility room and shower room with WC.

Sarah knew exactly how she wanted the conservatory to look and gave her builder, who had a good eye for period detail, a photograph of a simple Victorian design torn from a magazine. Together they worked out the floor plan for both the conservatory and an extension that would replace the outside boiler house (originally an outdoor WC) and coal bunker.

To retain sufficient ceiling height for the shower, the floor had to be lowered and the planned sloping roof converted to a flat roof. Sarah feared a flat-roofed extension would look too modern but, built with bricks from the

demolished outbuildings and the kitchen wall, the extension looks as though it has always been there.

Together, the original kitchen and new conservatory form a large cooking and living area, separated by an island unit housing a sink, dishwasher and storage. Sarah can now cook for guests while they chat to her from the conservatory.

'I love my house more than ever and this new project has transformed my life. The conservatory is a lovely place to relax when I get home from work, and my overnight guests can at last have the privacy of their own bedroom and en-suite bathroom. I now wonder why I waited all those years.'

Above *The simple Victorian-style conservatory, its exterior painted a traditional colour, looks entirely in keeping with the period of the house. Because it faces north, the conservatory never gets too hot, even in the height of summer. On the right, the extension was built using recycled bricks; simple four-pane windows help integrate it with the rest of the building.*

Below left *A blue-painted island unit, situated where the original outside wall stood, now houses the sink and dishwasher. A radiator is cleverly hidden inside it, behind a panel made from strips of dowelling.*

Right *A simple garden table and a pair of director's chairs, as well as the palms, suit the feel of a conservatory and give Sarah a place to enjoy a snack meal or just to relax and look at the garden. The wall is faced with MDF, grooved to resemble tongue-and-groove panelling and painted a soft yellow.*

Commissioning Architects and Builders

Who will supervise the building work? Do I need an Architect? A surveyor? The builders want paying up-front, what should I do? These questions can bring you sharply down to earth when you start to translate ideas into reality. Though most of us are happy to employ a decorator or have a go at a little light diy, commissioning a professional to carry out major structural work can be unnerving, and not only because the sums involved can exceed five figures. But there are ways to make it easy.

Why employ an architect?

Anyone can draw up plans but architects can do much more, finding extra light and space in small areas and suggesting sympathetic materials for an extension to your home. If all you want is advice, they'll provide that too, because you can pay for just an hour's consultation if you wish. More ambitiously, an architect can work on the concept, obtain planning permission and then hand the plans over to you or a builder to progress. If you want, and can afford it, architects can see the whole scheme through to completion, supervising the standard of building work and making sure that the contract is completed on time. Look for professional bodies and organizations that publish Plans of Work to help you to decide the services you need. Fees for a full service generally come to between 8 and 15 per cent of the total building cost. You can also pay by the hour, or for peace of mind, settle on a lump sum.

Choosing an architect

All architects are vetted by the professional bodies but word of mouth is a good recommendation. Whichever architect you choose, ask to see some examples of finished work and visit one or two sites. Make sure you're happy with the architect's approach at the initial meeting and, if you feel pressurized into approving ideas you have reservations about, or spending more than you can afford, find another one.

What happens next?

After discussing your ideas, budget and time scale, the architect will produce initial sketches for you to approve. Depending on the scope of your agreement, one of you will apply to the local authority planning for permission if necessary (it usually is if the project's big enough to involve an architect) and check that the proposed work complies with any building regulations. Once planning consent has been granted, the architect will draw up detailed plans and suggest a builder and a building contract if required. Of course you also need to sign a contract with your architect: again check with a professional body, as some publish Small Works forms designed for projects under certain amounts and supply an idea of charges.

Getting in the builders

Praise for builders is praise indeed so if a local firm is lauded, it's well worth considering. That said, you still need to protect yourself by seeking at least three written and itemized quotations; estimates are not the same. Contact the relevant trade association to check that the firm is a member – and if it's not, find out why. Ask what criteria members have to meet and if the organization offers an insurance-backed guarantee scheme and arbitration for any dispute. You should ask to see examples of the builder's work, but make as sure as you can that they belong to bona-fide paying customers.

What about sub-contractors?

Small builders almost inevitably employ 'subbies' and in theory you should check them out too, though that may be difficult when neither you nor your builder knows who will be available on the day. However, if you take on responsibility for finding and paying sub-contractors, check them out with the right trade association – depending on whether they are a plumber, an electrician or a gas fitter.

The small print

Your contract with the builder should specify the extent of the work, the materials used, its price and timings. Read the small print and do not sign if there are any exclusion clauses you think are excessive. Try to avoid changing your mind once work is in progress as this causes endless wrangles over inflated costs. Anything extra that you ask for - or agree to - should be put in writing and signed by both parties. Stage payments are usual. Never pay the full amount up-front (10 to 15 per cent is about right as a deposit) or employ a builder who wants cash to buy materials. And don't be tempted to pay cash in order to avoid tax. Legal aspects apart, there is every reason to avoid the black economy because if you pay by credit card, the finance company will compensate you if the builder lets you down.

Directory of suppliers

KITCHENS

Alternative Plans
9 Hester Road
London SW11 4AN
Tel: 020 7228 6460
Fax: 020 7924 1164
www.alternative-plans.co.uk

Belling Appliances Ltd
Talbot Rd
Mexborough
South Yorkshire S64 8AJ
Tel: 01709 579900
Fax: 01709 579904

Bulthaup
37 Wigmore Street
London W1H 9LD
Tel: 020 7495 3663
Fax: 020 7495 0139
www.bulthaup.com

Camargue Plc
Townsend Farm Road
Houghton Regis
Dunstable
Beds LU5 5BA
Tel: 01582 699122
Fax: 01582 609361

Febo Designs
1 Foxscombe
S. Harting
Petersfield
Hampshire GU31 5PL
Tel: 01730 825041
Fax: 01730 825053

Habitat
196 Tottenham Court Road
London W1P 9LD
For your nearest store call:
Tel: 0845 6010740
www.habitat-international.com

Humphersons
2nd Floor, Heal & Son
196 Tottenham Court Road
London W1P 9LD
Tel: 020 7636 1666
Fax: 020 7436 4738

IKEA
2 Drury Way
North Circular Road
London NW10 0TH
Tel: 020 8208 5600

Plain & Simple Kitchens
Studio 1
Filmer Studios
75 Filmer Road
London SW6 7JF
Tel: 020 7731 2530
Fax: 020 7731 3789
www.ps4kitchens.co.uk

SieMatic
Osprey House
Rookery Court
Primett Road
Stevenage
Herts SG1 3EE
Tel: 01438 369327
Fax: 01438 368920
www.siematic.com

FREE-STANDING KITCHEN FURNITURE

Aero
96 Westbourne Grove
London W2 5RT
Tel: 020 7221 1950
Fax: 020 7221 2555
www.aero-furniture.co.uk

Deacon & Sandys
Apple Pie Farm
Cranbrook Road
Benenden
Kent TN17 4EU
Tel: 01580 243331
Fax: 01580 243301
www.deaconandsandys.co.uk

The Dining Room Shop
62–64 White Hart Lane
London SW13 0PZ
Tel: 020 8878 1020
Fax: 020 8876 2367
www.thediningroomshop.co.uk

Robert Grothier
602 King's Road
London SW10 0TZ
Tel: 020 7736 6778
Fax: 020 7736 6360

McCord
London Road
Preston PR11 1RP
Tel: 0870 908 7020
Fax: 0870 908 7050
www.mccord.uk.com

Jerry's Home Store
163–167 Fulham Road
London SW3 6SN
Tel: 020 7581 0909
Fax: 020 7584 3749

SINKS AND TAPS

GEC Anderson
Oakengrove
Shire Lane
Hastoe
Herts HP23 6LY
Tel: 01442 826999
Fax: 01442 825999
www.gecanderson.co.uk

Armitage Shanks Ltd
Old Road
Armitage
Rugeley
Staffs WS15 4BT
Tel: 01543 490253
Fax: 01543 491677
www.armitage-shanks.com

Blanco Ltd
Oxgate Lane
London NW2 7JN
Tel: 020 8450 9100
Fax: 0800 282846

Brass & Traditional Sinks Ltd
Devauden Green
Chepstow
Monmouthshire NP16 6PL
Tel: 01291 650743
Fax: 01291 650827
www.sinks.co.uk

Carron Phoenix
Carron Works
Stenhouse Road
Falkirk
Scotland
FK2 8DW
Tel: 01324 638321
Fax: 01324 620978
www.carron.com

Kinetico Ltd
Hipley Street
Old Woking
Surrey GU22 9LQ
Tel: 01483 753400
Fax: 01483 726030

BATHROOMS

Armitage Shanks Ltd
Rugeley
Staffordshire WS15 4BT
www.armitage-shanks.co.uk

Aston Matthews Bathroom Specialists
141–147a Essex Road
London N1 2SN
Tel: 020 7226 3657
Fax: 020 7354 5951

Ideal Standard
The Bathroom Works
National Ave
Kingston-Upon-Hull
HU5 4HS
Tel: 01482 346461
Fax: 01482 445886

Triton Plc
Shepperton Park
Caldwell Rd
Nuneaton
Warwickshhire CV11 4NR
Tel: 01203 344441
Fax: 02476 349 828

B&Q Plc
Portswood House
1 Hampshire Corporate
Park
Chandlers Ford
Hampshire SO53 3YX
Tel: 02380 256 256

Abacus
681–689
Holloway Road
London N19 5SE
Tel: 020 7281 4136
Fax: 020 7272 5081

Bathroom City
Amington Road
Tyseley
Birmingham B25 8ET
Tel: 0121 708 0111
Fax: 0121 706 6561
www.bathroomcity.co.uk

The Bathroom Warehouse Group
Unit 3
Wykeham Estate
Moorside Road
Winnall
Winchester
Hants SO23 7RX
Tel: 01962 862554
Fax: 01962 840927

Bathrooms Direct
410–414 Upper Richmond
Road West
London SW14 7JX
Tel: 020 8878 2727
Fax: 020 8878 2225
www.bathstore.com

Colourwash Bathrooms
165 Chamberlain Road
London NW10 3NU
Tel: 020 8459 8918
Fax: 020 8459 4280
www.colourwash.co.uk

Just Bathrooms
Pembroke Ave
Denny End Industrial Estate
Waterbeach
Cambridge CB5 9PB
Tel: 01223 863631
Fax: 01223 576863
www.justbathrooms.co.uk

West One Bathrooms
45–46 South Audley St
London W1Y 5DG
Tel: 020 7499 1845
Fax: 020 7629 9311

Aqualisa Products
The Flyers Way
Westerham
Kent TN16 1DE
Tel: 01959 560000
Fax: 01959 560030
www.aqualisa.co.uk

Bedfordshire Bathroom Distributors
Unit 10A/5
Elstow Storage Depot
Kempston
Hardwick
Bedford MK45 3NS
Tel: 01234 741 441
Fax: 01234 741278

Galaxy Showers
Units 3 & 4
Holbrook Park Estate
Off Kingswood Close
Holbrooks
Coventry CV6 4AB
Tel: 02476 637635
Fax: 02476 637306

Caradon Bathrooms
Lawton Road
Alsager
Stoke-on-Trent
Staffs ST7 2DF
Tel: 01270 879777
Fax: 01270 873 864

Roca
Samson Road
Hermitage Ind. Estate
Coalville
Leicester LE67 3FP
Tel: 01530 830080
Fax: 01530 830010

Villeroy and Boch UK
267 Merton Road
London SW18 5JS
For your nearest store call:
Tel: 020 8871 4028
Fax: 020 8870 3720
www.villeroy-boch.co.uk

Heritage Bathrooms
Unit 1A
Princess Street
Bedminster
Bristol BS3 4AG
Tel: 0117 953 9762
Fax: 0117 953 5333

Showeristic
Unit 10
Manor Industrial Estate
Flint
Clwyd CH6 5UY
Tel: 01352 735381
Fax: 01352 763388

Vola
Unit 12
Ampthill Business Park
Station Rd
Ampthill
Bedford MK45 2QW
Tel: 01525 841155
Fax: 01525 841177

FURNITURE

Traditional/ Upholstered
Beaumont & Fletcher
261 Fulham Road
London SW3 6HY
Tel: 020 7352 5594
Fax: 020 7352 5546

Duresta Upholstery
Fields Farm Road
Long Eaton
Nottingham NG10 3FZ
Tel: 0115 973 2246
Fax: 0115 946 1028

Parker and Farr Furniture
75 Derby Road
Bramcote
Nottingham NG9 3GY
Tel: 0115 925 2131
Fax: 0115 925 9749

Recline and Sprawl
604 King's Road
London SW6 2DX
Tel: 020 7371 8982
Fax: 020 7371 8984

Wesley Barrell Ltd
Ducklington Mill
Standlake Road
Ducklington
Witney
Oxon
OX8 7UL
Tel: 01993 893100
Fax: 01993 702720
www.wesley-barrell.co.uk

Chairs and Stools
Back 2
28 Wigmore Street
London
W1H 9DF
Tel: 020 7935 0351
Fax: 020 7935 5293
www.back2.co.uk

The Classic Chair Company
Studio R
The Old Imperial Laundry
71 Warriner Gardens
London SW11 4XW
Tel: 020 7622 4274
Fax: 020 7622 4275

The Dining Chair Company
4 St Barnabas Street
London SW1W 8PE
Tel: 020 7259 0422
Fax: 020 7259 0423
www.diningchair.co.uk

Parker Knoll
London Road
Chipping Norton
Oxon OX7 5AX
Tel: 01494 557850
Fax: 01494 557898
www.parkerknoll.co.uk

Clock House Furniture
The Old Stables
Overhailes
Haddington
East Lothian EH41 3SB
Tel: 01620 860968
Fax: 01620 860984
www.clockhouse-furniture.com

Pine
Joyce Hardy Pine and Country Furniture
The Street
Hacheston
Suffolk IP13 0DS
Tel: 01728 746 485

Maison
Grand Illusions
PO Box 81
Shaftesbury
Dorset SP7 8TA
Tel: 01747 854092
Fax: 01747 851205

Contemporary Furniture
Aero
96 Westbourne Grove
London W2 5RT
Tel: 020 7221 1950
Fax: 020 7221 2555
www.aero-furniture.co.uk

Atrium
22–24 St Giles High Street
London WC2H 8LN
Tel: 020 7379 7288
Fax: 020 7240 2080
www.atrium.co.uk

The Conran Shop
Michelin House
81 Fulham Road
London SW3 6RD
Tel: 020 7589 7401
Fax: 020 7823 7015
www.conran.co.uk

Domain
83 Rusper Road
Horsham
West Sussex RH12 4BJ
Tel: 01403 257201
Fax: 01403 262002
www.domain.co.uk.co

Ligne Roset
95A High Street
Great Missenden
Bucks HP16 0AL
Tel: 01494 865001
Fax: 01494 866883

Liberty Plc
214 Regent Street
London W1R 6AH
Tel: 020 7734 1234
Fax: 020 7573 9876
www.liberty-of-london.com

Pure Living
The Ground Floor
1–3 Leonard Street
London EC2A 4AQ
Tel: 020 7250 1116
Fax: 020 7250 0616

Purves and Purves
83 Tottenham Court Road
London W1P 9HD
Tel: 020 7580 8223
Fax: 020 7580 8244
www.purves.co.uk

SCP
135–139 Curtain Road
London EC2A 3BX
Tel: 020 7739 1869
Fax: 020 7729 4224
www.scp.co.uk

Lakeland Ltd
Alexandra Buildings
Windermere
Cumbria LA23 1BQ
Tel: 01539 488100
Fax: 01539 488300
www.lakelandlimited.com

Oka
52 Beauchamp Place
London SW3 1NY
Tel: 020 7 581 0013
Fax: 0207 589 9309

Beds
And So To Bed
638–640 King's Road
London SW6 2DU
Tel: 020 7731 3593
Fax: 020 7371 5272
www.andsotobed.co.uk
Branches nationwide

Laura Ashley
FREEPOST P.O Box 5
Newtown
Powys SY16 1LX
Nationwide stockists
Tel: 0800 868100
Fax: 01686 621273

Big Table Furniture Co-operative
56 Great Western Road
London W9 3NT
Tel: 020 7221 5058
Fax: 020 7229 6032

Dreams
Knaves Beach
High Wycombe
Bucks HP10 9QW
Tel: 01628 520520
Fax: 01628 520333
www.dreams.plc.uk.

Habitat
196 Tottenham Court Road
London W1P 9LD
For your nearest store call:
Tel: 0845 6010740
www.habitat-international.com

The Iron Bed Company
Funtington Park
Funtington
Chichester
West Sussex PO18 8UE
Tel: 01243 778999
Fax: 01243 575760
www.ironbed.co.uk.

John Lewis
Oxford Street
London W1A 1EX
Tel: 020 7629 7711

Muji
187 Oxford Street
London W1R 1AJ
Tel: 020 7323 2208
www.muji.co.jp

The Futon Company
138 Notting Hill Gate
London W11 3QG
Tel: 020 7221 2032
Fax: 020 7792 1165

The Feather Bed Company
Crosslands House
Ash Thomas
Tiverton
Devon EX16 4NU
Tel: 01884 821 331
Fax: 01884 821328

Heal's
196 Tottenham Court Road
London W1P 9LD
Tel: 020 7636 1666
Fax: 020 7637 5582

Relyon
Station Mills
Wellington
Somerset TA21 8NN
Tel: 01823 667501
Fax: 01823 666079

Vi-Spring Ltd
Ernesettle Lane
Ernesettle
Plymouth PL5 2TT
Tel: 01752 366311
Fax: 01752 355108
www.vispring.co.uk

LIGHTING

Marks & Spencer
Michael House
Baker Street
London W1A 1DN
For your nearest store call:
0845 6031603

CTO Lighting Ltd
35 Park Avenue North
London N8 7RU
Tel: 020 8340 4593
Fax: 020 8340 4543

BHS
Euston House
132 Hampstead Road
London NW1 2PS
For your nearest store call:
Tel: 020 7388 0347

Habitat
196 Tottenham Court Road
London W1P 9LD
For your nearest store call:
Tel: 0845 6010740
www.habitat-
international.com

Beaumont & Fletcher
261 Fulham Road
London SW1 6HY
Tel: 020 7352 5594
Fax: 020 7352 3546

**Christopher Wray
Lighting**
600 King's Road
London SW6 2YW
Tel: 020 7736 8434
Fax 020 7731 3507
www.christopher-wray.com

John Lewis
Oxford Street
London W1A 1EX
Tel: 020 7629 7711
www.johnlewis.co.uk.

IKEA
2 Drury Way
North Circular Road
London NW10 OTH
Tel: 020 8208 5600

**Carlos Remes Lighting
Company**
10 New Quebec Street
London W1H 7DD
Tel: 020 7262 9963
Fax: 020 7262 9227

Aero
96 Westbourne Grove
London W2 5RT
Tel: 020 7221 1950
Fax: 020 7221 2555
www.aero-furniture.co.uk.

Ocean
FREEPOST LON811
London SW18 4BR
Tel: 0870 848 4840
www.oceancatalogue.com

Purves & Purves
80–81 & 83 Tottenham
Court Road
London W1P 9HD
Tel: 020 7580 8223
Fax: 020 580 9244

STORAGE

The Pier
161 Milton Park
Abingdon
Oxon OX14 4SD
For your nearest store call:
Tel: 020 7814 5020

Aero
96 Westbourne Grove
London WC 5RT
Tel: 020 7221 1950
Fax: 020 7221 2555
www.aero-furniture.com.uk.

**The Empty Box
Company**
The Old Dairy
Coomb Farm Building
Balchins Lane
Westcott,
Dorking
Surrey RH4 3LW
Tel: 01306 740193
Fax: 01306 875430

The Holding Company
241–245 King's Road
London SW3 5EL
Tel: 020 7352 1600
Fax: 020 7352 7495
www.theholdingcompany.
co.uk

IKEA
2 Drury Way
North Circular Road
London NW10 OTH
Tel: 020 8208 5600

McCord
London Road
Preston PR11 1RP
Tel: 0870 908 7020
Fax: 0870 908 7050
www.mccord.co.uk

Lakeland Ltd
Alexandra Buildings
Windermere
Cumbria LA23 1BQ
Tel: 01539 488100
Fax: 01539 488300
www.lakelandlimited.com

Muji
187 Oxford Street
London W1R 1AJ
Tel: 020 7323 2208
www.muji.co.jp

Habitat
196 Tottenham Court Road
London W1P 9LD
For your nearest store call:
Tel: 0845 6010740
www.habitat-
international.com

Index

Picture Credits and Acknowledgements

The publisher thanks the photographers and organisations for their kind permission to reproduce the following photographs in this book.

key

t = top of page, b = bottom of page, c = centre of page
l = left side of page, r = right side of page, rpt = repeat

prelims and chapter one – room planning

Good Housekeeping/National Magazine Company Limited:

1 Simon Archer (rpt); 2 Di Lewis; 4 Russell Sador (rpt); 6 Jan Baldwin (rpt); 7 Simon Archer (rpt); 10 Colin Poole; 12tl Polly Wreford (rpt);12bl Christopher Drake (rpt); 13 Debbi Treloar (rpt); 16, 17bl and 17tr Trevor Richards.

Other Sources:

8–9 Nick Carter; 11 Christopher Hill; 14tl, br and 15 Nick Carter.

chapter two – living rooms

Good Housekeeping/National Magazine Company Limited:

18 Di Lewis; 20 Trevor Richards; 21tr Trevor Richards; 21br Pia Tryde; 22 Christopher Drake; 23tr Nick Pope; 24 Chris Drake; 25tr Pia Tryde; 25br Peter Aprahamian; 30 tl, br and 31 (rpt) Di Lewis; 32tl and 33 Trevor Richards; 34tl, br and 35 Polly Wreford; 38 tl Simon Archer; 41tl Good Housekeeping; 41tc Good Housekeeping; 41tr Good Housekeeping; 41cl Good Housekeeping; 41c Good Housekeeping; 41cr Good Housekeeping; 41bl Good Housekeeping; 41br Good Housekeeping; 46tl Polly Wreford; 46bc Polly Wreford; 46–7 Jan Baldwin; 48cl Polly Wreford; 48–9 Jan Baldwin; 49tr Polly Wreford; 55tr Polly Wreford; 55br Polly Wreford; 56 Polly Wreford; 57tr Polly Wreford; 57bl Jan Baldwin; 58tr Mark Luscombe-Whyte; 58br Trevor Richards; 60tl, 60bl, 62tr, 62br and 63 Peter Aprahamian; 64 Trevor Richards; 66br Polly Wreford; 68 tr, 68c and 69 Polly Wreford, 71tl Pia Tryde; 71br Pia Tryde; 72 Lizzie Orme; 73tl Polly Wreford; 73br Trevor Richards; 74 Jan Baldwin.

Other Sources:

22tr Christopher Hill; 23tl Christopher Hill; 23br Nick Carter; 227tl IKEA UK; 26 Chaplin's of London; 27tc Wesley-Barrell/www.wesleybarrell.co.uk; 27tr IKEA UK; 27cl Wesley-Barrell/www.wesley-barrell.co.uk; 27c Beaumont and Fletcher; 27cr OKA Direct Ltd; 27bl Chaplin's of London; 27bc Wesley-Barrell/www.wesleybarrell.co.uk; 27br Chaplin's of London; 28 IKEA UK; 29tl IKEA UK; 29tc Chair Designs Ltd; 29tr Multiyork ; 29cl Hamilton Sofa by Beaumont and Fletcher; 29c The Hackwood; 29cr Wesley Barrell/www.wesleybarrell.co.uk; 29br Out There Communications; 29bc Kingcome Sofas; 29br The Raffles; 36tl, 36br and 37 Bernard O'Sullivan; 39 Abode; 40 Black and Decker; 41 bc Ewbank Products Limited; 42tl Abode; 42bl Lu Jeffery/www.elizabethwhiting.com; 43 Ian Parry/Abode; 44tl Nick Carter/www.elizabethwhiting.com; 44bl Nick Carter/www.elizabethwhiting.com; 45 Di Lewis/www.elizabethwhiting.com; 50 Chaplin's of London; 51tl Marks and Spencer; 51tc Marks and Spencer; 51tr Chaplin's of London; 51cl IKEA UK; 51c Muji; 51cr Marks and Spencer; 51bl Muji; 51bc Aero; 51 bl Muji; 52 Paul Ashley for The National Magazine Company Limited; 53tl Christopher Wray Lighting-the ultimate light source; 53tc Marks and Spencer; 53tr CTO Lighting; 53cl CTO Lighting; 53c CTO Lighting; 53cr Habitat; 53 bl CTO Lighting; 53bc Paul Ashley for The National Magazine Company Limited; 53br Marks and Spencer; 54 Tony Hall/Abode; 59 Abode; 65 DennisStone/www.elizabeth whiting.com; 66tl Graham Henderson/www.elizabethwhiting.com; 67 Neil Lorimer/www.elizabethwhiting.com; 70 Andreas Von Einsiedel/www.elizabethwhiting.com; 75tr Edina van der Wyck/Interior Archive (designer Jenny Armit); 75br Fritz Von der Sculenburg/ Interior Archive (designer John Stefanidis); 76tr Ian Parry/Abode;76br Di Lewis/Yvonne Hellin Hobbs/www.elizabeth whiting.com; 77 Nick Carter

chapter three – dining rooms

Good Housekeeping/National Magazine Company Limited:
96tl Debbie Patterson; 96br Lizzie Orme; 97 Russell Sador; 98
Russell Sador; 99tr Christopher Drake; 99br Harry Cory-Wright;100
and 101tl Gloria Nicol; 101tc Gloria Nicol; 101br Gloria Nicol;
102tl Lizzie Orme; 103 Lizzie Orme.

Other Sources:
78–9 Abode/Di Lewis; 80tl Brian Harrison/www.elizabeth
whiting.com; 80bl E.W.A/www.elizabethwhiting.com; 81 Dennis
Stone/www.elizabethwhiting.com; 82 Andrew Dee/Abode; 83 Tony
Hall/Abode; 84tl Mark Luscombe Whyte/www.elizabethwhiting.
com; 84bl Nick Carter; 85 Andrew Wood/Interior Archive (designer:
Babylon Design); 86tl Jan Baldwin/Jane Graining Library; 86bl Ian
Parry/Abode; 87 Nick Carter; 88 IKEA UK; 89tl Muji; 89tc Marks
and Spencer; 89tr Muji; 89cl IKEA UK; 89c Laura Ashley; 89cr
OKA Direct Ltd; 89br Aero; 89bc Maison at Grand Illusions; 89br
IKEA UK; 90, 91tr and 91bl AndreasVon Einsiedel/Abode; 92tl,
92br and 93 Paul Barker/Abode; 94tl, 94bl and 94–5 David
Brittain/The Jane Graining Library; 104 BODUM (UK) Limited;
105tl Marks and Spencer; 105tc Cucina Direct; 105tr Cucina Direct;
105cl BODUM (UK) Limited; 105c Mann and Man; 105cr Marks
and Spencer; !05bl BODUM (UK) Limited; 105bc Habitat; 105br
Mann and Man.

chapter four – kitchens

Good Housekeeping/National Magazine Company Limited:
108tl Polly Wreford; 108bl Polly Wreford; 109 Peter Aprahamian;
110tl Mark Luscombe-Whyte; 112tr Trevor Richards; 112br Peter
Aprahamian; 113 Jennifer Cawley; 117 Peter Aprahamian; 118tr
Helen Marsden; 119 Trevor Richards; 120tl Trevor Richards; 120bl
Peter Aprahamian; 121 Trevor Richards; 124 Christopher Drake;
125tr Helen Marsden; 126bl, 126t and 127 Helen Marsden; 128bl,
128–9 Peter Aprahamian; 130tc, 130 tr and 131 Christopher Drake;
132bl, 132tr and 133 Christopher Drake; 134br Polly Wreford; 135
Jennifer Cawley; 136tl Polly Wreford; 136bl Simon Archer; 137
Polly Wreford; 140bl Simon McBride; 141 Christopher Drake; 143tl
Good Housekeeping; 143tr Good Housekeeping; 143cl Good
Housekeeping; 143c Good Housekeeping; 143cr Good
Housekeeping; 143bl Good Housekeeping; 143br Good
Housekeeping; 144 Simon Archer, 145tr Nick Pope; 145bl Helen
Marsden; 146tl Trevor Richards (rpt); 146br Debbie Patterson; 147
Debbie Patterson; 148tl Debbie Patterson; 149 Christopher Drake;
152bl Lizzie Orme; 152tr Lizzie Orme; 153 Lizzie Orme; 155tr
Lizzie Orme; 155br Lizzie Orme.

Other Sources:
106–7 Nick Carter; 110br Fired Earth; 111 a/w Harper
CollinsPublishers; 114tl Nick Carter; 114bl John Gott; 115 Abode;
116 Marianne Majerus/Barbara Weiss Architects; 118br Rodney
Hyett/www.elizabethwhiting.com; 122 Abode; 123tr Spike
Powell/www.elizabethwhiting.com; 123br Neil Lorimer/
www.elizabethwhiting.com; 125br Rodney Hyett/www.elizabeth
whiting.com; 134tr Nick Carter; 138 Laura Ashley; 139tl
Littlewoods Retail Ltd; 139tc Marks and Spencer; 105tr Marks and
Spencer; 105cl IKEA UK; 105c Maison at Grand Illusions; 105cr
Littlewoods Retail Limited; 139bl IKEA UK; 105bc Laura Ashley;
105br Maison at Grand Illusions; 140tl Dennis Stone/
www.elizabethwhiting.com; 142 Belling Appliances Ltd;143tc Belling
Appliances Limited; 143bc Habitat; 148bl Spike Powell/The Jane
Graining Library; 154 David Brittain/The Jane Graining Library.

chapter five – halls and stairways

Good Housekeeping/National Magazine Company Limited:
160tl Trevor Richards; 171 Christopher Drake.

Other Sources:
158–9 Friedhelm Thomas/www.elizabethwhiting.com; 161 Mark
Luscombe-Whyte/www.elizabethwhiting.com; 162 Trevor Richards/
Abode; 163bl E.W.A/www.elizabethwhiting.com; 163tr Ian Parry/
Abode; 164c Abode; 164tl Rodney Hyett/www.elizabethwhiting.

com; 166 Andrew Dee/Abode; 167bl John Gott; 167tr Ian Parry/ Abode; 168 Marianne Majerus/Barbara Weiss Architects; 169tr Lu Jeffery/www.elizabethwhiting.com;169bl Abode; 170 Nick Carter; 172 E.W.A/www.elizabethwhiting.com; 173 John Gott.

chapter six – bedrooms
Good Housekeeping/National Magazine Company Limited:
174–5 Debbi Treloar; 178 Debbi Treloar; 179tl Trevor Richards; 179bl Mark Luscombe-Whyte; 180tr Colin Poole; 180br Debbie Patterson; 181 Debbie Treloar; 183tl Debbie Patterson; 190tl, 190br and 191 Simon McBride; 194bl Harry Cory-Wright; 194tr Trevor Richards; 195 Trevor Richards; 196bl Dennis Stone: 196tr Polly Wreford; 197 Simon Archer; 198tr Di Lewis; 198br Nadia McKenzie; 199 Simon Archer (rpt) 206bc Elizabeth Zeschin; 206tr Di Lewis; 207 Mark Luscombe-Whyte.

Other Sources:
176tl Abode; 106bl Mark Luscombe Whyte/www.elizabeth whiting.com; 177 Abode; 182 David Brittain/The Jane Graining Library; 183bl Reylon; 184tl Trevor Richards/Abode; 184bl Nick Carter; 185 Abode; 188tl, 188tr and 189tl Ian Parry/Abode; 192tl, 192br and 93 Andrew Dee/Abode; 200 Lakeland Limited; 201tl Marks and Spencer; 201tc Marks and Spencer; 201tr Aero; 201cl Maison at Grand Illusions; 201c Muji; 201cr Laura Ashley; 201bl Futon Company/www.futoncompany.co.uk; 201bc Maison at Grand Illusions;201 br Laura Ashley; 202 Chaplin's of London; 203tlMarks and Spencer; 203tc Maison at Grand Illusions; 203tr Muji; 203cr Aero; 203c Maison at Grand Illusions; 203cr Laura Ashley; 203bl Marks and Spencer; 203bc McCord; 203br McCord; 204 Marks and Spencer; 205tl Deptich Designs; 205tc Marks and Spencer; 205tr McCord 205cl Maison at Grand Illusions; 205c Marks and Spencer; 205cr Marks and Spencer; 205bl SCP; 205bc Maison at Grand Illusions; 205br SCP; 208 SCP; 209tl Futon Company/www.futoncompany.co.uk; 209tc Trevor Richards for The National Magazine Company Limited; 209tr Trevor Richards for The National Magazine Company Limited; 209cl Futon Company/www.futoncompany.co.uk; 209c Futon Company/ www.futoncompany.co.uk; 209cr SCP; 209bl Trevor Richards for The National Magazine Company Limited; 209bc Muji; 209br Marks and Spencer.

chapter seven – children's rooms
Good Housekeeping/National Magazine Company Limited:
220tl Nick Pope

Other Sources:
210–11 Ian Parry/Abode; 212tl Di Lewis/Maggie Colvin/ www.elizabethwhiting.com; 212bl David Brittain/The Jane Graining Library; 213 Abode; 214tl Shona Wood/www.elizabeth whiting.com; 214br Brian Harrison/www.elizabethwhiting.com; 215 Andreas von Einsiedel/www.elizabethwhiting.com; 216 Mark Thomas/www.elizabethwhiting.com; 217tl Ian Parry/Abode; 217br Ian Parry/Abode; 218 Fritz von der Schulenburg/The Interior Archive (designer: Juliette Mole); 219bl Abode; 219tr David Brittain/The Jane Graining Library; 220tr Abode; 221 Simon Upton /The Interior Archive (designer: Cath Kidstone); 222bl Abode; 222tr Nick Carter; 223 Andrew Wood/The Interior Archive (designer: Kate Blee).

chapter eight – bathrooms
Good Housekeeping/National Magazine Company Limited:
224–5 Di Lewis; 226tr Dennis Stone; 228br Simon McBride; 229 Wayne Vincent; 230tl Christopher Drake; 230bl Christopher Drake; 231 Polly Wreford; 232 Lizzie Orme; 233tl Jennifer Cawley; 233bl Polly Wreford; 234 Jennifer Cawley; 236tl Jennifer Cawley; 236br Simon McBride; 237 Nick Bolton; 238tl Christopher Drake; 239 Trevor Richards; 240tl Wayne Vincent; 240bl Dennis Stone; 241 Polly Wreford; 246 and 247 Trevor Richards; 248tl, 248tr, 248br and 249 Brian Harrison; 250tl, 250bl and 251 Trevor Richards; 252bl, 252tr and 253 Helen Marsden; 254tl Jennifer Cawley; 254br Polly Wreford; 255 Polly Wreford; 256tr Jan Baldwin; 256cr Polly Wreford.

Other Sources:
226br Nick Carter; 227 Marianne Majerus/Barbara Weiss Architects; 228tr Rodney Hyett/www.elizabethwhiting.com; 235 Ian Parry/Abode; 238bl Dominic Blackmore/The Jane Graining Library; 242 Colourwash; 243bl WestOne Bathrooms; 243 (rest of) Colourwash; 244 Aston Matthews; 245tl Carron Phoenix; 245tc Carron Phoenix; 245tr Carron Phoenix; 245cl West One Bathrooms; 245c West One Bathrooms; 245cr West One Bathrooms; 245 bl West One Bathrooms; 245bc West One Bathrooms; 245br West One Bathrooms; 257 Nick Carter.